EAST TO WEST

Arnold J. Toynbee

EAST to WEST

A JOURNEY ROUND THE WORLD

1958

OXFORD UNIVERSITY PRESS

NEW YORK   LONDON

PRINTED IN THE UNITED STATES OF AMERICA

CONTENTS

CONTENTS

PREFACE

The journey described in this book was the longest that my wife and I had ever made. We had the time to make it, because we had just retired from our posts at the Royal Institute of International Affairs in London. My wife had been on the staff of the Institute for thirty-four years, and I for thirty-three. So we had to start out on a new chapter of life, and the most promising start seemed to be to launch ourselves on a long journey, on which we should meet people and see places that were already familiar to us from our work, but only at second hand. To meet someone face to face, and to see a landscape with one's own eyes, is worth more than volumes of letterpress, photographs, and maps. The journey was a strenuous one, but it was rewarding. We came back with new friendships and new knowledge that will be precious possessions for us for the rest of our lives.

The account, here given, of some of the things that we saw and did is a collection of articles written, *en route*, for *The Observer*. This is a paper for which it is a pleasure to write. I am most grateful to the editor for the permission to republish the articles in a book.

A connected account of our journey, in summary form, will be found in the itinerary at the end of the volume and on the accompanying map. The book itself does not give a continuous narrative. There are experiences, such as that of passing through the Panamá Canal, that are interesting when one has not had them before, but that are too familiar to too many people to justify another description of them. One's first sight of Canberra and New Delhi is interesting too, but all the world now visits these two recently laid out capital cities. One might as well give a description of Washington, D.C. For the same reason, Riyadh—a remarkable new city still fast going up—is the only capital city, out of a number visited on this journey, that I have attempted to describe, apart from a few sentences about Quito and Bangkok. On the whole, the capital cities of the present-day world are much of a muchness, and are fast becoming harder to distinguish from one another. Damascus, new as well as old, is a brilliant exception; but Damascus, too, is familiar. So are Petra and Palmyra, but not, perhaps, Borobudur or Angkor; so I have left the first two undescribed and have given accounts of the other two, though, for my wife and me, who had never seen any of these four wonderful places before, it would be difficult to say which of them we found the most fascinating. On the whole I have passed lightly over the towns and have dwelt on the countryside, which is mostly less well known and is, I should say, much more interesting.

Our journey was made financially possible by a grant which the Rockefeller Foundation of New York had given to us jointly for the purpose of travelling with a view to revising my book, *A Study of History*. On this grant we had previously visited Mexico, and we look forward to making further journeys, thanks to it. On the present journey, our first objective was to visit Asian countries and Latin American countries which, like Mexico, have a predominantly non-European population.

I had also had the honour of being invited by the Australian Institute of International Affairs and the Australian Universities to be one of their annual lecturers on the Dyason Trust, and by the American University of Beirut to be a visiting professor on its campus. These two invitations fitted in happily with our plans for travel on the Rockefeller Grant. This grant, together with the Dyason Lectureship and the visiting professorship at Beirut, made it possible for us to go round the World. We travelled from east to west. This way round lengthens one's nights instead of shortening them, and that is an important consideration when one is travelling hard. We timed our journey so as to be in Australia during the southern hemisphere winter, and in India during the northern hemisphere one.

In both planning the journey and carrying it out, we owe more than we can say to the British Council. Without the help of the Council's central office in London and of its representatives and other officers overseas, it would have been impossible for us to accomplish what we did. In every country in which the Council operates, it made the wheels go round for us. If we managed to stand up to the strain of a formidable programme, that was thanks to the kindness, hospitality, and efficiency with which the Council came to our aid. I hope that the lectures that I had the pleasure of giving under the Council's auspices were a partial *quid pro quo*. We cannot express the gratitude that we feel. If I set out merely to name the members of the Council's staff whose individual acts of kindness we remember gratefully, the list would fill several pages. But I cannot refrain here from thanking Mr J. B. S. Jardine, the Council's representative in Baghdad, for his goodness to us when my wife fell ill while we were his guests.

We are also very grateful to a number of other people, institutions, and governments for hospitality and facilities: for instance, the governments of Ecuador, New Zealand, Indonesia, Vietnam, India, Pakistan, Syria, and Jordan, the Casa de Cultura Ecuatoriana, the Peruvian Corporation, the International House of Japan, the Indian Institute of World Affairs, Aramco, the United Nations Relief and Works Agency, and an array of distinguished universities.

It is perhaps invidious to single out the names of individuals, when so many others have also done so much for us. Yet I cannot publish this book without here thanking Señora Escallon Villa, in whose hospitable house I stayed in Cartagena; Mr Louis Stumer, who was my genial host and travelling companion in Peru; Miss Nance Dickins, the Secretary of the Australian Institute of International Affairs; Miss Budiardjo of the Cultural Department of the Ministry of Education in Djakarta; Mr and Mrs Shigeharu Matsumoto of the International House, Tokyo; Professors Nabih Amin Faris and Zeine Zeine of the American University of Beirut; and Professor Yar Shatir of the University of Tehran, who was my travelling companion on a number of memorable expeditions in Iran.

But words of thanks are inadequate. The best way for us to show our gratitude will be by trying to turn to some account all that we have learnt through the disinterested help that we have received from a very large number of people all round the World. The memory of this kindness is the most precious part of the mental cargo that we have brought back with us to England.

I. Cartagena de Indias

I had seen famous Venetian fortresses in the Levant—Modon and Coron, Napoli di Romania and Negroponte—but these examples of the work of a sixteenth- and seventeenth-century school of Italian military engineers had not given me an inkling of the magnificence of their chef d'œuvre: the mighty South American fortress of Cartagena de Indias. Sixteenth-century Venice still commanded considerable resources, and she lavished these on building strongholds that still cling like limpets to the rocks of an alien coast. But Cartagena was designed to be the shield for a whole continent, and the far vaster resources of the Spanish Empire were placed at the disposal of those Italian masters whom the Spanish Crown employed to fortify this gateway into Spanish South America. The work went on for years and swallowed up fabulous sums; but the result was to justify the effort. The fortress of Cartagena still stands intact today, and, during the three hundred years that have now passed since it was completed, it has made history.

Imagine a huge deep-water harbour in the tropics, with a narrow spit dividing its still surface from the sounding waters of the Caribbean Sea. The inner city stands with its back to the Caribbean; the outer city is protected by the harbour and an adjoining lagoon. The bridge leading into the outer city from the mainland is dominated by the massive fort of San Felipe, crowning a natural ridge of rock which springs, surprisingly, out of the marshy flats. And, far away westward, hidden by intervening headlands and islands, the 'Little Mouth' of the harbour, the Boca Chica, is defended by two forts between which a chain used to be stretched at night to prevent pirates—Dutch, English, or French—from stealing in. As for the 'Great Mouth', the Boca Grande, the Spaniards made it permanently impassable by building a submarine wall across it—a death-trap for enemy ships whose captains were unaware of what was lying in wait for them. The fortifications of this immense perimeter are all built of the finest hewn stone, compacted with cement that is the envy and despair of modern engineers. They have tried, without success, to discover the lost secret of its composition. They have no recipe of their own to match it.

Cartagena was fortified after Sir Francis Drake had seized and sacked the city; and, when the King of Spain met the bill for these tremendous works, he may have felt that he was paying dear for being wise after the event. But the expenditure proved far-sighted when, in the eighteenth century, the English came again, and this time with more ambitious intentions. In 1586 Drake had been content to pocket a ransom and slip away. In 1741 Vernon was bent on permanent conquest. The fall of Cartagena was to be the first step in the forcible conversion of a Spanish Empire into a British one. From Cartagena harbour an artificial channel leads into the Magdalena River; the Magdalena opens up the interior (or did open it up till river navigation was replaced by air transport, only the other day). Up the Magdalena's tributary, the Cauca, one can make one's way to the coast of the Pacific Ocean. So, if Vernon had succeeded in taking Cartagena, all the Spanish dominions in South America, from the coast of the Caribbean to the vale of Chile and the estuary of the River Plate, would have been at the mercy of the British to occupy at their leisure.

Every British schoolboy knows the story of Walpole's gloomy comment on the public enthusiasm over the War of Jenkins' Ear: 'Now they are ringing their bells, but soon they will be wringing their hands.' American schoolboys ought to know it too; for Admiral Vernon's disaster was an Anglo-American one, since part of the land forces was contributed by the Thirteen Colonies. A brother of George Washington served under Vernon and lost his life, and his British commander's name was immortalized by being given to George Washington's new house in Virginia.

The foiled British invaders did make their way into South America in the end; but they had to wait another eighty years, and then they came, not as military conquerors, but as merchants and civil engineers doing their peaceful business with the goodwill of Creole populations that had now liberated themselves from Spanish rule. In the nineteenth century the British held an economic empire in South America. They linked her, by bonds of trade, with the great world from which the Spanish Crown had jealously insulated her. They built harbours for her and railways. Today, this economic British empire is being nibbled away by North American competitors and by South American apprentices who have been learning the 'know-how' of a mechanized world in the United States, at M.I.T. or Cal. Tec. But, though this economic empire may be changing hands, the work that the British entrepreneurs started in South America more than a hundred years ago is continuing, *accelerando*, under new management.

This enterprise is the audacious one of taming Nature in a continent where she still has the upper hand over Man. The Indians won a livelihood from Andean Nature by propitiating her. The Spanish conquistadores and their horses have been the only living creatures, up to date, who have defied Nature with impunity in her Andean stronghold. Even the alliance of Italian art with Spanish courage might have failed to defeat Admiral Vernon at Cartagena if Nature had not sent a pestilence to slay more of his men than were slain by Spanish hands. In South America today, Nature is being assaulted by tropical medicine and by aircraft and by a road-building apparatus that can raze mountains and fill up valleys. But Nature is still making a savage fighting retreat. When the aeroplanes soar over her snow peaks, she springs at them and claws some of them down. When the engineers push their roads through her gorges, she buries them—and their builders with them—under avalanches. She is being tamed, here too, at last, as she has been tamed long ago in Egypt and in Holland; but in South America one still feels her terrible power. Here one finds oneself in the awful presence of the fierce feline goddess—the puma of the desert, the jaguar of the forest—who is one of the perennial motifs of pre-Colombian art in Peru. A wild beast is never so dangerous as when it is at bay. So, rash visitor to the Andes, beware.

2. Ecuador

'So this is Quito,' I said, as the plane came down between the mountains on a flat, green expanse with an overflowing river wriggling across it. Putting on my overcoat to meet the highland temperature at 8,000 feet, I found myself sweltering as I walked over to the airport through the rain. Where were the friends who were going to meet me? In grotesque Spanish, I asked the young woman at the information desk to put me through to the Casa de Cultura Ecuatoriana. 'But this isn't Quito,' she said. 'You are back again in Colombia, at Cali.' Next morning, when the plane did succeed in landing at Quito, I understood why the pilot had turned back the day before. The surroundings of Quito are like those of Sedbergh, on a rather larger scale. Quito, too, lies in a cup whose walls are steep, green fells; and certainly no pilot in his senses would ever try to land in the north-west corner of Yorkshire when the weather was foul.

Quito itself, of course, is not like Sedbergh at all. The city is dominated by the churches of the religious orders: Franciscans, Dominicans, Augustinians, Jesuits; and the fathers are still in possession. The Compañia (i.e. the church of the Society of Jesus) was crowded with young women listening attentively to an eloquent sermon. It was a special mission for maidservants, and there must have been more of them gathered together in that single church in Quito than the United States, the United Kingdom, Australia, and New Zealand can muster between them. So, in the highlands of Ecuador, the upper and middle class is still enjoying amenities that are now legendary in the English-speaking world.

The high point of Quiteño art and architecture is the

church and cloister of San Francisco, with its fine collection of pictures of the imperial age. In the days of the Spanish Empire of the Indies, Quito was the home of a school of religious painters whose works are still prized today as far afield as Bogotá. Their only rivals were at Cuzco. But what is passing through the minds of these Indians from the countryside who are swarming through the streets of Quito and entering the churches to pray? Their devotions are whole-hearted, but what do those ultra-baroque Christian sanctuaries mean to them? Can the four-centuries-old gulf between Indians and conquerors ever be bridged? Of course, the townspeople of Quito, too, are partly Indian in blood; but the mestizo, and even the full-blooded Indian, who enters our Western world through its Spanish door, is apt to repudiate his Indian past. So the gulf remains; the Hispanicized Indian has crossed it without diminishing it.

If the highlands were the whole of Ecuador, and Quito were the country's only city, the bridging of the gulf between the Hispanicized townsmen and landowners and the Indian peasantry might be postponed till the Greek kalends. But the sierra has to reckon with the coast, and Quito with Guaya-quil. For physical health, come to the sierra. On the road to Guayaquil from Quito, we passed bus-loads of people on their way aloft to recuperate, in the sierra, from the harshness of the coastal heat. Guayaquil is like a hothouse in Kew Gardens with the heat turned on full blast; and, at the first encounter, one is not much attracted by a modern city in the tropics. This, however, is a city that grows upon one quickly. Drive north towards the rock that overhangs the town, and you come upon a great modern hospital. It is an expression of the citizens' public spirit, and the country people of the whole Ecuadorian coast resort to it for treatment. And then, beyond the hospital, you come to a fringe of shacks, built of split bamboo and matting, that are in violent contrast with the rectangular streets of modern concrete buildings which constitute the present town. A few years ago, Guaya-quil was all shacks, and it used to be swept by devastating fires. Fighting the fires, fighting the heat, fighting the

insects, fighting the yellow fever, the people of Guayaquil
have been tempered to an indomitable spirit, and the effects
of this are now making themselves felt far beyond the point
where the concrete buildings end. More building is going on
busily, and this work is drawing in labour. Italians come to
build Guayaquil from Europe, and Indians come to build
her from the Ecuadorian sierra. The wages paid in Guayaquil
are high, compared with an agricultural labourer's wage in
the sierra; and this migration of labour from the sierra to
Guayaquil is now raising the rates of wages in the sierra as
well, and is consequently forcing the landlords in the sierra
to modernize their methods by introducing agricultural
machinery. Guayaquil may be the vibrant flame which
will eventually weld into a national unity the disparate
elements of the country's population.

From Quito to Guayaquil is a long way in every sense. I
was to make the journey by road; and, as the new road is still
unfinished and I was booked to give a lecture in Guayaquil
at 6.30 p.m. that day, we were to start at 6 in the morning. It
had been raining the night before; but, when I looked out of
my bedroom window at 5 a.m., the stars were shining
bright; and, when daylight came abruptly, it was a lovely
morning. What a thrill to see the perfect cone of Cotopaxi,
with its snow cap, and the rugged snow-sprinkled thighs of
still taller Chimborazo. What would have been the use of
having learnt their names by heart at the age of seven, if,
at sixty-six, one had been robbed of the long-deferred sight
of them by a barrage of clouds? And now we are turning
right, on to the new road that is being built by an Italian
construction company with Ecuadorian labour and British
plant. Up we wind, heading for the western cordillera of the
Andes. Now we are on the Paramo, the treeless moors, and
'Arkengarthdale' is on the tip of my tongue when I sight my
first llama (say 'yama')—my first, that is, outside the London
Zoo. Then the good surface abruptly ends, and we crawl
and bump through a tangle of tufa mountains whose fertile
slopes are intensively cultivated. As the angle is quite sixty
degrees, the beanstalks, potato plants, and sheep stand in

tiers like the spectators in a precipitous-sided stadium. We pass through a cloud, register an altitude of 12,000 feet, and begin to descend among trees that are not yet quite tropical, but that already signal to me that we are leaving the temperate zone behind. Within an hour and a half I sight my first banana palm (bananas and llamas are mutually exclusive; a llama would feel much less at home at this altitude in Ecuador than he does in Regent's Park). As we corkscrew down into the tropical lowlands, the banana plantations envelop us for miles and miles, till at last they give way to sugar-cane and rice-fields. In eleven hours on wheels, we have passed from the climate of Westmorland, through the climate of Iceland, to the climate of West Africa; and, at each descending contour, I have stripped off a layer of clothes: first my woollen muffler, next my cloth cap, then my tweed coat, then my woolly waistcoat, till I am left panting in a shirt and trousers that I cannot get rid of till I reach the hotel. So this is Ecuador: a whole world within the compass of one country.

3. Man and Water in Peru

We were standing at the head of a bay on the south side of the Parácas Peninsula, which juts out into the Pacific from the coast of the fifth valley south of Lima. If it had not been for the sea it might have been the Moon. The beauty of the landscape was unearthly. The pale gold desert undulated like the back muscles of a titanic puma. The sky, bay, and ocean were pale blue. Sharp lights and shadows flickered over the cliffs and headlands. The tops of the jagged guano islands gleamed white. I had seen nothing like this since I once steamed out of the Persian Gulf between Baluchistan and Jebel Musandim. How could this landscape support life? Yet in the National Museum at Lima, two days before, I had been gazing at the marvellous embroideries that had been recovered from graves only a mile or so from this spot.

As I marvelled, my eye was caught by a cormorant on a rock and a fisherman hauling in his line. Sea and desert were not utterly lifeless after all. We climbed into the land-rover, and my friend who was conducting me—an archaeologist whose chosen field is this central section of the Peruvian coast—manœuvred our dauntless steed over the steep sandy slopes. In a few minutes we were poking about in the sand among the graves from which the embroideries had been retrieved, and the mystery began to solve itself. The sand was streaked white with the shells of the shell-fish which the spinners and weavers had eaten; and there, down on the opposite shore of the peninsula, the water's edge was alivē with thousands of sea birds eating their fill. Among the shells in the settlement site there were also corn shucks, and these carried my eye to the green fields of the Pisco Valley, between the sea and the mountains. When those embroideries were woven, perhaps 2,500 years ago, that valley was already irrigated and cultivated; and the Parácas embroiderers, who managed to fetch their alpaca wool all the way from the sierra, could far more easily find their cotton and their corn in the valley at their feet.

Coastal Peru is a tawny desert slashed, at right angles to the coastline, by sinuous ribbons of green. In the plane, travelling to Lima from Guayaquil, I had seen the pattern below me like a flat map in two alternating colours. Now, on the ground, the desert looked like a relief map in the hard light, and the fields ranged themselves in tiers at different levels. The art of valley irrigation is to carry the life-giving water to the maximum altitude, and this means leading it out of the river-bed into irrigation channels starting far up the river's course. The yellow desert soil is rich in the chemicals that will nourish vegetation. Nothing but the magic touch of water is needed in order to make crops spring into being. Up to the limit of the irrigator's reach, these southern valleys are thick with cotton, bananas, figs, and vines (a marriage of the tropics with the Mediterranean). But the line between the desert and the sown is dramatically sharp. At life's edge you can stand with one foot in fertile mud and the other in desiccating sand. Every drop of water must be channelled to its destination, for, down here, the rain never falls, though, as one looks up the valley towards the source from which the river descends, one always sees the leaden rain-clouds lowering over the farthest visible range of peaks. Up there, they say, the mountain sides are terraced into fields that are watered, not by Man, but by Heaven. But I have still to see that lofty homeland of the potato and the llama.

The waters that make life possible for plants and animals, and therefore for Man, make work difficult for the archaeologist. Whether they flow in Man-made rills or fall in rain, these waters are all waters of Lethe. But, one yard away from the rigid frontier of the rainfall or the irrigation, the desert immortalizes all the acts of man and beast, from the most trivial to the most sublime. This horse-dung, in the courtyard of the Inca viceroy's palace at Tambo Colorado, 'the Painted Station', may have been dropped last week; but this llama-dung, lying beside it, must have been dropped more than four centuries ago; for, at this low altitude, the llamas came and went with the Incas, and the Incas went when the Spaniards arrived. Is it possible that those Parácas tapestries, which I saw in the museum, were woven 2,500 years ago? The threads are as sound, and the colours as fresh, as if they had come off the loom only yesterday. Yet the carbon test, which registers their antiquity, is believed to tell the truth with no more than a century or two's margin of error. In Lima the date seemed incredible; but here at Parácas, among the graves, I pick up a scrap of embroidery which is just as well preserved as the magnificent museum pieces. Grimmer things are immortalized too. Out of this grave pit comes a head of perfectly intact human hair; out of that one a hand with the flesh as well preserved as if the corpse had passed through the 'funeral parlour' of an Ancient Egyptian mummifier.

And now I am climbing the side of a vast mound—natural rock and sand below, but the rubble of millions of sun-dried adobe bricks above—which was the capital of the local kingdom or confederation, covering this group of coastal valleys, in the last chapter of history before the Inca conquest. By comparison with the cost of empire-building in Mexico and in the Old World, the cost in Peru was not very high in bloodshed and devastation. The ruler of Chanchán, the capital of the Kingdom of Chimú in the North, capitulated when the invading Inca army cut off the water from his irrigation channels. But here, in the Cañete Valley, the local people resisted, and the Incas had to take the great city by storm. Panting up the sandy side of the hill, we reach the lowest of the successive brows and find ourselves advancing towards the first line of adobe fortifications over a scene of wholesale slaughter: skulls and skulls and skulls, with fragments of spear-shafts and spear-throwers and stone mace-heads, but no funeral gear such as one finds in the graves at Parácas. The dead—and the soldiers died here in their thousands—must have been shovelled into shallow common graves. The dry sand faithfully preserves the record. The Pax Incaïca, like the Pax Romana, had to be purchased at a price.

Standing on this stricken field and turning back to look at the green plain out of which I have climbed, I can see, perched on the last spur of an isolated ridge of desert, the fortress that the Incas built in order to hold the valley that they had conquered. In the Chincha Valley, between here and Parácas, I had seen just such another—'The Sentinel' —standing guard over the palace mound of the subjugated local ruler. The heart of the plain and the neck of the valley were the two positions that the Incas usually chose for building their forts and planting their garrisons. 'The Painted Station' guarded the road down the valley from the highlands where the Incas were at home. 'The Sentinel' and its sister fortresses in the plain were strung along the imperial trunk road down on the coast (revived today as the Peruvian section of the Pan American Highway). Next month I shall be climbing up to the highland home of these Romans of the Andes—up there under the clouds in a country where the rain does fall. The coastal valleys never felt the rain, but they did feel the hand of human conquerors who fell upon them from the rainy country—and this at least twice over in the long history of the Andean Civilization before the Spanish conquest from the sea.

4. Purgatorio

Man is always his own worst enemy. Travelling southward from Lima, along a coast where the valleys are narrow and life is hard, one is astonished at Man's genius for wringing beauty out of Nature. Travelling northward, the impression subtly changes. There is the same rhythmic alternation of valley and desert, and the same cool breeze blowing inland off the Humboldt Current. But the valleys gradually grow broader and more fertile, till, in the sixteenth valley north of Lima, one almost loses sight of the bounding mountain walls. And here, among fields of sugar-cane and rice, rise mountains made by human hands: the stupendous towers of sun-dried bricks which the builders' Christian descendants today call 'Purgatorio'.

These piles do, in truth, recall Dante's vision of a pre-cipitous-sided mountain in the Antipodes, except that Dante's Purgatorio could be reached only on board Charon's barque, while the man-made mountains in the Lambayeque Valley have to be approached from Lima along nearly 500 miles of Pan American Highway. This Peruvian Purgatorio is a monument to Man's pride in his own power. And Pur-gatorio is far surpassed in area, though not in height, by Chanchán, the capital of the Chimú kingdom, which controlled the water, crops, and man-power of the next half-dozen valleys to the south, till North and South and Highlands and Lowlands were all incorporated in the world-empire of the Incas. Chanchán is an assemblage of vast quadrangular courts, with sides three or four hundred yards long and with a labyrinth of buildings embraced within each quadrangle's double or triple walls. Since Chanchán and

Purgatorio met their doom, there has been time for their
massive brickwork to be ravaged by the rains, though, here
on the coast, these fall only once in every 25 or 30 years.
Yet those furrowed walls and mounds still tell their tale of an
imperious minority who once organized the labour of the
peasantry, on those fertile plains, to minister to the minority's
pride of life and lust for power.

The lust for power bred war, as is witnessed by the
fortress of Paramangas. This scientifically planned military
work commands the Highway at its southern exit from the
unusually broad belt of desert that was the limit of the
Chimú kingdom in this direction. The bastions, flanking
and covering the curtain walls, strangely anticipate the
seventeenth-century style of military architecture in Europe.
It made me think of the fortifications of Padua and Verona,
and of inconclusive sieges and battles on the plains of
Lombardy and Flanders. But in Peru the clash of local
powers led up to a climax when the Inca Power, based on
the highlands, vanquished all the rest.

This organization of human industry to produce wealth
and power for a privileged minority is not mere ancient
history in the coastal valleys of Peru. Turn left off the
Highway and enter the domain of this immense hacienda
with its private railway and private city housing thousands
of workers in field and factory. It is a veritable *imperium in
imperio*, and one day there will surely be a mighty clash
when this unrepentant feudal power collides with the demand
for social justice that is sweeping over the face of the World
in our time. Chimú and Inca will be contending again under
other names. The strong man armed will be meeting a
stronger than he.

Though the valleys are broader along this northern
stretch of Peruvian coast, the desert dominates the landscape
here too, and the desert is savage and sinister. These fantastically coloured hills are bare of life. The pink is the stain
of iron ore; the green is the stain of copper ore. In the desert,
these colours do not spell blossoms and grass. The frowning
yellow mountains above seem to be waiting for Man to

falter or fail. At the first opportunity they will pounce and will crush the life out of him with their stony paws. And now, on the rough road home from Purgatorio to Lima, we are approaching the stretch where a sandy mountain falls sheer into the sea. The road is cut into the mountainside half way up, as if a giant had run his finger along it and so made a ledge for mannikins to coat with tarmac and to sweep with brooms in a fight to keep the road clear of the perpetually encroaching sand. The sun is sinking; a mist is rising from the sea. This stretch of road is a death-trap at night-time in a sea-fog; and, travelling south and driving on the right, we now have to take the side of the road that overhangs the precipice. If Dante had been with us, this terrifying section of the Pan American Highway would have been immortalized in his picture of Purgatory. My friend who is driving, skilful and hardy though he is, breathes more freely now that we are past the cliff and are dropping down into the plain. Another valley, another desert, and then suddenly the hovels and sky-scrapers of Lima loom up. We will collect our mail at the post-office and then go home and have a bath. But, as the landrover is enveloped in a crowd pouring out of a cinema, the dust of the desert, which has been stealthily insinuating itself into the ignition, brings us abruptly to a halt. The desert has pounced, but fortunately just too late to work its wicked will.

5. Arequipa

With our feet dangling over the edge of a terrace, and our heads shaded by a leafy tree, we were talking about the philosophy of history. It was a spot which Plato might have chosen for the scene of one of his dialogues; and, as my eyes involuntarily drew my mind away from our academic subject to the living landscape, I felt grateful to my Arequipeño friends for their considerateness in agreeing to hold our discussion under the open sky. They had proposed a round table (mesa redonda) under the University of Arequipa's hospitable roof; but I had only the inside of two days for feasting my eyes on this enchanting landscape. So I had asked for a carro redondo (a round car) instead, and my fellow professors had amiably agreed. So here we were, sitting on the heights of Jesús (Hayssooss, with the accent on the second syllable), with the oasis of Arequipa at our feet.

Have you ever set eyes on the oasis of Damascus, with a line as sharp as a knife-edge dividing the green irrigated land from the tawny desert, and with a white city nestling under the lea of a mountain chain? If you have seen that Syrian landscape, you can begin to imagine what Arequipa is like; and yet the half of it has still to be told. At Arequipa the oasis is not all on one plane, as it is in the Ghutah of Damascus. The skill of the Peruvian water-masters has tapped the river Chili high up among the mountains and has led off the life-giving conduits at two or three different levels, so that here you have an oasis in several storeys. And then, how could Antilebanon, for all its majesty, hold up its head in face of the symmetrical trinity of mountains that towers above this oasis in Peru? In the centre the volcanic cone of Misti ('the White') soars up into the brilliant blue sky (the sky here is azure blue in the daytime and ultramarine at night). On the left rises the still higher mass of Chachani, and on the right stands Picchu Picchu ('Peaks and Peaks'), which makes up by its jagged skyline for its lower altitude. Take Mont Blanc and increase its height by about a quarter, and you have the altitude of Misti; increase it by about a third, and you have the altitude of Chachani. Even at Jesús, which cannot be more than a paltry 8,000 feet above sea-level, one feels that only the thinnest of stratospheres intervenes between the human soul and pure space. Sunlight and starlight shine through here with their original brightness almost undimmed.

As one's eyes range round the oasis to Misti and its two attendant mountains on the highland side, and to a line of rosy cliffs in the direction of the Pacific coast, one is tempted to suppose that life in this miniature world must be idyllic.

But where there is life there will always be trouble, and even a paradise has its problems. Arequipa's chief problem today is that it is a veritable paradise for the Quechua and Aymara Indians of the Altiplano that hides up there behind Misti's back. In the days before Arequipa was equipped with modern means of communication, this oasis was a preserve for the Mestizo descendants of the Spanish founders of the city. But audacious Englishmen from Doncaster have built and operated a railway from the coast which, not content with climbing up to Arequipa, climbs on over a 14,668-feet-high pass into the highland basin of Lake Titicaca; and a route that carries foreign goods up is now carrying Indian migrants down.

The Indians are arriving in Arequipa by bus-loads and by train-loads, and are squatting in the outskirts of the city. This mass-immigration is causing the Arequipeños dismay. It is, indeed, the Indian counter-offensive to the Spanish conquest of Peru, and it is not the less effective for having been delayed for more than 400 years and then taking the form of peaceful penetration. A foreign observer, who has no personal interest at stake, will view this portent with mixed feelings. No doubt it is the highland Indians' ultimate destiny to become members of our modern Western society, and the mestizo cities—Arequipa and Lima in Peru, and Guayaquil in Ecuador—are the melting-pots in which the fusion is taking place. The squalor in which the Indian squatters live is ease and luxury for them by comparison with the hardness of their previous life as husbandmen, herdsmen, and fishermen. Yet it is also a pity for them and for the World that the vortex of our modern civilization should be sucking them in. For the Indians' home-grown civilization, arduous though it be, is admirable in its self-sufficiency. Two days later, when I was rolling on train-wheels over the Altiplano and was catching glimpses of the Indians at home, I had the same impression that I once had when I drove out into the countryside from Quebec. If the modern civilized world should ever manage to wipe itself out by a perverse combination of technology, folly, and sin, these earth-bound peasants would still be there to multiply and replenish the Earth when the flood of poison-radiation had subsided. It would take perhaps barely a thousand years for the southernmost French Canadian peasant pioneers to run into the northernmost Quéchua Indian peasant pioneers among the ruins of Miami, Florida, or Houston, Texas; and on that day the New World, at any rate, would have been re-populated.

This fantasy of the self-destruction and self-re-creation of civilization was familiar to Plato. He pictured it as having happened already, over and over again. Well, once would be once too much for us. Let us hope that this is one of thóse bad dreams that are not translated into reality.

6. Altiplano

'Am I really awake or still dreaming?' I asked myself as, at dawn, I peered out of the window of the sleeper. 'This is unmistakably the Anatolian plateau, and, if the train is not approaching Konia from Karaman, it must be approaching Eskishehir from Inönü. This level expanse pocked with tufts of coarse grass and with incrustations of whitey-grey salt; these villages built of mud brick; these patches of cultivation in the waste, and these children herding the flocks: where could this be but Turkey? Yet, in those Turkish flocks and herds, I never saw these llamas or alpácas, and I do seem to recollect that, at 10 p.m. last night, the place where I entrained was Arequipa in Peru?' Well, so it was. Yet I might be forgiven for having fancied myself in Turkey when I was still only half awake, for the similarity of the two landscapes is extraordinary. Lift the Anatolian plateau to about four times its actual altitude, and then shift it about twenty degrees nearer to the Equator, and you have the Altiplano of Peru and Bolivia. Even the people look alike, for the Spanish Government did to the Indians of the Altiplano what the United Kingdom Government did to the

Scottish highlanders after 1745. They compelled them to give up wearing their native dress; and the sixteenth-century Spanish peasant garb, with the twist that the Indians have given to it in the course of four hundred years, is not unlike the Phrygian costume that the highlanders of Turkey used to wear before Ataturk forcibly put them into modern Western cloth caps and reach-me-downs.

As I watched the sun rise above the mountain rim of the plain, I realized that I had come sleeping over the highest point on the railway (14,668 feet) without having been waked up by mountain sickness or having been constrained to suck the oxygen-container that was standing ready by my berth. The station that we were approaching was neither Konia nor Eskishehir. It was the Peruvian railway town of Juliáca, and the altitude, measured in feet, was here 12,551. And now we trans-shipped from our sleepers into the coach that the railway authorities had generously placed at our disposal. It was a home on wheels, complete with two bedrooms, a kitchen, a veranda, a major-domo, Señor Justo, and his mate; and we were free to hitch this house on wheels on to any train that we chose. So we headed first for Puno, the port on the westernmost bay of Lake Titicaca, and by 9 a.m. that morning we were travelling in a car along the road that skirts the lake's south-western shore.

The surface of Lake Titicaca is 12,500 feet above sea-level, and the steamers that ply on it had to be carried up from the coast in the smallest pieces into which they could be dissected. The first steamer came up piece-meal on mule back, the rest piece-meal in railway trucks after rail-head had reached the lake shore. If you travel by the Southern Railway of Peru from the Pacific port of Mollendo via Arequipa to the capital of Bolivia, La Paz, you traverse Lake Titicaca on board one of the railway company's steamers. Our car ride along the lake shore was a thrilling experience.

Lake Titicaca provides the necessities of life for man and beast. The cattle wade out, breast-deep, to crop the tender shoots of the totóra reed; their human masters cut the tough stalks to make rafts from which they catch the fish with which the lake teems. We watched a family building one of these balsas, as the fishermen's rafts are called. They take two days to build and they last for two months before becoming waterlogged. The raw material is inexhaustible and the construction simple. Two large bundles of reeds, bound with plaited straw, are tied tightly together at each end. Two smaller bundles are tied on top to serve as gunwales. Add a wooden paddle, wooden mast, and reed sail, and your fishing craft is complete. The fishermen do not trouble to learn to swim; for the water of this sky-high lake is so icy cold that anyone who has the misfortune to fall in out of his depth will be paralysed by cramp in five minutes, even if he is one of the best swimmers in the World.

And now we are travelling over a steppe screened from the lake by a line of low hills. Little girls are shepherding vast flocks of llamas, alpácas, guanácos, sheep, and goats. Here and there we pass patches of cultivation. Perhaps you would not have thought that a potato patch could be romantic; yet it does give you a thrill when you see it in the homeland of potatoes, and when you notice that, on the Altiplano, this Peruvian staff of life is cultivated with all the care that, in Europe or North America, we lavish on an asparagus bed. And then there is the quiñoa: a cereal, looking like a rainbow-coloured foxglove, that will produce edible grain at an altitude that defeats not only maize but even oats. We linger on the bridge over the Ilavi River, twin brother of Anatolian Sangarius, winding its sluggish way towards the lake through shoals of sand. We ford another river, pass through Juli, with its seventeenth-century churches, and then, as the road climbs the shoulder of a mountain, the main body of the lake springs into view. The ethereal blue of the water is indescribable. It reflects the colour of empty space undimmed by veils of intervening atmosphere. In the centre, beyond the tip of the Copacabana Peninsula, lies the sacred Island of the Sun, one of the holy places of the Andean World in its pre-Christian age. And in the background of the north-eastern shore rise the Bolivian Nevadas, seventy-five miles of them

in an unbroken line, with their glistening teeth biting
savagely into the pure blue sky.

As I stare over the neck of the Copacabana Peninsula, I
can see, with my mind's eye, the Altiplano stretching away
south-eastward across Bolivia, with the mighty masonry of
Tiahuanáco standing solitary in the bleak plain. The
excruciating moment in travel is when the time comes for
turning back, with some notable landmark still just hidden
below the horizon. Well, at least I have set eyes on the lake,
and Lake Titicaca is a sight for the gods.

7. Inca Land

'At Curve One Hundred and Four you will see the landscape change,' said the English traffic inspector, as he bade
us goodbye on the watershed between the basin of Lake
Titicaca and the basin of the Atlantic Ocean. Here, at La
Raya, we were 14,153 feet above sea level; and, if Mr Le
Tourneau, the famous Californian engineer, had transported Pike's Peak from the Rockies on one of his fabulous
machines, he could have stowed it away below the railroad
tracks with a clearance of fully eight feet between the summit
of the buried mountain and the ballast of the permanent
way. In the Rockies or the Alps, La Raya would have been a
famous peak; but in the Andes it is a lowly valley, with snow
caps and glaciers looking down on it superciliously from
both sides. Just on the Atlantic side of the watershed, hot
springs—so hot that one cannot hold one's hand in them—
well up out of the tundra with loud gurgles and groans.
These are the headwaters of the Vilcanota River (known
lower down its course as the Urubamba), which joins with
the Apurimac to form the mighty Ucayali River; and the
Ucayali, in its turn, joins with the Marañón to form the still
mightier Amazon. A hundred yards or so below the springs,
an infant volcano is poking its snout up skywards through
the grey bent. 'If that thing goes on growing,' said the

Inspector ruminatively, 'it may become quite a nuisance to the Company.'

After the passenger train, travelling from Cuzco to Arequipa, had passed our goods train at the summit, we began the descent of the Vilcanota valley; and at Curve One Hundred and Four, sure enough, the landscape did begin to change. The tundra now gave way to fields of beanstalks and oats. The mountain sides, which had been naked higher up, began to clothe themselves in a film of green, and cultivation terraces, set at fantastically steep angles, were soon grooving the mountains' flanks like the contours on a relief map. As we plunged down and down, the valley opened and closed and opened again. We did the last part of the downward journey in an autocarril (a motor car on railway wheels) in which another official of the railway was travelling behind our train. By the time we had reached Huambutio, we had descended more than 4,000 feet from the head of the valley. But here we left the main stream to our right and began to climb a broad and fertile side-valley in the fading light. We had regained 1,000 feet before we slid into Cuzco station in the dark.

At dawn next morning I looked eagerly out of my bed-room window to catch my first glimpse of this famous city. In front stood the cathedral, and on its right the two domes of the church of the Compañia (the Society of Jesus). Craning my neck to the right again, I could look down the Cuzco valley and across the course of the here invisible Vilcanota to a distant snow-peak. Turning left, I found myself facing the green hill that is crowned by the massive fortress of Sacsahuamán. The location of the Inca capital, at the head of a short but fertile vale, reminded me of the location of Boghazqalé, the Hittite capital in the heart of Asia Minor. But at Cuzco, as at Quito in Ecuador, the colour and texture of the landscape are those of the English Lake District.

Here, then, was the spot from which the Inca conquerors had gone forth to unite and organize the whole Andean World in their Empire of the Four Quarters. When the

Spaniards made their calamitous appearance out of the blue, the Incas' dominions stretched from Southern Colombia through Peru and Bolivia into North-Western Argentina and Central Chile. Yet the Incas were upstarts. They had started on their empire-building enterprise less than a hundred years before the Spaniards' arrival, and even the valley of Cuzco had not been theirs before the thirteenth century of the Christian Era. From the summit of the Inca fortress of Sacsahuamán, a professor of Andean archaeology pointed out to me the site of the pre-Inca city during the Tiahuanacoid time of troubles, and the site of the pre-Tiahuanacoid city during the still earlier period of Andean cultural florescence. The Incas had been interlopers who had had to fight hard in order to conquer the fertile vale that was the germ cell of their immense empire. Well, they might be parvenus, and they might be destitute of the artistic sense displayed by the more cultivated peoples whom they subdued. Yet they could look the Chimú and the Ica in the face; for they had done for them the service that the Romans once did for the Greeks. They had imposed peace on warring communities that would not voluntarily live at peace with one another.

As we stood on the top of Sacsahuamán, they pointed out to me the four roads along which the imperial messengers and administrators had sped to and from the capital. The westward road ran via Arequipa to the distant Pacific coast; the eastward road ran to the dangerously close Amazonian montaña, with its warlike independent tribes; the northern road ran to Quito; the southern to Chile. And all four roads ran straight; for they were built, not for wheels nor even for mule hooves, but for human feet; and, where the mountain flanks were steep, the pavement simply changed into a staircase.

And how can I describe the Inca masonry; the polygonal walls of Sacsahuamán and Ollantaytambo, and the rectangular dressed blocks of the palaces of the Incas in the city of Cuzco itself? The cyclopean blocks weigh many tons. Yet they were levered into position by human muscle-power at an

altitude at which the lowlander's heart goes pit-a-pat if he
climbs a flight of stairs; and then these huge stones were
fitted together so exactly that you cannot insert the blade of a
pocket-knife between them. As for the dressed masonry of the
palaces, it is proof against the earthquakes that have made
havoc of the baroque superstructures that the Spanish
conquerors piled upon it. The Incas' reign may have been
brief, but they built for eternity.

8. Machu Picchu

As I climbed the steep flight of steps to the Cuzco terminus
of the Santa Ana Railway, I could not imagine how we were
going to find our way over the mountain and into the
Vilcanota valley, which we had left behind us on the last
stage of our journey to Cuzco two days ago. We did it by
zigzagging, with an agile young man leaping out of our
autocarril and back again to re-set the points each time that
we doubled back. Looking down the mountain-side up which
we were climbing, we could see the steam-train that was
following us puffing and blowing several flights below us on
this giant staircase. And now we are over the top and are
travelling across a green level savannah, a sky-high water-
meadow teeming with cattle. The Inca, in his day, is said to
have kept his herds of llama here. Then, suddenly, the
sluggish rivulet, alongside of which we are ambling, begins
to swirl, and we are diving, side by side with it, through a
gorge between the mountains. I have travelled through the
Cilician Gates, twice by rail and once by road, but this
Peruvian gorge beats Alexander's highway hollow in the
literal meaning of the word. Down here, at the bottom, with
just room for the torrent and the rails, we cannot see the sky;
but, far above us, we can just make out a fearsome bridle-
path hugging the mountain's flank and picking its way over
the brow of a precipice. At last, the gorge spews our train
out as suddenly as it had sucked it in, and we are being shot,

like a bullet, into the Vilcanota valley, far down below the altitude at which we had left it when we swerved out of it into the Vale of Cuzco.

As the Vilcanota river foams and roars in its headlong descent towards the distant Atlantic, and our autocarril races the water neck and neck, a subtle change begins to come over the landscape. At each successive twist of the valley, the flanks of the mountains become greener and more furry. Leafy trees are now finding a footing on fantastically steep slopes. We have passed out of the sierra into the semi-tropical montaña, which runs in a belt all the way along the eastern flank of the Andes from the southern shore of the Caribbean to the Bolivian yungas. 'How far north-westward does the river run through the montaña before it breaks its way into the level Amazonian jungle?'—'O, just about another two hundred kilometres,' is the reply. The Andean World is built on a titanic scale, and we cannot reach the Amazonian selva by train; for the line runs on only 20 or 30 kilometres beyond Machu Picchu, which is our journey's end today. Look, here are the buses waiting to haul us up aloft; but, once again, how do we get there? As we drive over the bridge with about an inch to spare on either side between us and the turbulent river below, a precipice rises to the left of us and another to the right of us, and we begin to zigzag up a slope, between them, that would count as a precipice too in a less precipitous country than this.

What is Machu Picchu? Strictly speaking, it is 'the great peak' in which the left-hand precipice terminates; but nowadays the name is used to designate the Inca city that crowns the saddle between 'the great peak' and the little one. 'Little peak'! Huayna Picchu! It soars into the sky like the spire of some giant's cathedral. And the city poised between the two peaks matches its natural surroundings in grandeur, while surpassing them in mystery. Never reached by the Spanish conquerors of the Inca Empire, it was laid bare in our own day by a North American explorer, Hiram Bingham. He broke through the city's jungle-screen and brought it to light like a sleeping beauty. But neither

Bingham nor the younger generation of archaeologists have been able to ascertain the city's age or function. Was it a fortress? And, if so, was it a frontier fortress of the Inca Empire against the independent tribes of the montaña, or was it a city of refuge from the Spanish invaders who broke the Inca Empire up? The city is fortified with a dry ditch and a wall on the 'great peak' side, where the approach would be easiest for foot-soldiers with legs like mountain goats; and this suggests that it was built to serve a military purpose. But, of the skeletons found in the graves on the slopes below, all but a tiny percentage are those of women; and this suggests that the inhabitants were not warriors, but were virgins dedicated to the worship of the Sun. The enigma baffles us, and an analysis of the architecture does not solve it, since all styles of Inca architecture, from the roughest to the most exquisite, are represented here.

From the summit of this city you can look down on both sides to the Vilcanota River wending its way far below; for the river writhes round the foot of Huayna Picchu, so that peak and saddle together form a lofty peninsula. The sunset over this scene was indescribably grand, and the sunrise would have been grander if the clouds had not descended on the city during the night. In a white mist we drove cautiously down the zigzag that we had driven up the day before, and then we began to rattle back up the line— taking care, as we swung round the curves on this Sunday morning, not to run over the peasants who were plodding along the permanent way to Mass and then to market. We did not even run over a calf, a pig, or a fowl. The only casualty was a hawk, who was so intent on pouncing on a wild pigeon that he made a head-on collision with the bows of our autocarril.

On this return-journey we changed, at Ollantaytambo, from rail to road. The masonry here rivals in magnitude the stones of Sacsahuamán; but Ollantaytambo is an enigma, like Machu Picchu. Was it a fortress? Or was it a temple? The experts disagree; but there can be no dispute about the Inca village that lies at its foot: a miniature Cuzco, without the Spanish superstructure. And now we are on the long trail back to Cuzco up the Vilcanota valley and over the hills from Pisac. The fireworks that celebrate the climax of the Mass are followed by the buzz of the market place. In an upland glen, within a few miles of Cuzco, we stumble on a massive Inca retaining-wall with a spring of water gushing out of it. The Inca used to take his pleasure here, and nothing in this charming scene has changed since his day. Last of all, within sight of Cuzco itself, we tarry at Kkencu (be sure to pronounce both K's) and I rub my eyes. For, as I thread my way through the clefts in this labyrinth of numinous rocks, I cannot believe that I am not in the heart of Yazili Kaya, 'the scrivened rock', within sight of Boghaz-qalé, that was once the Hittites' holy of holies. In Anatolia and in Peru, the same weird shapes of rock have awakened the same sense of awe in human hearts. What a testimony to the uniformity of human nature.

9. The Selva

The selva at last! The oxygen had stopped streaming into my lungs out of the nozzle, like the mouthpiece of a hookah, that I had been sucking greedily during our flight over the Andes. The plane was bearing down upon a level carpet of trees that spread eastwards to the horizon. But no man-made carpet ever had so thick a pile or so close a texture. The texture was so close that the dead trees had no room to fall, and their erect white skeletons gleamed like lace-work among the many shades of green. From Pacific desert to Atlantic selva in a flight of one hour and three-quarters! A few minutes after we had become air-borne at Lima, we had risen above the fog-belt that hangs over the city; and, when the World had become visible again, it had still been the arid world of the coast, a world of bone-dry mountains with ribbons of green, down below, along the banks of the trickling rivers. Next had come highland villages and cultivation terraces at apparently inaccessible altitudes; and then the sierra blanca, the snow-clad chain of the Andes. This dwarfs, in its magnificence, the panorama of the Alps on the flight from Milan to Zürich; but what caught and held my eye, as the oxygen faded out of the tube, was, not the receding sierra, but the approaching selva. Here, at last, was the sight that had eluded me on the journey to Machu Picchu.

We landed at Pucallpa, the only point in South America, so far, at which a 'route carrossable' from the Pacific coast meets the navigable waters of the Amazon Basin. We had converged on this road as our plane came down to earth, and, from the air, the straight red scar, cleaving the dark green jungle, had looked impressive. It belied its looks now that we were jogging along it, and I learned that it was carrossable with a reservation. If your truck or car were to be caught by the rains in one of the mountainous sections, you might have to wait three months before getting through to your destination. However, the road is a going concern for at least six months in the year, and the River Ucayali is a permanent reality. From the air at Pucallpa it looked about the size of the Thames at Richmond, and it gave the impression of ambling along as gently; but, when I landed on its surface next day in one of the Linguistic Institute's hydroplanes about forty miles below Pucallpa, I found that the Ucayali was as broad, and also as masterful, as the Danube at Ruschuk. In the last three weeks, it had eaten away 150 yards of the Indian village on the bluff that we were visiting.

The Linguistic Institute is a North American Protestant missionary enterprise that has the blessing of the Peruvian Government because it is introducing the Amazonian Indians to the rudiments of modern civilization and is thereby preparing them for gradual incorporation into the national life of the country of which they are legally citizens. This is indeed a devoted band of men and women. They go out by twos—a husband and wife or a couple of girls—to live with the Indian tribes, learn their languages, teach them a smattering of Spanish, and translate the New Testament into the vernaculars. The out-stations may be 50 miles, 100 miles, 400 miles from the base at Yarinacocha. Nowadays the workers travel out and back in hydroplanes and keep in daily touch with the base by radio. But, when they began operations ten years ago, there was no radio and not one hydroplane. They had to travel by canoe and to remain marooned at their posts for six months or a year on end.

The enlistment of the hydroplane in the service of religion has been a stroke of genius. In the selva you cannot walk two yards without being stopped dead either by wood or by water, and waterways are the only ways along which one can travel, unless one takes to the air and uses the water just for ascending and descending. Fortunately there is plenty of water for the purpose. The rivers find the flat selva dull after having fought their way through the montaña, so in the selva they amuse themselves by perpetually changing their courses, cutting themselves new loops and abandoning the old ones. Yarinacocha stands on the shore of an abandoned loop of the Ucayali, and this makes it an ideal taking-off place for the Institute's hydroplanes. It was less ideal to land on when it was infested by fifteen-feet-long crocodiles basking awash, since one big crocodile's back might shatter a one-engine hydroplane's floats. But the crocodiles have now been exterminated and the alligators intimidated, and members of the Institute, with their tiny children, bathe in their lake every evening with impunity. I was introduced to a Plymouth Brother from Philadelphia, Pennsylvania, living between Yarinacocha and Pucallpa, who was finding the necessary protein for his fowls by feeding them on boiled-down alligator meat. To be converted into chicken-feed is a humiliating end for even a minor carnivorous reptile.

At what level in the hierarchy of civilization do these Amazonian Indians stand? The answer depends on the criterion that one takes. If the criterion is our modern technology, then, of course, the Indian has no standing at all. At Tourna Vista, on the Pachitea tributary of the Ucayali, I saw at work the Californian engineer, Mr Le Tourneau's, terrific machines: for instance, the tree-stinger, which digs its tail into the ground and then pushes a tree over with its steel arm. The tree in the selva has no more chance of defeating the tree-stinger than the bull in the bull-ring has of defeating the toreador; and, as it topples over to its death, its spirit flies to Hades as indignantly as the hero Turnus's in the last line of the Aeneid. The Amazonian Indian could no more build a tree-stinger than he could fly; and, by comparison with Mr Le Tourneau's two-storeyed houses on wheels, the Indian's thatched roof on poles makes a poor showing. But change your standard of comparison from the field of technology to the field of art, and the Indian can look the Gringo in the face. Observe the gracefulness of the pattern of that cloth that this Indian woman is weaving and the sureness of the touch with which her neighbour is painting this beautifully moulded pot. We could not improve upon this in New York or Paris or Florence. Perhaps we could not equal it. So what is civilization? Which of us has the last word?

10. North Island

Before we were clear of the southern suburbs of Auckland, the sheep had begun. They were a welcome sight to sea-weary eyes, for we had boarded our friend's car at the quay-side, and these were the first four-footed creatures that we had seen since we had sailed out, three weeks before, from the Panamá Canal into the vast Pacific. For readers of *Kon-tiki*, it is tantalizing to travel in that romantic balsa-raft's wake, yet see none of the lovely horrid monsters with which Thor Heyerdahl and his companions made such an intimate acquaintance. The only life that we had seen had been flying fish and petrels and albatrosses. And now here were sheep again, and such eloquent sheep too. Their English cousins are often noisy; they bleat and baa because they feel anxious and plaintive. These New Zealanders had no time to express their feelings vocally. Why waste your breath when you

have luscious green grass to crop for twenty-four hours a
day all round the calendar? Their eloquence was in dumb
show. 'We thoroughly approve of these pastures,' they were
telling the World; 'and how clever we have been to find
our way to this sheep's paradise from the other side of the
globe.' Billowy waves of self-satisfaction radiated from their
fleeces. Evidently it had not occurred to them that Man had
had a hand in their migration from the fells to the Elysian
fields.

By English standards these North Island sheep were
incredibly thick on the ground. But these exuberant pastures
had not been waiting, ready-made, for four-footed British
immigrants to occupy them. They had been won from the
bush by arduous human labour; and, in the course of our
journey from Auckland to Wellington, we saw something of
the second stage of Man's conquest of a livelihood from
Nature. The first wave of settlers cleared and improved the
flatter country in the river valleys. But New Zealand's
physiographical make-up is like Japan's. Nine-tenths of its
area, in its natural state, are occupied by a tangle of bush-
covered hills, so inaccessible from the ground that, in the old
days, reclamation was impossible or at any rate would have
been prohibitively expensive. Today the Government is
bull-dozing the trees and then laying a top-dressing on the
shorn slopes by dropping it from the air. The new hill-farm
is handed over to the farmer with the heaviest of the pioneer-
ing work already done. He can put his sheep on the sprouting
grass, and go to it. In this way New Zealand, with the aid of
modern chemistry and technology, is extending her effective
area; and this achievement is of immense importance to a
couple of islands that are marooned in the Pacific and are
not well endowed with minerals.

It is a fascinating spectacle to watch two floras contending
for the possession of the same land. The defeat of the native
flora is a foregone conclusion, because the intrusive grass and
pine and poplar have Man for their ally. It is only when the
road takes one within sight of precipitous gulleys and ravines
that one sees New Zealand as she once was. These remnants

of terrain that Man still cannot turn to account are filled,
chock-a-block, with an impenetrable 'cold jungle' of ever-
greens. The giant tree-ferns catch the English observer's
eye. I had seen the like in Colombia a month or two back;
but there, next-door to the Equator, this vegetation did not
descend below an altitude of 9,000 feet, whereas in New
Zealand one finds it at sea-level.

In the North Island of New Zealand, 'dominion over palm
and pine' can be had without conquering an empire on
which the sun never sets. They grow, side by side, in the same
garden, to the perpetual astonishment of the visitor from
Northern Europe. Just when he is succumbing to the
illusion that he is travelling through the English countryside, a little palm tree pops up to disconcert him. The
kaleidoscopic North Island landscape is, indeed, constantly
evoking illusory reminiscences of the Old World and the
Americas. The green pastures of England give way to the
crater lakes of Etruria (Lake Taupo is a second Lake
Trasimene) and to the volcanoes of South America (Ngauru-
hoe, with its two flanking mountains, all under snow, is the
twin of Misti in Peru). The volcanoes, in turn, give way to
downs as one approaches Wellington. These downs, though,
are more knobbly and more crinkly than the downs in
Sussex; and Wellington, when the harbour bursts on one's
view on a sunny day, turns out to be a second San Francisco
—till wind and rain transform it into a second London or
Shanghai (the weather at Wellington can be as raw as that).

The characteristic fauna of the North Island are neither
sheep nor men, but chthonic gods. At Rotorua their breath
rises in clouds of steam from the bush, and their mouths
gape to spit out boiling, sulphurous spume. At Wairakei
they roar and rage in an agony of frustration. They have
fought their way here so near to the surface, yet have just
lacked the strength to heave their mighty limbs clear of the
ground. Surely this region must have been Father Zeus's
principal interment ground for the vanquished Titans.
We know, of course, that he buried a batch of them alive
under Mount Etna and another batch under Mount

Vesuvius, but those blow-holes in Italy and Sicily are peril-
ously close to Mount Olympus; so the Olympian victor
deposited the rest of his foes in New Zealand, at the antipodes of Greece. Whatever the future of sheep and man may
be, the Titans beneath Wairakei will go on raging till the
end of time.

11. Australia in the Tropics

We are familiar on the map with Australia's long rhinoceros
horn that beckons so invitingly to the teeming millions of
East Asians, up there to the north. Towards the root of the
horn, about 180 miles north of the bridge of Australia's
enormous Roman nose, the little town of Cairns looks out
over the Barrier Reef towards the Pacific. Here I am; and,
if you were to travel this far towards the Equator from
Europe, you would find yourself in Senegal or the Sudan.
Yet this patch of Northern Queensland is authentic Australia
still. Cairns is, on a small scale, a typical Australian east-
coast city, complete with wharves, shopping centre, banks,
hotels, airport, and railway station. The railway, which runs
to Cairns without a break from Brisbane and the other great
cities of the South, here climbs from sea-level on to the
Atherton tableland and splays out into little branches along
which the agricultural produce of the hinterland is carried
down to the port. On the tableland, Nature has made an
apparent concession to far-faring Nordic Man. In the same
latitude in Peru, one has to hoist oneself up to an altitude of
eight or ten thousand feet to obtain a temperate climate. In
Northern Queensland, twelve or fifteen hundred feet do the
trick. There was a sharp frost on the tableland the other day
in this winter month of June, and the district is farmed by
Australians of British and Irish origin—leaving Italian
Australians to do the cane-cutting in the sugar-producing
country down below. Nordic Man in Northern Queensland
has made fewer concessions to Tropical Nature. He does

drape a mosquito-net over his bed, and does build his
house on stilts, so that he can at least observe the invading
white ants, even if he cannot stop them. But he is still
eating beef-steak pie and suet pudding, like his forebears in
the British Isles.

Tropical Nature is generous with one hand, though
treacherous with the other. She is lavishly generous below
sea-level, as you will see if you take the trip from Cairns
to Green Island on the Barrier Reef (the distance is four
miles less than the passage from Dover to Calais). After
visiting the aquarium on this coral island, you can go down
into an aerium, anchored among the coral on the sea bottom,
and can give the fish their turn to look at you through the
portholes. Here you find yourself in the submarine world
described by the crew of the *Kon-tiki*; but it is being revealed
to you in miniature, and without its deep-sea horrors. Here
it is a vision of all things bright and beautiful. The fish and
the waving vegetation—which sways on the coral like a
magnificent head of hair—are unimaginably brilliant and
varied in their colours; and the fish, which dart about in
incredible numbers, do not prey on one another, though they
range in length from about a foot to perhaps less than a
quarter of an inch. They are not tempted to become cannibals
because, in spite of the density of their population, there is
plenty of plankton here for all. In Cairns, for the same reason,
the human visitor leaves his bedroom door unlocked in his
hotel. The human equivalent of plankton is consumer goods,
and there are enough of these in circulation in Northern
Queensland to remove the temptation to commit those petty
larcenies that became so frequent in Britain in the hard
times at the end of the war. Nordic Man's inborn honesty is
not, I suppose, greater in Australia than it is in his original
habitat; but in Australia, if he does turn predatory, he preys
on the shark's scale and not on the parrot fish's. Now and
then and here and there, an Australian politician may
misappropriate a million acres of still undeveloped public
land; but such things are done at the expense of a state or the
Commonwealth. Meanwhile, the private citizen in Northern

Queensland does not have to stand on guard over his safety-razor or his fountain pen.

What is the future of this fascinating corner of the Earth? The volcanic soil on the tableland is almost as rich as the alluvial soil in the valley bottoms, and the present production of milk, maize, peanuts, and sugar is considerable in absolute figures. Yet, when these are compared with the country's potentialities, the use that Nordic Man and Mediterranean Man have made of Northern Queensland so far cannot seem impressive to those millions of East Asians who are now peering over the mountains of New Guinea at this trans-equatorial land of promise. What is the future? Let us put the question to the termites who have dug themselves in on that section of the Atherton tableland that one encounters first as one travels by road from Cairns to Kuranda.

This stretch of country is inhospitable to trees as well as to men, so the social insects have made it and kept it their own. Their apartment-houses are thick on the ground, and they soar to heaven. Most of them would dwarf the Empire State Building, if Man and his works were to be reduced to termite stature. The termite population of these few square miles is perhaps as great as the human population of present-day China. Let us ask the termites about Northern Queensland's destiny. For the last million years, the social insects have been waiting for Man, that aggressive but undisciplined parvenu in the social insects' ancient domain, to make the inevitable blunder that will eliminate him. This blunder might well take the form of a war to the death between European and Asian Man for the possession of desirable lands to which European Man has staked out a claim without having made this claim good by entering into effective possession. Between the termites' stronghold and the village of Kuranda, there are some sinister portents: the abandoned runways of fighter and bomber bases and some rows of war graves in the local cemetery. During the Second World War, the Australian Army and the United States Air Force were present here in strength, as a precaution against the risk of a Japanese invasion.

'Next time,' the termites, no doubt, are saying to themselves today, 'the human intruders on our Earth are going to wipe themselves out. After less than a million years of existence, these ingenious creatures have discovered a way of committing mass-suicide.' Alas, poor termites, you have overlooked one material point in your calculations. If Mankind did destroy itself in an atomic war, it might also destroy you and your neighbours, the tropical fish and the coral-building animalculae and the plankton. It might destroy all life on this planet. And therefore, O termites, you had better line up with Mr Nehru and work with all your might for compromise and coexistence. The potential wealth of Northern Queensland is a glittering prize, but it would be bought too dear if the price were to be annihilation.

12. The Elusive Continent

I have been in Australia five weeks today, and yesterday I saw Australia for the first time. I am speaking, of course, of Australia the producer, the great mother of wool and wheat. Australia the consumer is impossible for the visitor from overseas to miss. He will find her, almost larger than life, in any one of the six state capitals. These are all on tidewater, and he can hardly avoid making his landfall at one of them. He will be amazed at the size of even the smallest of them, even if he has been properly instructed at school that Australia is the most highly urbanized country in the World in our day. I had imagined, for instance, that Sydney, big though it might be, would be dwarfed by the vast expanse of Sydney Harbour, and I was astonished to see the city encircling, with its octopus-tentacles, not only the Harbour, but Botany Bay as well. These immense cities lie basking on the beaches of the continent like whales that have taken to the land again. What do these great, sleek, well-fed creatures live on so sumptuously? That is the

question that intrigues the visitor from overseas on his
arrival at this elusive continent's rim.

I expected to read the answer when I took the air from
Sydney airport, travelling north. Surely, as soon as the
suburbs ended, the pastures and the wheat-fields would
begin. But what did begin, when at last the suburbs abruptly
faded out, was an uninhabited expanse of bush, without a
road or a house in view. And this wilderness of trees looked as
if it might be left in its virgin state for all time; for the
country that it covered was a maze of hills dissected by
steep-sided, winding ravines. Now, though, we were crossing
the dividing range, somewhere near the head of the Hunter
Valley. This was, I had been told, one of the historic routes
into the interior that had been followed by the first generation
of pioneers; so in a moment, surely, I should be setting eyes
on the real Australia. This real Australia, out of which the
six capital cities make their living, is shaped like the cradle
of civilization in the Middle East. It is a fertile crescent,
bounded on its concave side by the Central Desert and on its
convex side by a loop of mountains bending round the
contour of the East Australian coast all the way from Cape
York to the hinterland of Melbourne. This boomerang-
shaped Australia, on the western slope of the mountains,
produces most of the continent's wool and wheat and much of
its minerals too. And, sure enough, when we crossed the
divide, the livestock and the fields came into view as our
little plane flew on over the landscape. When we came to
earth on a landing-strip on an open plain, I felt that I was at
last seeing Australian life. If it was as real as this at Gun-
nedah, it must indeed be the real thing at Tamworth, which
was our destination. So you can imagine my disappointment
when, on taking the air again, the plane swung round,
fluttered back to the foot of the hills, and shot us into a car
which transported us back to the eastern slope of the watershed.

From then on, the real Australia continued to dodge us.
Baulked of meeting her on the western plains, we hoped to
catch her on the New England plateau, which is also a

notable sheep and cattle country. A hospitable invitation took us from Armidale to a famous upland sheep station; but, as we arrived, the rain came down in a deluge which reduced visibility to zero. Even the luminous white countenances of the Herefordshire cattle hardly glimmered through the downpour. Our next opportunity seemed to be coming when, a week later, we found ourselves in a car travelling from Cooma towards the southern foot of Mount Kosciusko. Turn the corner and we should be entering the basin of the Murray River, which is the greatest of Australia's western waters. But in that instant our car swerved to the right and diverted us to the headwaters of the Snowy River, which flows, not into the interior, but down to the Pacific coast. In a year or two the magnificent engineering works that we were being taken to see would have made the waters of the Snowy flow inland instead of coastward, to irrigate rich but thirsty soils in the Riverina after providing, on its descent, enough hydro-electric power to supply the whole of New South Wales. But, since the tunnels that were being driven through the mountains were not yet complete, we were still on the coastal side of the watershed. Canberra, of course, is on the inland side; but the lovely skyline of the circle of hills in which the city is set most effectively debars one here from catching even a glimpse of the great western plains towards which the local river is racing.

By this time I was beginning to fear that the nearest that I should ever come to a sight of the real Australia would be the spectacle on the top floor of Dalgety's wool-warehouse by the riverside at Brisbane. Wandering through the rows of opened sample bales, I had been reading on their tickets the romantic names of the sheep stations in the Queensland 'outback' from which these golden fleeces had been gathered in. On the concave edge of the fertile boomerang, where it shades off into the desert, there might be sustenance for only one sheep per acre, but, at that minimal density of sheep population, there were acres enough to fill this capacious warehouse, and others like it, in Brisbane; and Brisbane is only one of Australia's wool-marts. Here I was fingering the

provender on which one of the six capital cities lived; and
even here I was catching the clip only just before it was
going to vanish over the Equator. A few minutes earlier, in
the Brisbane wool exchange, I had been listening to the
buyers bidding against one another at greyhound speed for
these precious lots. The bids rose by one farthing a time, and
each time thousands of pounds might have been gained or
lost. Here, in the warehouse, by the bales, stood presses,
waiting, like guillotines, to reduce the bales to half their
present size; and there, across the road, at the quayside, lay
the ships that were then to carry this cargo to the English or
French or Japanese manufacturers, for whom the buyers had
been acting. I had learned how Brisbane throve; but here,
on the brink of the Ocean, I felt nearer to Bradford than to
Longreach.

When, yesterday, on Canberra airfield, I climbed into
the plane under an overcast sky, I was in a mood of resigna-
tion. Before the plane deposited us at Melbourne, it would
have carried us over the south-west corner of the Australian
fertile crescent, but, no doubt, we should fly blind. Even
this unpressurized plane would fly high enough to make
certain of that. And, indeed, we lost sight of the ground after
one tantalizing glimpse of the Murrumbidgee River seeking
its way through the hills. We crossed the dividing range in a
blanket of cloud; and more than half our journey was already
behind us when suddenly the cloud parted and dispersed;
and there, under a clear blue sky, was the Murray River
pouring out of the Hume Reservoir, past the town of Albury,
into a level plain that stretched away and away to the
northern horizon.

In an instant my mind's eye had travelled on, over
steppeland and downland, to Longreach and beyond. I
had set eyes on the fertile crescent at last. But, even now, the
elusive continent was doing its utmost to cheat me of my view.
The plain that is normally a thirsty land, crying out for an
extra dole of water for its parched fields and pastures, was
half submerged yesterday under floods of an unprecedented
volume. Though our south-westerly course quickly bore us

away from the Murray River at a wide angle, one could see the river's swollen reaches gleaming in the sunshine, miles out in the plain, while, below us, there was a tragic spectacle of waterlogged paddocks, half-drowned farmsteads and townships, and vehicles immobilized on the Hume Highway, which is the main road between Melbourne and Sydney.

Nature in Australia may not be so terrifying as she is on the Amazon or in the Andes; but, though she is not grim, she is obstinately disobliging. On this side of the South Pacific, as on that, she is determined not to let herself ever just be taken for granted.

13. Overland

How is one to take the measure of a country? Certainly not by flying over it. The more competent the plane, the more effectively it defeats your purpose by hoisting you into the stratosphere and quite breaking your contact with the Earth. The best measure is a pair of human legs; the next best is the back of a mule; and these are grand ways of making oneself intimate with, say, Greece. But Australia is a continent, and man and mule power have their limits; so let us compromise by taking the trains from Adelaide to Perth: 'trains', not 'train', because en route one changes, *diminuendo*, from South Australian broad gauge to Commonwealth standard gauge, and from that to Western Australian three foot six.

At Adelaide one is already about two-fifths of the way from east to west; and, as one slides out of the station there, it is exhilarating to reckon that one has still nearly a two-days' journey to go before running up against the Indian Ocean. Take New Zealand's top dressing and spread it on an Australian landscape. This gives you a picture of the country as far as the broad-gauge terminus. The vast undulating green expanses are packed with sheep almost as

tight as the little New Zealand paddocks. The South
Australian farmer has made a fine art of cultivating delectable varieties of grass, and it is fascinating to watch the grass-
crop rippling in the breeze with the afternoon sun lighting
it up and the ewes and their lambs revelling in it. On the
map of Australia this paradise is a minute oasis. You could
whizz over it by plane without even being aware of its
existence. But the revealing railway journey takes a whole
afternoon, and the sun is low by the time one reaches the
standard-gauge railhead at Port Pirie. By the time we are
off again in the Commonwealth transcontinental train, the
light is fading. Will it hold out long enough to let one see
where and how the grass dies away?

As we make from Port Pirie for Port Augusta, the sun is
setting over a long narrow gulf of the southern sea. The sky
turns crimson; the water turns the blazing blue colour of the
fringes of the coral along the Great Barrier Reef; and at that
moment the pastures shrivel. On the left they change into a
salt marsh, on the right into a blasted heath. And now,
between sunset and moonrise, all the ways are dark. One
might as well have dinner and go to bed.

What will the Moon bring to light? The endless bare
plain, of which one has heard so much? The Moon is up
when I wake from my first sleep; and, as I look out eagerly
I feel a pang of disappointment at seeing, not desert, but
bush. True, this bush holds out a promise of the desert, for
the trees are sparse and squat. Yet, every time that I wake
and look out again expectantly, the bush is still with us, till,
in disgust, I let sleep conquer me, and miss the dawn.
When I wake next, it is already broad daylight, and here,
at last, is what I have come to see: flat red earth stretching
away to the horizon, with tufts of grey-green growths
flecking it here and there, but not a tree in sight—not even a
stunted one. The learnèd pioneer who gave this plain its
Latin name 'Nullarbor' was not romancing.

Nothing is less monotonous than empty space. It soothes
the senses and sets the imagination free. The Pacific Ocean,
the Siberian forest, the Lincolnshire fenlands all have this

magic influence. And now I am feeling it once more on the Nullarbor Plain.

Through the whole of the morning and half the afternoon, the tufted red expanse went on opening out in front of us and fading away behind our rolling wheels. Nothing changed except when, once in every hour or two, we passed a row of half-a-dozen houses and a water tank. 'Cook', 'Hughes', 'Reid', 'Haig': such monosyllabic place-names are just the right ones for these pin-points of human life on the map of the wilderness. The rhythm of the journey is so regular that it begins to have an hypnotic effect. But something must be going to break the trance, for this evening we are to reach Kalgoorlie, and to-morrow we shall be in Perth. What is that, far away over the plain, that is catching my eye and knocking at the door of my consciousness? The object that stands out so portentously against the void is a shrub, not much more than twice the height of the ever-lastingly recurrent grey-green tufts. But that shrub is the beginning of the end. Within ten minutes we have passed two more shrubs, within seven minutes more a bush, five and a half minutes later a dwarf gum tree, and now, all around us, the bush is asserting itself again. It has swallowed up the plain before the Sun sets for the second time upon our journey. The Nullarbor is undoubtedly now behind us, and we feel a pang of regret. The inside of one day is not nearly long enough to give us our fill of this enchanting experience. If we had a second day and a third day of the Nullarbor to look forward to, we should not complain. But these nostalgic thoughts are suddenly cut short by a characteristically Australian transformation scene. The nocturnal bush abruptly gives way to arc lights, sidings, gasometers, and hotels, and we are in Kalgoorlie station, changing from four foot eight and a half to three foot six.

These changes of gauge are one of the amenities of railway travel in Australia for anyone whose aim in travelling is, not to arrive, but to see what lies on his way. An aeroplane would never dream of being so obliging. Between trains we have time to walk out into the broad streets of this extraordinary mining town, which lives on water pumped through a pipe from reservoirs more than 350 miles away to the westward. In 'the golden mile' at Kalgoorlie, every other building is a bank with 'licenced purchasers of gold' engraved on a gigantic brass plate.

The builders of the three-foot-six-gauge rolling stock are magicians. They have built sleeping-berths, crosswise to the train, that give comfortable head and foot room for a five-foot-ten-and-a-half man. My feet must be sticking out beyond the rails on one side and my head on the other; yet I have never slept more soundly. So I wake up late, to find myself among green fields again. How tame. What a pity. If only I could have yesterday morning back.

14. A Radiant Wilderness

'A town like Alice?' No, Alice herself is the little town that spreads out below us as we mount the top of Anzac Hill. Just half a dozen parallel streets, flanked on one side by a belt of trees that marks the course of the Todd River (Todd was Alice's surname). On the surface the river flows only once or twice a year; but the trees declare that there is perennial water not far below the sands of the now dry river-bed. Alice Springs is a tiny town, yet it is a miniature capital, complete with residency, public library, schools, hotels, and shopping centre. It is, indeed, the metropolis of all the southern half of Australia's huge Northern Territory; and the Territory's thin-spread and far-flung inhabitants come into 'the Alice' from hundreds of miles away to do their business and to see the world. The majority of Australians are, of course, huddled together in the six state capitals on the coast, and for them this oasis in the heart of the continent is as legendary a name as it is to the visitor from England. Most Australians live and die without ever setting eyes on Alice Springs—though quite a number of them will have managed to see San Francisco, New York,

London, Paris, and Florence. One is always tempted to leave the sights in one's own country till the last. I myself, for instance, had seen the Great Wall of China before seeing Salisbury Cathedral or Stonehenge, though I went to school at Winchester and have lived all my life in London.

As I lift my eyes from the town to the surrounding ring of mountains, this morning's bleak drive, before a winter's dawn, to Melbourne airport from the Menzies Hotel seems like a dream. That dawn might have been in London, while this oasis might be in Sa'udi Arabia. Only in Australia could the Alice and Melbourne lie in the same continent, and within one short day's flight of one another. The mountains are not Alpine or Andean, but they make up for their diminutive stature by their brilliant colour and arresting outline. In the sunlight they shine bright pink, in the shade they glow deep blue, and their gaunt bare shoulders and serrated crests rival the shapeliness of the mountains of Greece. As we approached them, against the sun, this afternoon, driving into town from the local airfield, a gap opened in the deep blue wall, to let us into the charmed circle within which 'the Alice' lies. And now we are driving towards the sunset along a dusty winding bush-road—the real Australia at last. We are racing the sunset, but we have eighty-five miles westward travelling to do; and, though the N.T.A. Government's representative, who is conducting us, has the skill to traverse bush-roads at an average of forty miles an hour, the night has overtaken us before we draw rein at Hermannsberg Mission.

This work of Christian charity for the Australian aborigines was started by the German-Australian Lutherans in South Australia. Their forefathers left Germany about 120 years ago, in protest against the Prussian Government's high-handed amalgamation of the Lutheran Church in Prussia with the Calvinist Church. The present generation— including the Pastor at Hermannsberg and his family—are still bilingual. Theirs is a labour of love, and its visible fruits are the well-established school and the newly rising hospital. It is a deed of mercy to break the impact of our

steam-roller civilization on the natives by giving them
something of the Western World's gentler side. The children,
dancing along merrily through sun and sand, tell the tale of
the Mission in dumbshow. Their bodies look frail, but their
spirits are merry. In supporting the Hermannsberg Mission's
work, one could be quite sure that one was doing active
good.

The next day's drive takes us in a two-hundred-and-sixty-
mile sweep—west, north, and east—from Hermannsberg to
Aileron on 'the bitumen'. That is the local name for the
tarmac road that, during the Second World War, was laid
down all the way from Alice Springs to Darwin, the Northern
Territory's capital city and principal port. But today we are
still travelling along bush-roads via Haast Bluff and the
Derwent River and Mount Wedge. This Derwent's dry bed
recalls none of its English namesakes, but the radiant carpet
of wildflowers that stretches away in all directions to the
horizon outshines the colours of an English spring. The
prevailing colour here is the yellow of the 'daisies' (a larger
kind and a smaller). The rest is everlastings (some a glistening
white, some a delicate pale purple). This field of the cloth of
gold—spread on a bright red ground—stretches away and
away through the parkland of scattered gum trees, and the
bright red bush-road twists and turns to dodge, here a
mountain and there just a tree, and then dips to cross the
bed of a creek. We have indeed been lucky in our timing;
for in the wet season any one of these now dry creek beds
might be filled by a roaring torrent, while in the dry season
there might be nothing but grey green spinifex grass under
the trees. The flowers are the gift of a gentle shower that
blessed this thirsty soil a few days ago. A week from now they
will have withered, perhaps not to appear again for another
five or six years. But we have seen them in their glory today.
To Melburnian or Adelaidian eyes, they are a less familiar
sight than an English bluebell wood.

This is a living desert; for, though sustenance for life
is spread very thin on the ground, the ground itself is so
incredibly extensive that the total of its insect, reptile, bird,

and mammalian population tots up to surprisingly large figures. One mosquito every cubic foot, one lizard every five square yards, one flock of startled whirring budgerigars every acre, one quarter of a head of cattle every square mile, one homestead at thirty-mile intervals along the road: ascertain the overall area of the Northern Territory and work out these sums. The result will take you aback.

This twisting turning journey through the sunshine and the flowers is intoxicatingly beautiful. 'The bitumen', running dead straight for hundreds of miles without a swerve, is an impressive symbol of the modern world. Yet, as our wheels take to it joyfully on the morning of the third day, our hearts leave the bush-road with a twinge of regret. May I live to make that entrancing two-days' journey once again.

15. Crossing the Line

In this Wanderjahr 1956 I have crossed the Equator six times between the 12th March and the 14th September: twice in South America, once in mid-Pacific, and three times within one week in Indonesia. But there is nothing in that, for the two sides of the Equator are as monotonously like one another as a pair of identical twins, in whatever longitude you may happen to be making your transit. Nor am I talking here of 'the Wallace line' between the gum trees and marsupial mammals of Australasia and the standard flora and fauna of the rest of the World. This dramatic line has, I have been told, now been diffused into a graduated zone by the researches of later naturalists who may not have possessed Alfred Russel Wallace's genius, but who have outtopped that Victorian giant by standing on his and one another's shoulders. I did cross this 'Wallace Zone' on the flight about which I am writing; but this is not the line that made me aware of its significance that morning. The line that hit me in the eye and made my heart leap up was the boundary between the New World and the Old World. In the New

World, civilization, which is now five generations old in the latitude of Sydney, is still no more than three generations old in Northern Australia. But Indonesia, where the Old World sags down into the Southern Hemisphere, has yielded one of the earliest yet known specimens of the human race; and Java Man has been followed on his inviting island by representatives of all subsequent stages of human culture. The line that I was crossing was a cultural divide. To the south of it, civilization is still only 150 years old; to the north of the line its age is numbered in millennia.

In an airliner the passage of the intervening straits is extraordinarily swift. After rising from Port Darwin airfield and losing sight of the northern coast of Australia I settled down to read the first four chapters of the Gospel according to Saint John and then to write three short letters of thanks for hospitality. There is plenty of time, I was thinking, before I need look out of the window again, when, to my astonishment, I saw that we were treading on the toe of Timor, the easternmost island of the main Indonesian chain. With a backward glance I could see the grassy slopes of the Timor mountains drifting away behind us to the north-east, just as they had been described to me by a countryman of mine who had had the good fortune to explore them. I must have been looking right across the frontier between the Indonesian Republic and the Portuguese Empire, which divide Timor between them. How dully flat, by comparison, is the islet named Roti on our left. But soon we are passing between Sumba and Flores—a row of mountain tops, rising out of the sea, where the local Indonesian princes still wear six-teenth-century Portuguese morions as part of their gala dress. And now on our right, visible between Flores and Sumbawa, a perfectly shaped volcano rises sheer out of the sea—one of the many bearing the name Gunung Api ('mountain of fire'). We are passing over one of the most tormented sections of that world-encompassing chain of folded and erupting mountains that runs from New Zealand via the Himalayas, Alps, and Appennines to Cape Finisterre.

But are we yet in the Old World? As we skim over the great

bay in the bosom of Sumbawa, the visibility is providentially clear (I am now viewing the scene from a point of vantage in the aircraft's cockpit). Sky and sea are of an ethereal blue, half drowned in golden sunlight; and I observe, to my surprise, that the island below me is as bare and lifeless as Central Australia. Where, then, do we cross the historic line between the untamed wilderness and the cultivated fields that Homer calls 'the Works of Man' *par excellence*? As we slide between the peak of bare Sumbawa on our right and the higher peak of inaccessible Lombok on our left, the blanket of tropical cloud begins to close in. Far to the left, over there, a lofty volcano is just lifting its nose above the cloud fleece, and I know that I am setting eyes on Gunung Agung in Bali. Shall I set eyes on Java too before these malicious clouds quite veil the landscape? For an age— so I feel it, in my impatience—we head across open waters, and then suddenly the low-lying fields of Madura spread themselves out on our right, and the plane flits over the Javanese port and city of Surabaya.

A great city and a busy port: one can see half a dozen to match these in Australia. But the hinterland of the Australian cities is the desolate bush, while the hinterland of Surabaya is a web of rice-fields embroidered with villages embowered in cocoanut-palm plantations. Here are 'the Works of Man' again at last. It is four months now since I had my last air-sight of the terraced mountain-sides of Peru; and now I find myself once more in a world in which Man coaxes Nature with inexhaustible love and labour, instead of coercing her as he does in Australia and North America. In Java I am in the same world as in Lombardy or in Holland.

I feast my eyes on those tiers of rice-trays, with the hurrying clouds reflected in their still waters. This ancient land is oozing with water and teeming with life. Here come two broad, sluggish rivers, writhing out of the southern mountains of Java like gigantic boa-constrictors. The dividing line between wet and dry is as sharp, and as apparently capricious, as the line between Ancient and Modern. At

Tennent Creek, only the day before yesterday, they drove us seven miles out of town just to look at two stagnant pools of water standing in the elsewhere empty creek-bed. Tennent Creek is a town whose 1,300 inhabitants extracted minerals worth £4,000,000 (Australian) within the last calendar year. If they could buy a tithe of Eastern Java's surplus water, it would be worth their while to pay for it with half the gold that they dig out of Noble's Knob for a futile re-burial in the bowels of Fort Knox. Perhaps, one day, Man will harness atomic energy to the Aeolian task of pulling the clouds about more rationally, for human purposes, than Nature's caprice misdirects them. And then Indonesia may make a comfortable living by watering vast Australian rice-fields. But this is 'music of the future'. The line across which I flew on the 23rd August, 1956, is still as real a frontier as ever it was for both culture and cultivation.

16. The Land where the Religions are Good Neighbours

For the young Republic of Indonesia, life is not easy in this first chapter of her experience of independence, and Indonesians in responsible positions speak frankly to the foreign visitor of the problems with which they are having to cope. Eleven years ago Indonesia suddenly took her place as one of the sovereign independent states of the modern world. But, unlike India, for example, she had to assume this exacting rôle without previous apprenticeship or preparation. By the time when India attained full independence in 1947, Indians had already had the benefit of 30 years of 'Indianization'. The British decision to give India self-government had been taken in 1917, and, since then, the British Government had been progressively transferring power and responsibility from British to Indian hands. The Dutch, on the other hand, seem never to have intended or expected to give up their rule

over Indonesia. At any rate, they did little to help the
Indonesians to equip themselves in advance for the task of
managing their own country. So Indonesia has had to start
life woefully understaffed. Administrators, engineers, doctors,
teachers—all are in short supply; and consequently a heavy
burden is now weighing upon the few pairs of shoulders that
are competent to carry it. This handful of leading men and
women have to do double work. They have to keep the
country going from day to day, and at the same time they
have to train up the rising generation to assist them and
eventually to replace them. There is a thirst for education.
The young people and their families make great personal
sacrifices for the sake of obtaining it; and this is auspicious
for Indonesia's future. But it adds to the load that the
leaders are bearing now.

This problem of personnel would be enough in itself for
any nation to wrestle with, but it is by no means the only
grave difficulty confronting Indonesia today. There is also
the problem of the uneven distribution of her population.
Perhaps as much as five-eighths of the country's eighty
million inhabitants are huddled together on the com-
paratively small island of Java. The congestion here is
becoming worse as the improvement in public hygiene
brings down the death-rate. Can the Javanese and Balinese
peasantry be induced to migrate to Borneo or Sumatra?
And, if they can, how is this migration to be organized and
financed? Then, again, there is the very controversial issue of
administrative centralization versus devolution. In non-
Javanese Indonesian eyes, centralization means a Javanese
hegemony, and there is an active revolt against this on some
of the islands—in Sulawesi (Celebes), for example, and at the
north-western end of Sumatra, in Atjeh. Most formidable,
perhaps, of all is the problem of the Chinese middleman and
shopkeeper, a problem that Indonesia shares with Malaya,
Thailand, Vietnam, and the Philippines. It is therefore
fortunate that a country which is beset by so many difficulties
is at any rate free from one of Mankind's worst evils: religious
strife.

The world religions—Buddhism, Christianity, Hinduism, Islam—have conferred immense spiritual benefits on the human race during these first few thousand years of their presence among us; and we may guess that the future, too, will belong to them and not to Nationalism, Communism, Fascism, Socialism, or any of our other modern secular ideologies. But in one respect the 'higher' religions have brought calamity on the World and discredit on themselves: they have seldom been content to live and let live, side by side; and their attempts to eliminate one another have been responsible for some of the bitterest conflicts and cruellest atrocities that have ever disgraced Man's history. In this, the two world religions of Jewish origin, Christianity and Islam, have been the worst offenders; but Hinduism, and even Buddhism, have not been guiltless. It is therefore remarkable, and encouraging, to find three of these religions living together amicably in Indonesia today.

At least ninety per cent of the total present population of Indonesia is Muslim, with the remaining ten per cent divided between Christianity, Hinduism, and a remnant of primitive paganism. For a considerable time past, Indonesia has contributed the largest of the national contingents to the annual Muslim pilgrimage to Mecca and Medina; and the costliness of the performance of this religious duty is evidence that the pilgrim takes his religion seriously. Yet, for a devoutly Muslim country, Indonesia is most unusually tolerant. When you walk about in Djakarta or any other large Indonesian city, the most conspicuous places of worship are Christian churches, not Islamic mosques (the mosques are hidden away in the side-streets, as the Catholic 'chapels' are in Dublin). Then, when Friday comes, you find that this is only a half-holiday; the weekly whole-holiday is not the Muslim day of rest; it is the Christian Sunday; and the Indonesian national language is written in the Roman alphabet of the vulgate and vernacular Bible, not in the Arabic alphabet of the Qur'an. The Indonesian national airlines call themselves Garuda, not Boraq. What other Islamic country has been as easy-going as this? And why is

Indonesian Islam so bright an exception to the prevalent
Islamic spirit and practice?

Part of the explanation lies in the historical fact that
Indonesia became a Muslim country, not through a military
conquest, but by a peaceful and gradual process of conversion—and this no longer ago than the sixteenth and
seventeenth centuries of the Christian Era. Islam settled
here as a thin top-dressing on a deep rich soil of Hinduism,
and the older and more catholic-minded religion still shows
through. An Indonesian Muslim's first name will be Arabic,
but his second name will be Sanskrit. Even in so self-
consciously Muslim a district as Minangkabau, in the
highlands of Central Sumatra, the habit of taking Sanskrit
second names survives. Indonesian Muslims celebrate the
Prophet Muhammad's birthday (if you refer to it as the
Mawlid, they know what you mean, though they themselves
call it by a Malay name). But the celebration here takes the
rather shocking form of an all-night puppet-show in which
the figures and the scenes are taken, not from the Prophet's
biography, but from the Mahabharata. Arjuno and Krishna,
not Hamzah or Khalid, are the heroes that have the hold
upon Indonesian Muslims' feelings and imaginations. These
are indeed unconventional adherents of Islam; and you
have only to cross the narrow strait between the eastern
end of Java and Bali to find Hinduism still on the surface
without even a perfunctory Islamic veneer. Here every house
has its family temple and every village its community
temple. There are shrines to house the images of the Hindu
gods, and tabernacles to receive their worshippers' offerings.
The Balinese Hindus are a tiny minority; but their Muslim
fellow-countrymen have never sought to coerce them. In
this vital matter of religious tolerance, Indonesia has set
an example that the rest of us would do well to follow.

17. Borobudur

There, there it is—that consummate work of Buddhist art which I have so often gazed upon longingly in photographs. The obliging pilot of the Garuda plane has gone out of his way to wheel round the stupa-crowned hill of Borobudur en route from Djakarta to Jogja. Though he is travelling as slowly as he can, the vision has come and gone in a flash; yet, even if I had been condemned to enjoy no more than this single Pisgah-sight, that would have repaid me for having come more than half-way round the World. Thanks, however, to the hospitality of the Gadjah Mada University at Jogjakarta, I am to see this Wonder of the World again, and this time from the ground; and when, two mornings later, we take the northward road by car, I find myself keyed up to a more thrilling sense of expectancy than at any moment on my present pilgrimage since my approach to Cuzco over the Andean watershed.

For the first four-fifths of our forty-kilometre drive, the cottages, nestling among cocoa-nut palms, jostle one another so closely along both sides of the road that one can hardly catch a glimpse even of the rice-fields behind their backyards. But at last we swerve leftwards out of the great north road that runs on to Semarang. The plain begins to undulate; and we are heading towards a range of mountains that rivals anything in Central Australia or in Greece for the beauty of its outline. The professor who is conducting us suddenly points towards the middle distance. And there is Borobudur again, standing in its natural setting, which neither air-view nor photograph can display, though the harmony between Man's architecture and Nature's land-scape is the making of this masterpiece of artistry.

Borobudur is a four-sided pyramid, built up in tiers of balustraded terraces round a natural eminence. Each terrace runs between two continuous bands of reliefs, depicting scenes from the legend of the Buddha. Some of these are old and familiar friends—for instance, that square-rigged ship scudding before the breeze. But the reliefs must wait. Before I pore over them I must mount to the summit and view the whole monument as the architect meant it to be viewed, with the green lawns at its foot, the forest-clad mountain for a drop scene at the back, and the glassy rice-fields embroidering the fertile plain to the east. Wild Nature; Nature tamed by Man; the genius of the architect and the sculptor; the earthly life of the blessed Redeemer of all sentient beings: here is a comprehensive poem about the mystery of the Universe, a symphony of the inaudible music of the spheres.

How am I to convey this ineffable poetry to your mind's eye? If your native city is Peking, try to imagine the Altar of Heaven magnified manifold without forfeiting any of its beauty. If you are a Londoner you must attempt a more difficult feat of imagination. You must transfigure the Albert Memorial by magnifying it, too, manifold and also trans-figuring its hideousness into loveliness. Yet, do what one will, no prescription of mine can convey to you the interplay between the monument and the landscape. If only I could exchange soul and body with one of those Hindu-minded Javanese Muslims who spend night after night here in contemplation. Then I might be able to incorporate Borobudur into my innermost being and carry it with me as 'a possession for ever'—in defiance of the precepts of the Buddhist philosophy that Borobudur expresses. Which shall I choose? The detail of the reliefs or the panoramic view? Well, I can always go on studying the reliefs in a picture-book in my study in Kensington, so I will spend the rest of this all too brief half-morning in gazing alternately, from the summit of the stupa, at the rising mountain and the reclining plain.

Do you challenge my adoration of Borobudur? Do you tell me that its rhythm is ultra-baroque? Do you prefer the classic severity of the neighbouring Buddhist shrine at Mendut, or the animation of the reliefs round the Shaiva temple at Prambanan, where the hero is, not Gautama, but Rama? You might perhaps convince my mind, but you could never change my feelings. Borobudur holds my heart: it is a holy of holies for me, on a par with the Sacro Speco and the Sainte Chapelle. As the stupa-crowned hill disappears behind the palm groves, I crane my neck round to take a wistful farewell look at it. In a trice I am engulfed among the 8,000 university students and the 40,000 secondary schoolchildren of Jogjakarta, all mounted, Dutch-wise, on bicycles. 'Fled is that music: Do I wake or sleep?'

18. The Island of Hope

We had risen early to catch our plane, and, after peering down at a fascinating fretwork of islets below us, and then gazing out into the open ocean through a break in the land to our left, I must have fallen asleep. When I woke again and looked out of the window, I wondered whether I was dreaming still. For what could be more unlike Java than the scene that now met my eyes? An interminable flat jungle, with the timber standing so thick that the white skeletons of the dead trees had no room to fall. And then those broad, sluggish, curving rivers, with some of their older loops capriciously abandoned and converted into crescent-shaped lakes. Where could this be but in the Amazon basin? Was I once again approaching the Peruvian river-port Pucallpa, with a transit of the Andes just behind me? No, I had merely made the transit from Western Java to South-Eastern Sumatra; and that short flight across the sea had carried me from an old world of congested cities and rice-fields into a new world whose only present human tenants are a few tiny hunting and food-gathering tribes living the primitive life of the Amazonian Indians.

For a rash moment, I longed for engine-trouble to bring our plane fluttering down among the tree-screened savages, chimpanzees, rhinoceroses, tigers, crocodiles, and boa-constrictors. It was tantalizing to realize that I was within just a few thousand feet of all this hidden wild life. But on second thoughts I was relieved to find us holding our north-westward course over the unchanging jungle, hour after hour. Unchanging? Just when I was beginning to feel that the trees might never end, the landscape opened up, and 'the Works of Man' reasserted themselves. What are those great straw-gabled buildings set at regular intervals at an acute angle to the road? Are they the community-houses of some antique people? They turn out to be prosaic modern tobacco-drying barns, and in a moment we are skimming over the city of Medan and coming down to earth, not among the jungle fauna, but in a modern airport near the north-west end of this vast virgin Indonesian island.

'This is the island of hope,' said the official of the provincial government who received us. 'It has only ten million inhabitants, and already it produces nearly half the total revenue of the Indonesian Republic.' This officer was a Batak, from the highlands that I was to visit next day; and, when we exchanged cards, we found, to our mutual surprise. that we had been baptized with the same Christian name. The Bataks are one of three notable peoples whose home is the hill-country overhanging Sumatra's south-west coast. They are Protestant Christians; and, though there are only two and a half million of them, I was told by a representative of the Church of England in Singapore that the Batak Church has more theological students in training than are to be found in all the Anglican theological colleges in Britain. The Bataks' north-western and south-eastern neighbours are ardent Muslims. The north-western tip of Sumatra is the redoubtable fastness of Atjeh, where the Dutch never succeeded in establishing themselves, and where the Indon-esian Government's writ does not yet run. The Atchinese are formidable fighters. The Muslims of Minangkabau, in the highlands of Central Java, are efficient and enterprising businessmen. They are the one element in the Indonesian nation that holds its own in business against the Chinese. At

Bukatinggi, the chief town of Minangkabau and the provincial capital of Central Java, you see few names in Chinese characters over the shops. The Minangkabau Muslims and the Batak Christians might become the nucleus of a native Indonesian commercial middle-class; and this is one of Indonesia's crying needs.

When one takes the road from Medan westward to Lake Toba in the Batak highlands, one travels for a whole morning through neat and prosperous plantations of tobacco, sugar-cane, rubber trees, and vegetable oil palms, with factories on the spot for processing the produce. This region was opened up by Dutch pioneers some eighty or ninety years ago, and there seems to be no reason why the whole of the low-lying north-eastern side of Sumatra, over which I flew from Djakarta to Medan, should not likewise be transformed from a wilderness into a garden. At the south-eastern end of Sumatra, this transformation has already begun. Here, round Palembang, are Indonesia's principal oil-fields, and the neighbouring forests and marshes are being reclaimed for agriculture by peasant immigrants from Java and Bali. Sumatra's destiny is to become a greater and more prosperous Java, with a lower density of population and a higher tension of human energy.

In the Batak and Minangkabau highlands there is a fascinating mixture of modern activities with traditional manners and customs. The Batak family house is a Noah's Ark perched on massive scaffolding, with sharply upward-curving gable-ends. A Minangkabau family house may have as many as six gable-ends if the lady-mother has four married daughters living with her. In Minangkabau the inheritance of property is through the female line—a remarkable survival of customary law in a self-consciously Muslim country—and the bridegroom is housed by his mother-in-law. Those curving Minangkabau and Batak roofs used, once upon a time, to be thatched with straw; but, today, thatch is almost as rare in Sumatra as it is in Australia, and these two great south-sea islands have now come literally under the same roof. The typical Australian and Sumatran roof today is made of sheets of corrugated iron; but the Sumatran architects have coaxed this drab material into shapes which would enliven the cities of Australia if the Australian architects were to take this leaf out of modern Sumatra's book. In Sumatra the artists in corrugated iron have learnt how to follow every twist and turn of the carpenter and the thatcher whom they have superseded. They can even turn you out a corrugated-iron dome for your village mosque. Tomorrow, no doubt, they will be reproducing the same traditional motifs in plastics.

The south-west Sumatran highlands are not high by Central or South American standards. Yet, as you wind your way up the forest-clad gorges on to the cultivated plateaux, overhung by craters and interspersed with crater lakes, you pass out of the tropics into the temperate zone. Here is the breeding ground of the active and upstanding race that could do much for the whole of Indonesia. Oil, soil, and toil are the three blessings of 'the island of hope', and toil—the energy and enterprise of her highlanders—is the greatest blessing of the three.

19. The Chinese Tide in South-East Asia

How long do restorations last? Well, the restored Stuarts in England lasted twenty-eight years; the restored Bourbons in France,.fifteen; the restored French in Indochina, eight (in so far as they made any headway at all against the Vietmin resistance movement); the Dutch restoration in Indonesia lasted no time at all (it was called off before it had got under way). So what is the expectation of life for the British restoration in Singapore and Malaya? These thoughts coursed through my mind as I found myself, for the second time in my life, crossing the causeway between the island and the continent. My first trip from Singapore to Johore had been made twenty-seven years ago, and meanwhile those two initial letters—'H.D.'—had entirely changed their meaning. In 1929 'H.D.' had spelled 'Homo Dominator', alias 'Homo Occidentalis Invictus Kiplingi'. But, since I first passed this way, the same causeway has witnessed the military débacle in which 'H.D.' had his great fall; and all the king's horses and men cannot set Humpty Dumpty up again permanently. They have managed to put him back on his perch for the moment, but how long can this precarious restoration be expected to last?

Like Napoleon and other militarists in the past, the Japanese in the Second World War made history, not for themselves, but for unintended beneficiaries; and, in all the countries temporarily included in the short-lived Japanese 'Co-prosperity Sphere', the sixty-four-dollar question today is: Who are going to be those foiled Japanese conquerors' eventual heirs? The Japanese made history by demonstrating to the rest of the human race that the Western rulers of Asian and African empires were not the invincible demigods that they had been deemed to be for the last two centuries. British, Dutch, French, and Americans, we all went down like ninepins; and the Americans alone salvaged their military honour out of the common defeat thanks to their dogged defence of Corregidor. The three European Powers were defeated ignominiously. The Portuguese alone kept the West's flag flying over Macao and North-Eastern Timor. The fall of Singapore, after the capitulation of an entire British army, is one of those historic events that are irreversible and ineffaceable.

What was my errand when I was traversing the Singapore-Johore causeway on the 16th September, 1956? I was on my way to attend the opening meeting of a congress in Johore in which a delegation from Indonesia was to confer with a Malay delegation from Malaya. The purpose of the conference was to make progress towards unifying the Malayan and Indonesian variants of a standardized form of the Malay language. Union is strength. Dialects of a common Malay mother-tongue are spoken all the way from the Philippines on the north-east to Madagascar on the south-west. If a hundred million Malay-speakers could stand together, they might perhaps have some chance of holding their ground against 600 million Chinese. But can they? That was the underlying question on the agenda of this Indonesian-Malayan Language and Literature Conference.

'The meek shall inherit the earth.' Military conquerors, Central Asian and European, come and go, but the Chinese shopkeeper perpetually advances without ever receding, and, sooner or later, he brings the Chinese peasant in his train. Three thousand years ago, China was a patch, no bigger than, say, France, astride the lower course of the Yellow River. Five hundred years later, her frontier had reached the southern watershed of the Yangtse. Before the beginning of the Christian Era, 'peaceful penetration' had carried this frontier to Canton. And today, under our eyes, we can watch the ever-flowing Chinese tide rising, inch by inch, over South-East Asia. Singapore may have been founded by British enterprise, but today it is a Chinese city: the future capital of a Chinese 'Co-prosperity Sphere' which is likely to last, because it will have been established by business ability and not by military force. These Chinese shopkeepers are no swashbucklers. They live on the defensive, behind iron shutters and bars, in 'China towns' that are the counterparts of the ghettos of medieval Western Christendom. They are in constant fear of frantic reprisals on the part of the economically incompetent South-East Asian peoples whom they serve and at the same time exploit. They have some anxious moments, but they survive and prosper. Their magnificent schools and tombs are built for eternity, and neither pogroms nor discriminatory legislation can halt the flow of this gentle but persistent Chinese flood.

Vietnam—the anti-Communist southern half of that partitioned country—is perhaps the most gravely threatened of all the states of South-East Asia, and the Vietnamians are a strong-willed people who are determined to survive. Not long ago they passed anti-Chinese laws that remind one of the anti-Jewish laws of Visigothic and medieval Spain.

After a period of from six to twelve months' grace, the Chinese residents in Vietnam are to be excluded from the practice of eleven scheduled professions, and all Chinese born in the country have already been turned officially into Vietnamian nationals. But is not this drastic Vietnamian legislation likely to have a Spanish result? In Spain, when the Jews were forcibly baptized, the result was that, in no time, one out of every three officially Christian Spanish archbishops and grandees was a crypto-Jew. It seems probable that in Vietnam the shopkeeping business, and bigger commercial affairs than that, will remain in the hands of officially Vietnamian crypto-Chinese. European empire-builders and Japanese conquerors and South-East Asian nationalists alike, we have all been working, in spite of ourselves, to further the interests of the insinuating Chinese huckster.

20. A Glimpse of Half Vietnam

As we dropped down-river from Saigon (say 'Say-Gaw'), the twin spires of the Cathedral continued to hold my eye. At each bend of the channel they shifted to and fro along the horizon. But they remained in view till the rice-fields had given way to the virgin jungle-swamp that must have been the Mekong delta's original state of nature. And, when at last their tips disappeared below the wall of trees, the holy mountain of the Caodai religion—an isolated volcanic cone more than a hundred kilometres deeper in the interior—rose up out of the plain. It offered me an alternative land-mark which did not fade out into the dusk until we were dropping our pilot at the headland which flanks the mouth of the Saigon river's estuary.

Those seventy hours in Vietnam had been a gift of the gods; for, not knowing when we were to arrive or how long we were likely to stay, I had not made any arrangements in advance, and the contacts that I did make at the last moment were the result of a happy accident. 'Are you a

diplomatist?' asked the Japanese architect by whose side I
found myself sitting after we had boarded the Messageries
Maritimes S.S. *Cambodge* at Singapore. 'No,' said I, laughing:
'I am an historian.' 'So am I,' said my French neighbour.
'And where?' 'Why, at the Vietnamian National University.'
We exchanged names; my French friend sent off a radio-
gram; and at Saigon, a few hours later, I was being wel-
comed by a representative of the French Mission for Cultural
Co-operation and found myself the guest both of the National
University and of the National Government. Thanks to this
hospitality, I was able to turn those seventy hours to good
account in meeting some notable people and driving out
into the countryside—one day to the Caodai temple at
Tây-Ninh, and another day to a camp of Roman Catholic
Vietnamian refugees from the northern half of the country,
which is now under the Communist régime of the Vietmin.

In Vietnam, pedestrians carry loads in a pair of panniers
slung from the two ends of an elastic wooden yoke balanced
on the bearer's shoulder, and this contrivance has provided a
graphic image of the geographical structure of the country.
One pannier is the delta of the Red River (Tongking); the
other is the delta of the Mekong River (Cochin China).
Most of the population is concentrated in one or other of
these two giant rice-fields. The yoke is represented by a
string of isolated little plains along the intervening coast
(Annam), where the south-easternmost of Asia's mountain
ranges runs north and south along the seaboard. Since peace
was patched up in Indochina the year before last, the northern delta has been relinquished to the Communist World
and the southern delta relinquished to ours. For Vietnam,
as for Korea and for Europe, the partition that has saved the
World, so far, from an atomic war has been a local tragedy.
Yet in Vietnam, as in Europe, the present dividing line is in
accord with both Nature and History. In Europe the line
coincides with the eastern frontier of Charlemagne's empire
and with the western limit of the winter blanket of snow.
In Vietnam it coincides with the climatic boundary between
the tropics and the temperate zone and with an ancient

cultural frontier between a Chinese and a Hindu civilization.

In South Vietnam the only seasonal variation is between
a wet season and a dry one. But North Vietnam, like Europe
and North America, has a winter and a summer, and the
winds that blow from the plateaux of Tibet and Yunnan make
the North Vietnamian winter a severe one. Hence the energy
that once led the northerners to work their way down along
'the Yoke' and capture the Mekong delta for the Vietnamian
race and for the East Asian civilization. The same energy is
being displayed today by the refugees from the North who
have come south, a million strong, to escape from the
Communist régime. About two-thirds of these northern
refugees in the South are Roman Catholic Christians, and the
spirit in the settlement that I visited was remarkable. The
biggest building was the church, the next biggest the school,
the third biggest the silk-weaving factory through which this
community of 11,000 souls now earns part of its living.
The will to live, and to live by self-help, was very evident.
The presiding genius was the curé, who had led his flock on
their trek from their northern home, 1,200 miles away.

The Roman Catholic Church must be proud of what it has
done, and is doing, in Vietnam; for here it has successfully
shaken off its transitory association with the Western World
and has recovered its universality. In Vietnam, Catholicism
is not an instrument of Western ascendency. It has become
what it is in Western Europe: part of the native spiritual
heritage of the indigenous population. The popular religions
of the majority of the Vietnamian peasantry are the Mahayana form of Buddhism and the cult of one's ancestors. In the
past, Vietnam, like China, was administered by Confucian
scholars educated in the Chinese classics. In the tolerant
atmosphere of Eastern Asia the followers of these diverse
religions and philosophies live side by side without rancour.

The Caodai Church is a strange product of the blending of
cultures in a country that has been played upon by influences
from all directions. This is a syncretistic religion, which
recognizes Buddhism, Taoism, Christianity, Islam, and the

philosophies (Greek besides Chinese) as being stages on a
spiritual journey leading up to Caodai-ism as its goal. In
its organization the church is imitative. It has a pope (today
in exile in Cambodia), a college of cardinals (one of them a
woman), and, until last year, it also had a private army (as
the Roman See had till 1870). The road from Saigon to
Tây Ninh (the Caodai Church's Rome) had been put on the
map for me by Graham Greene in an agonizing passage of
The Quiet American; and, as we drove back in the dark,
between French-built blockhouses blown up by Vietmin
guerrillas, I felt glad that I had not attempted to do this
journey in the days before the Vietnam National Army had
re-established law and order. South of the line of partition,
Vietmin and other anti-governmental forces have now
been more or less effectively quelled; and, with French,
American, Canadian, and Australian aid, the young republic
of Vietnam has a chance to show what the Vietnamian
people is capable of accomplishing under a non-Communist
régime.

21. Mercurial Manila

Few cities can have suffered worse than Manila in the
Second World War. The city was taken, and eventually
liberated, by force. The old walled town, Tramuras, a
miniature reproduction of Cartagena de Indias, has been
laid flat. The Cathedral is a shell—San Agostin is the only
one of the principal churches that has survived intact; and,
even there, the beautiful cloisters—reminiscent of the sister
house at Quito—have been sadly knocked about. We were
not unprepared for this spectacle; for, earlier in the morning,
our ship had taken us between blood-soaked Batan Island
and grim Corregidor. Since 1945 we had seen the post-war
plight of Calais and Candia and Vienna and Viterbo, not to
speak of frequent visits to Amen House among the ruins of
the City of London, west of St. Paul's. Such physical havoc

is the fortune of war—though it is a malicious stroke of Fortune's to take so heavy a toll from cities like Manila and Rotterdam, which had no direct concern in the struggle between Great Powers. But in Manila the material destruction was the least horrifying memorial of the savagery that war evokes from the hideous underworld of the human soul.

In Manila the sights that made us shudder were the mass-grave under the pavement of San Agostin and the casemates in Fort Santiago. In San Agostin one can read the long tale of victims: Augustinian and Dominican and Franciscan friars and still more numerous lay men and women and children. In the casemates in Fort Santiago a crowd of civilians was herded together by the Japanese troops during the last hours of their reign of terror. This was a cold-blooded affair. The victims had been told they were being brought here for shelter against the American bombardment of the city, but they had actually been brought in order to be massacred with hand-grenades. On that terrible day one of our two Filipino hosts had been in charge of a hospital in which women and children had taken refuge. Japanese soldiers had burst in and bayoneted every human being whom they could find. There were eighty victims and seven survivors. Our host had been saved through being screened from view by the back of his office desk. Such meaningless and purposeless barbarities are no monopoly of any one race or civilization. While the Japanese were disgracing Asia, the Germans were disgracing Europe by committing identical atrocities. This brutal irrational spirit is the Original Sin that is the common heritage of all Mankind; and our never-ending common task of struggling against it ought to make all the peoples of the Earth humbly aware that they are kinsmen of like passions with one another.

What has been the effect of these awful experiences on the Filipino people? Another nation might have been crushed, but this American-minded Asian nation seems to be irrepressibly resilient. A few days ago the scars of war were reopened by a cyclone which ravaged the South. When we were received by the President, he had just been conferring with the mayors of the devastated districts, who had come to Manila to ask for the National Government's help. The Philippines have also suffered most of the major trials that have afflicted other Asian countries that have been temporarily conquered by the Japanese. The anti-Japanese resistance movement, followed by post-war disorganization and distress, has given an opening to the Communists in the Philippines as well as in Malaya, Vietnam, and Indonesia. President Magsaysay rose to eminence by proving himself to be the man who could quell the Communist movement in the Philippines by a statesmanlike combination of compulsion and persuasion. The Philippines are also faced with the common Asian population problem, and the other common problem of finding the capital for developing the country's latent natural resources (in the Philippines, chromium is one of the most promising of these). The problems are uniform, but the reactions are not. While all the recently liberated Asian countries that I have visited so far are making the same effort to become effective members of the family of modern nations, one is conscious in the Philippines of a vivacity and an optimism that are not so much in evidence in some of the neighbouring countries.

What is the explanation of such striking differences in outlook and spirit? It cannot be a matter of race; for the Filipinos are a branch of the great Malay race to which the Indonesians and the Madagascans also belong. Are the apparent differences in national temperament perhaps due to differences in the cultural influences that have played upon different parts of the far-flung Greater Malayan archipelago? Indonesia has been played upon by Hinduism, Buddhism, Islam, and the Netherlands; the Philippines by Roman Catholic Christianity, Spain, and the United States. The Philippines' cultural history has been both singular and fortunate.

Ever since the maritime nations of Western Europe made themselves temporary rulers of the World by mastering the oceans, the Catholic Church has shown a marvellous capacity for fusing together people of different races. The

Church has done for the Philippines what it has done for the chain of 'Indian American' countries that stretches from Mexico to Peru inclusive. One might describe the Philippines as a Latin American country that has been torn away from the Americas and been swept off to the opposite side of the Pacific by some legendary tidal wave or fabulous hurricane. But the Philippines are unique in having a North American as well as a Spanish chapter in their history—unique and also lucky, because Spain and the United States are complementary to one another as representatives of different elements in the Western Christian civilization.

In their appetite for education the Filipinos outdo even the Vietnamians and the Indonesians. In Manila ten universities, with a total of at least 68,000 students, have re-arisen from the war-time ruins. So there is a demand for all the educational aid that both Spain and America can give. The University of San Tomas has been staffed by Dominican fathers of the Spanish province since its foundation in 1611. The Americans, since 1898, have not only fostered higher education but have also spread primary education throughout the land.

In spite of my affection for America, I have sometimes felt a touch of the same irritation as my fellow Dutchmen, Frenchmen, and Britons at hearing my American friends confidently assert that America has done better by the Philippines than the rest of us Westerners have done by those Asian and African countries that have been temporarily under our rule. My glimpse of the Philippines has changed my feelings about this. The American boast is a proud one, but I believe it is no more than the plain truth.

22. Hongkong Revisited

Yes, here it is again, the faerie landscape that first printed itself on my mind's eye twenty-seven years ago. As I step out on deck, the sun springs up, like a jack-in-the-box, over the eastern horizon and instantly lights up the unforgotten maze of islands, headlands, and channels, with the mountains of the South China mainland bounding the view to the north. That fantastic sky-line is even more jagged than the wave-crests of the choppy sea on the outskirts of tornado 'Ivy'.

On the political stage, this last quarter of a century has been full of sound and fury in these parts. When I passed through Hongkong in 1929, the colony had been in British hands continuously for eighty-seven years, and the rest of China had just been reunited under the rule of the Kuomintang. Between then and now the Japanese conquerors have come and gone; the mountains of Kwantung Province have officially been dyed red; and the fallen British régime in Hongkong has been set up again. But the landscape, as it spreads out before me, looks quite unconscious of Man's vagaries. The changes of political colour have made no physical mark, as far as I can see.

I had no sooner jumped to this conclusion than our ship slipped through the eastern entrance into the harbour; and, as soon as I saw round the corner, it became clear that I had been mistaken. In the amphitheatre between the Peak and the Nine Dragon Mountains, the play of politics had effectively transformed the landscape by trebling the population and consequently setting the builders to work like beavers at Psyche's task. Last time, I had walked off the quay at Kowloon into a tangle of hills with nothing on them but a few tombs here and there. Today those hills are covered with blocks of tenements, and the mushroom city on the mainland stretches away and away, beyond Boundary

Road, into the New Territories, in waves of new buildings
which finally break against the foothills of the Nine Dragons
in a spray of human termite-heaps, ten or fifteen storeys
high. The mainland, as I knew it, is now unrecognizable,
and, when I turn my head, the island is unrecognizable too.
I had remembered a waterfront of three-storey buildings,
arcaded in a sixteenth-century Portuguese style. Today the
remnants of these antediluvian structures are overshadowed
by American-style high buildings with flat faces and simple
lines: apartment houses, office blocks, and, above all, banks.
The Bank of China is 'above all' in the literal meaning of
the words. It has taken care to overtop its neighbour, the
Hongkong and Shanghai Bank; and this is an eloquent
assertion, in dumb show, of a change in the international
balance of power that has been brought about by the
Second World War and its sequel.

Part of the sequel has been the piling of Shanghai on
Hongkong, as Mount Pelion was piled on Mount Ossa in
the legendary battle of gods and giants. For Chinese businessmen who found life impossible under a Communist régime
and unattractive in Formosa, Hongkong was the inevitable
city of refuge. Why stay at home to be taxed out of existence,
and why migrate to Formosa to vegetate there like Rip Van
Winkle, if, in Hongkong, one can still do business, more or
less as usual, under the British flag? So legions of Chinese
'displaced persons' have been flocking into the colony; and
this huge influx of population has been driving the local
architects up the precipices and into the sea. The ribbon of
reclaimed land between the foot of the Peak and the shore-
line of the harbour has been doubled or trebled in width
since I saw it last. The shore's encroachment on the water is
going forward in Hongkong today about as rapidly as in
Chicago; and the new buildings that can find no parking-
place for themselves down below on the piles are winning
standing-room on skilfully shored-up ledges perched from
foot to head of the Peak.

The architects of Hongkong (they are, most of them,
Chinese) have to start every operation by solving technical

problems that would daunt their confrères in most of the
World's other great cities. And their problems are not only
technical ones, either. In a rising textile town on the mainland, I visited a block of modern flats built to house a couple
of villages that had been moved to make way for a new
reservoir. This block was crowned by a temple, dedicated
to the villagers' ancestors, which had to be oriented in their
previous temple's direction, exactly facing one particular
peak on an island across the water. If this requirement had
not been met, the villagers would not have budged, and
Hóngkong's inadequate water-supply would not have been
increased. Could the temple be oriented as required without
making havoc of the new town plan? The architects managed
to satisfy both the town-planning authorities and the village
priest. This was a characteristic feat of Chinese ingenuity.
It was also a characteristic incident in the re-minting of
of Chinese life in a Western mould. And this is Hongkong's
staple industry.

23. Past and Future in Japan

'And great was the fall thereof.' These biblical words
reverberate in a Western traveller's ears in Japan, eleven
years after the catastrophe. The earth-shaking event of
which the visitor is aware is not the fall of the Japanese
empire and not the explosion of the atom bombs over
Hiroshima and Nagasaki. These, too, were historic events.
The Japanese empire had lunged out, before it fell, into
China, the Philippines, Indochina, Malaya, Indonesia, and
Burma. The dropping of the two bombs on Japan opened a
new chapter in the history of the institution of war and of
the destinies of the human race. But something else, besides,
fell in Japan in 1945, and that was the Japanese ideology
of the Meiji Era. This is the fall that is still echoing through
the land. Nagasaki has been rebuilt; in 1956 you could not
have guessed what had happened there in 1945 if you had

not known. But the collapse of the Japanese people's pre-war mental world has left a spiritual vacuum that is still a blank. You cannot be unaware of its existence, and you cannot help speculating on what is going to fill it. That it will be filled seems certain, since Nature abhors a spiritual vacuum as well as a physical one.

A clean sweep of some past outlook on the Universe is a hitherto unknown experience for the Japanese people; for Japan lies in that half of the Old World that has drawn its religion and philosophy from Indian and Chinese sources. Up till now, she has not been much affected by religions of the Jewish family. Wherever Judaism, Christianity, and Islam have penetrated, they have tried to wipe the slate clean; and, though traditional religious practices and beliefs have been apt to steal back, thinly disguised in an Islamic or a Christian dress, the conversion of the western half of the World to these intolerant Judaic religions has made breaches of mental continuity which Japan never suffered before 1945, nor China before 1949. In Eastern Asia down to our day, the traditional method of disposing of some new art, institution, or idea has been, not substitution, but juxtaposition. Instead of effacing the old thing and installing the new thing in its place, the East Asian peoples have always preserved what has already been there; they have always found room for things new and old side by side.

Suppose, for example, that the place called Bromsgrove had happened to be in Japan instead of being in England. In England today, 'Bromsgrove' is a mere place-name and nothing more. Even the people who live there are not conscious of the word's etymology, and there is nothing in the present-day life of Bromsgrove to remind them of it. But, if Bromsgrove had happened to be in Japan, everything that is recorded in the name would still have been alive today. The grove would still be standing and still be holy in the present-day inhabitants' eyes. In the midst of the grove, the timber-built shrine of the local war-god BRON would still be intact, in exactly the same form as at the time of the arrival of a world religion fourteen hundred years ago.

Pious hands would have replaced the timbers, one by one, as they rotted away. Of course, side by side with this primeval shrine, there would now be a medieval Christian church— or, to be more exact, a medieval Buddhist temple, if we are to imagine Bromsgrove being translated into a Japanese setting. But temple and shrine would be in a friendly state of co-existence. The Buddhist missionary who first brought a world religion to Bromsgrove would never have dreamed of hewing down BRON's grove or overthrowing the local god's image (if such there had been). He would have told his converts that their ancestral god was really a manifesta-tion of one of the minor figures of the Mahayanian Buddhist pantheon who had been sent on in advance to prepare the Buddha's way before Him. The god of the ancient local shrine would have been given the official status of an honor-ary guardian of the younger local temple; and the priest of the shrine and the parson of the temple would be on excellent terms with each other. Long ago it would have been tacitly agreed that the financial proceeds of the performance of religious ceremonies should be divided fifty-fifty. Weddings would be celebrated at Bron's shrine and the fees would go to the priest; funerals would be celebrated at the temple and the fees would go to the parson. Paganism and Buddhism would be living happily side by side.

When, a hundred years ago, the leaders of the Japanese people decided to abandon their predecessors' policy of seclusion and to adopt unreservedly all the practical side of modern Western civilization, they were not ready to jettison their traditional spiritual life. What were they to do with this stratified deposit of paganism (Shinto), Buddhism, and Confucianism? They fused together their Confucian ethics and their Shinto ritual into a rather artificial new amalgam, in which the centre point of devotion was the cult of the Emperor. Ancient fairy stories telling that Japan was 'the land of the gods', that she could never be invaded, and that she was destined one day to rule the World, were given the status of official doctrine. This worship of Japan's supposed national destiny fitted the mood of Japanese militarists in the nineteen-thirties, and, during the first year or two after the attack on Pearl Harbour, even the most extravagant of these political fairy tales seemed to be coming true. The reversal of military fortunes that ended in utter defeat therefore gave the Japanese the greatest shock that any living people has yet had. Legend was refuted by fact. The Japanese strong man armed had provoked, and succumbed to, a stronger than he. The Emperor himself told his people that he was not divine. Within the space of a few days, a whole mental world had dissolved into thin air. What new mental outlook was to replace it? This is the spiritual problem with which the Japanese are still wrestling today.

24. Religious Outlook in Japan

Post-war Japan is an interesting country for many reasons. One reason is that some of the post-war world's main problems are exercising Japan in acute forms that bring these problems' inner nature to light. The whole World today is in spiritual distress as a result of having lost touch with its ancestral religious traditions. Japan is suffering from this world-wide malady to an unusually high degree. The three traditional faiths of Japan—Shinto, Buddhism, and Confucianism—seem all to have lost their grip on Japanese minds and hearts.

Shinto is a primitive religion which started as a cult of fertility and was afterwards commandeered to serve as a kind of religious cement for political loyalty to the Japanese state incarnate in the Emperor. A Westerner who has been educated in the Greek and Latin classics will find both aspects of Shinto familiar. An accurate picture of the agricultural religion of the Japanese village can be found in Saint Augustine's celebrated account of the corresponding stratum of Roman religion. The worship of the Japanese state, which suffered its great fall in 1945, was an almost exact counterpart of the worship of the goddess Rome and the god Caesar which was rejected by the martyrs of the primitive Christian Church. Shinto as a cult of fertility is still an integral part of Japanese rice-cultivation. In Japan, growing rice is not just an economic operation; it is also a religious rite which has to be practised for its own sake, whether or not rice happens to be the most remunerative crop to raise in this or that locality. So long as rice continues to be cultivated by a Japanese peasantry, the agricultural form of Shinto will continue to be practised in the village shrine and on the farm-house holy shelf. However, nowadays a majority of every Japanese peasant's children have to leave the land and to earn—or half earn—their living in the cities. Year by year the land-workers in Japan are becoming a smaller and smaller percentage of the country's total population. And, when the land-worker turns into a town-worker, his practice of the agricultural religion soon ceases. So, in the more and more urban and industrialized Japan of the future, the outlook for agricultural Shinto is not promising.

The political version of Shinto is already far more deeply discredited. It was bound up with the political régime that brought Japan to disaster in 1945. But, even if it had not inflicted this calamity on the Japanese people, political Shinto might have found it hard to survive. Its mythology is in contradiction with the modern scientific spirit; and, when once Japan had opened her mind to this, it would hardly have been possible in the long run for her to keep her political ideas and ideals insulated in an antique watertight compartment. Indeed, it would not have been feasible to impose this ideology on the Japanese people after the Japanese reception of modern civilization in the nineteenth century if political Shinto had not been part and parcel of an unbroken national tradition. The new version of this old tradition that was furbished up after the Meiji Restoration in 1868 was, at best, rather artificial. Anyway, the tradition—genuine or spurious—was broken in 1945. It seems most improbable that it could now ever be re-established in cold blood.

The downfall of political Shinto has compromised
Confucianism, since political Shinto, on its ethical side, was
virtually Confucianism in Japanese dress. Confucianism
inculcates a sense of absolute and unquestioning duty
towards the senior members of one's family, particularly
towards the father as the head of the household and towards.
the Emperor as the head of the larger family represented by
the state. During the period of Japanese history that came
to an abrupt and disastrous end in 1945, the Confucian code
of ethics, applied to political Shinto, made sacrificial
demands on the individual. When events proved that the
sacrifices had been in vain and that the ideology was a
fairy-story, the individual asserted his human rights for the
first time in a thousand years of Japanese history. He
demanded life and happiness for himself. This reaction
towards individualism may have gone rather far for the
moment, but this is something normal and healthy, and,
even if the pendulum swings back, it will never re-approach
its pre-1945 position. Neither the head of the Japanese
household nor the head of the Japanese state will ever again
be revered as a demi-god. The Japanese family of the future
will be held together, not by a conventional code of duties,
but by natural affection. The central figure and focus will
be not the father but the mother.

The prospects for Buddhism in Japan might be expected
to be brighter. Here is a rational philosophy which, unlike
Christianity, is fully reconcilable with the modern scientific
outlook. It is the faith of more than half Ceylon and of nearly
the whole of Burma, Siam, Cambodia, Tibet, and Mongolia;
and it is one of the faiths of China, Vietnam, and Korea, as
well as Japan. Japan has been partially Buddhist for 1,400
years (rather longer than England has been Christian).
Every Japanese family is officially affiliated to one or other
of the innumerable Buddhist temples in Japan. On the other
hand, Buddhism was officially dissociated from political
Shinto when this was refurbished after the Meiji Restoration
in 1868. So Buddhism, was not directly implicated in the
downfall of the Meiji ideology in 1945. Cannot Buddhism

fill the spiritual vacuum produced by the collapse of Shinto mythology and Confucian ethics? It is surprising to find that Buddhism counts for little in Japan today, except among a small minority who follow the Zen sect's spiritual discipline. No doubt, during these last 1,400 years, the Buddhist outlook has moulded Japanese minds, but this has been an unconscious process. The practical role of Buddhism in Japanese life today is to usher one out of this world by giving one a Buddhist funeral. This practice is still the rule. Japanese agnostics will be cremated with Buddhist rites, just as Western agnostics will be buried with Christian ones. But this is about all, and it is not very much. Buddhism in Japan today is not providing the spiritual bread for which the Japanese people are hungry.

Their spiritual hunger is revealed in the rise of a multitude of new sects. There are said to be 600 of them, and, though Japan is not a rich country, they all seem to be flourishing financially. Their most numerous and active supporters are middle-class women, and many of them have had women for their founders. The oldest and most noteworthy is TENRI ('The Religion of Heaven'), whose foundress proclaimed her gospel before the end of the nineteenth century. This was soon after Japan officially reopened her doors to Western influences; and it is significant that Tenri believes in one almighty personal creator god. We may guess that this belief derives, however remotely, from Christianity. We may also guess that this belief has been the secret of Tenri's success; for here we have something that Buddhism cannot offer.

Then what about the prospects for Christianity itself in the new Japan that is now painfully struggling to be born? Japanese Christians occupy eminent posts today, but they are, of course, no more than a tiny minority, and it seems improbable that there will be further conversions on any large scale. At the same time it looks as if the spirit of Christianity were permeating Japanese life and were beginning gradually to replace or transform the traditional influence of Buddhism. On the conscious surface of the mind the present painful groping may long continue. But deeper down, at the subconscious level, the Japanese people may already be finding the bread of life.

25. Hokkaido

The northernmost island of an archipelago seems always to have some special virtue. Sumatra is Indonesia's island of hope; Hokkaido is Japan's island of expectation. In Hokkaido today one can already see the Japan of the future.

In Japan the tension between future and past is unusually sharp. Japan has been a pioneer among Asian countries in deliberately opening her doors to the modern civilization of the West. At the same time she is a country in which the hold of tradition is particularly strong. But in Hokkaido, alone among Japanese islands, the tradition built up by 1,300 years of pre-Western Japanese civilization has never existed in its original uncontaminated form. Until after the Meiji Restoration in 1868, Hokkaido was merely a Japanese possession, not yet a Japanese country. The Japanese foothold on the island was confined to a few military posts which had been planted there belatedly to stake out Japan's claim against an acquisitive Russian Empire. The rest of Hokkaido was then still an uncultivated wilderness, in which the only representatives of the human race were a few wandering bands of hairy Ainu (distant relatives of the hairy Australian blackfellow and hairy Nordic Man).

The Westernization of Japan gave Hokkaido a new destiny. One of the effects of Westernization was to put an end to the practices that had kept the population of Japan at a constant figure for a quarter of a millennium. The population started to increase at an accelerating rate (it is still increasing today, though re-stabilization is now in sight). The colonization of Hokkaido was the most obvious first recourse for relieving the population pressure in the other three Japanese islands. The movement was promoted by the Imperial Government from the eighteen-seventies onwards, and today Hokkaido is a Japanese-inhabited land. Its capital, Sapporo, is the largest city in Japan north of Tokyo. In Hokkaido a new Japan has been called into existence; but this new Japan is not just a reproduction of the old Japan. There is nothing Japanese here that antedates the beginning of the Westernization process. The vanguard of the pioneers who opened up this northern waste-land were not Japanese, but Westerners. The Japanese Government invited Dutch and Danish farmers to settle there for a term of years in order to show the Japanese settler how to grapple with a country that was more like Northern Europe than it was like the main island of Japan. These North Europeans have gone home again long ago; but they have left an abiding memorial of their former presence in the Teutonic build of Hokkaido farm-houses and barns. The Japanese settlers who came in at the Teutons' heels found by experience that this strange type of building suited the new country better than the less massive Japanese style. So they took it over and reproduced it. The revolution was not merely an architectural one. It was a psychological one too.

We were able to visit three characteristic present-day Japanese farms in Hokkaido: an onion farm on the outskirts of Sapporo; a rice-farm in the irrigated country to the east of the city; and a dairy-farm in rougher country farther south-eastward. In talking with the farmers and their families, one was struck both by the breach with Japanese tradition and by the effort which this breach had cost. In terms of physical distance the fathers or grandfathers of these Hokkaido farmers had not migrated very far—not much farther than the distance from, say, Wessex to the Scottish Highlands. But the psychological strain of pulling up and replanting their roots had been as great as if they had emigrated from Yorkshire to New Zealand. They were proud of the achievement and were pleased to find themselves enjoying a prosperity that would still be fabulous in those districts of old Japan from which their families came.

Yet the rice-farming family, at any rate, still clung rather anxiously to the past.

Rice is not at all the obvious crop for Hokkaido. In this harsh northern clime the rice-harvest has to be gathered in at least a month earlier than in regions where rice is at home. The agricultural department of the University of Hokkaido has devoted much research to breeding special varieties of rice that can mature in a short growing-season. Even so, the raising of rice in Hokkaido is an economic tour de force. Yet it is tacitly agreed in Hokkaido that, wherever rice cultivation is just possible, the land shall be used for raising rice in preference to any other product. If rice-growing were banned in Hokkaido, and if the whole utilizable area were turned over to rye and oats and pasture, the total food-production of the island could probably be increased substantially. This would enrich Hokkaido and cut down the imports of food into Japan from elsewhere. But it is high treason, or rather blasphemy, to make this utilitarian suggestion. The cultivation of rice is something like a religious obligation in Japanese eyes; and, for a rice-cultivating people, dairy-farming is not just an economic innovation; it is a rather shocking activity, verging on outright impiety.

Sure enough, the dairy-farmer was the greatest radical of the three farmers whom we visited. The rice-farmer had built himself a fine house in an ultra-traditional Japanese style with a holy shelf for the Shinto gods and a miniature chapel for the Buddhist bodhisattvas and a row of enlarged photographs of revered ancestors. The dairy-farmer had built himself an American two-storeyed house with a barrel roof in corrugated iron, and he and his family sat on American-like chairs and ate their meals at an American-like table. He had taken the impious plunge of making cheese and butter instead of cultivating a paddy-field, and he was not going to make the mistake of looking back.

That revolutionary dairy-farmer's grandchildren will be as modern as their contemporaries in Wisconsin and Minnesota. We left his farm at dusk and, after driving for an hour or two through desolate marshes, without a house or human being in sight, we sped past a huge paper-mill and arrived in the dark at an Ainu fishing-village. The bearded patriarch's noble countenance wore a pitying smile of forgiveness for the modern world that was sweeping his antique way of life out of existence. Hokkaido spans the ages, but the one age that is conspicuous here by its absence is the age of the traditional civilization of Japan.

26. The Battle of Trees and Men

A traveller to Cambodia from Mexico will not be much impressed, at first sight, by the forest that enfolds the massive ruins at Angkor. Like Palenque and the other Maya sites in south-western Mexico and Guatemala, Angkor is a forest-girt assemblage of public buildings. There is an unmistakable affinity between these two groups of deserted monuments in the tropics, though they are sundered from one another geographically by the breadth of the Pacific Ocean, and there is no evidence of any historical connexion between them. But the encircling forests do not look very like one another on first view. The forest on the mountains overhanging Mexican Palenque feels like a sinister hot-house cathedral. As soon as you step inside the outermost row of tree-trunks, the sky is blotted out by the matted roof. On this roof's invisible sunny upper surface, monkeys groan and roar like lions and tigers, but you never see them, and not one ray of sunlight pierces its way through; instead of descending shafts of light there are downward-dangling creepers that threaten to seize the human intruder in a snake-like grip. The air is still and stifling, and one gasps for breath. Compared to this Mexican nightmare, the Cambodian woods seem innocent. This is no primeval forest; trees here are mere second growth, and they confess themselves to be parvenus by the openness of their array. At Angkor you can see right through the tree-tops to the sky; and the carpet of brown autumn leaves underfoot in cool December gives the North European an illusory sense of being at home again, so long as one of the rare palm trees does not happen to be in sight. In Mexico you can almost see the creepers in the act of crawling over the road and smothering the masonry. At Angkor the principal monuments appear to be holding their own with ease.

But this first impression at Angkor is an illusion, created by the magic touch of the modern archaeologist who has recently come to the rescue of these works of Medieval Man. The archaeologist has performed a miracle that, in his technical jargon, he calls 'anastylosis'. This is a Greek word meaning 're-erection', and a series of devoted archaeologists have in fact re-erected the Cambodian monuments stone by stone. It is as fine an art as the fitting together of the bits of a jig-saw puzzle. Juxtaposed photographs of the same monument, before and after this labour of love has been wrought on it, make one rub one's eyes. Can these really be two pictures of the same object? One's amazement gives one a hint that the realities must be different from the appearances. Let us visit one of the temples at Angkor to which the art of 'anastylosis' has not yet been applied. What do we find? We find a savage battle in full swing.

Look at that gigantic tree which has leapt, like a panther, on to this unhappy building's back and is tearing its victim to pieces with its cruel claws. That tree is a veritable carnivore in slow motion. Keep it continuously exposed to the lens of a film camera for a hundred years, and then speed up the apparatus till you can display a century's action in one minute. You will see this panther-tree leaping swiftly and savagely to its kill. And now look at this outer gateway of a temple-enclosure. A seedling has planted itself on the crown of the gatehouse roof and has swollen into a boa-constrictor with as many bodies as a Hindu god has arms and legs. Here come half-a-dozen roots pouring vertically, straight into the ground, where there was once a passage-way for ox-carts and elephants. Other roots have writhed round the walls and are crushing them into a shapeless mass of rubble. Others are pouring right through the walls, forcing their way between the once closely fitted stones. Others have wrenched single stones out of their place and are holding them in their coils like prey that they are waiting to devour. It is a terrible spectacle; the struggle is so savage, and the wild-beast trees are so manifestly getting the better of these stones that have been humanized in their passage through the mason's and the sculptor's hands. The course of the battle testifies to the power of Nature; but this testifies, in turn, to the power of Man; for the present battle is Nature's counter-offensive; she is avenging a defeat that was once inflicted on her by her human adversary.

Now that the latent savagery of the seemingly innocent Cambodian forest has been unmasked, it is plain that the Khmer civilization's achievement in South-East Asia was as great as the Maya civilization's in Middle America. The makers of these mighty buildings had to be fed from a surplus of agricultural production; and the fields and building-sites had first to be cleared, and then to be perpetually kept clear, of the irreconcilable jungle. As soon as Man relaxed his efforts, the jungle reclaimed its own and buried Man's works in the oblivion from which they have been rescued by the archaeologists in our time.

But why did Man relax his grip? If he could drive the jungle back and open up these fields and plan and construct these magnificent buildings, why did he not go on from strength to strength? The answer is given in the friezes that cover all four outer sides of the outermost quadrangle at Angkor Wat and at the Bayon (the centre-point of the quadrilateral city of Angkor Thom). These lovely bas-reliefs depict a few scenes of everyday life and a few more of religious ceremonial and political debate. But the dominant theme is war. From the two ends of the enormous wall, armies come marching in opposite directions. At the first stage everything is still calm and orderly: files of infantry, trains of chariots, horsemen, and elephants. But, when the opposing forces clash, the scene becomes wild and the warriors' faces grow distraught. And here are gangs of prisoners being clubbed by the king or, worse still, being tortured to death. Nails are being driven in all over their bodies and they are being crucified. The king who ordered this tell-tale piece of sculpture, and the artist who executed it, evidently took the same simple-minded pleasure as their Assyrian counterparts, 2,000 years earlier, in immortalizing their own atrocities. The Khmer civilization, like so many other civilizations before and after it, wrecked itself by indulging in these mad crimes. Man's sinfulness gave the predatory trees their chance of taking their revenge on Man's genius.

27. Angkor

Man is a born geometer. Even when he is expressing himself in curves, as he has done in the undulating roofs of Eastern Asia and in the flowing sculptures at Borobudur, his lines follow mathematical laws that are unknown to Nature; and he is frankly defying her when he works in rectangles. Angkor is perhaps the greatest of Man's essays in rectangular architecture that has yet been brought to light. One must use cautious words, because there is said to be a still larger and more magnificent example of the same style of work lying hidden in the jungle of Northern Cambodia; and, when this sleeping beauty is revealed by the hand of some liberating archaeologist, Angkor may have to take second place. Meanwhile, it has no visible peer in the World.

The Buddhist stupa at Borobudur in Central Java is a lyric poem in stone, flowing round the crown of a hill to the musical accompaniment of a jagged mountain range on one side and a green expanse of rice fields on the other. Angkor is not orchestral; it is monumental. It is an epic poem which makes its effect, like the Odyssey and like Paradise Lost, by the grandeur of its structure as well as by the beauty of the details. Angkor is an epic in rectangular forms imposed upon the Cambodian jungle. The two largest of these are a pair of artificial lakes, the eastern and the western Baray, which balance one another without being quite symmetrical. The second largest is the four-square city of Angkor Thom—a vast quadrangle with two axial roads and four gates, on the same plan as a Roman camp or the Imperial City at Peking. The third largest, and the chef d'œuvre of the marvellous design, is the principal temple: Angkor Wat. The whole ensemble is so huge that it takes three and a half days on mechanized wheels just to make a first reconnaissance. There is one temple—Phnom Bakhêng—on the summit of a little mountain, overhanging the road from Angkor Wat to Angkor Thom, that gives one a bird's-eye view of the Wat's mounting terraces and soaring pinnacles. But an all-embracing view of the whole lay-out would be obtainable only from an aeroplane, and then only if the second growth of jungle that now envelops the ruins had been cleared. No doubt, when these buildings were in their glory, they stood like islands in an ocean of industriously scythed green lawns. It is difficult to imagine how any town-planner could have executed so enormous a design without having been able to circle above his surveyors in a plane and give them their instructions by radio.

If the present-day visitor wants to take the measure of Angkor from the ground, he can do it by driving to the south-west corner of the western Baray. A vast lake stretches away before his eyes, turning an opal colour in the fast dwindling evening light; but, when he consults the map, he will find that this body of water is only a fraction of the original. The easternmost three-quarters of the oblong have long since silted up and relapsed into rice-fields. The eastern Baray is now wholly dry, and one drives through it without being conscious of traversing a lake-bed. On this side the water-filled rectangles are represented today by the Srah Srang, an artificial lake that would seem huge in any other setting, and the Néak Peân, a basin with four subsidiary tanks at the cardinal points of the compass which would dwarf the fountains at Versailles if it were caught up on a magic carpet to be deposited beside them.

These water-filled rectangles are not, however, the most frequent of the variations on the standard form of architecture at Angkor. In most of the monuments the water-surface is confined to a rectangular moat; and the square or oblong area of dry land inside provides the campus for a structure of massive masonry. In some of the monuments the stone-work is all on ground level, and the genius of the work lies in a gigantic axial corridor through which one peers as if one were looking down a ride through the forest (this illusion is heightened in those ruins that have not yet been cleared of invading trees). In other monuments the masonry rises in rectangular tier above tier till it pierces the sky in a quincunx of sugar-loaf-shaped pinnacles—four of them at the angles and the tallest in the centre. The queen of these man-built four-square mountains is Angkor Wat. If the Tower of Babel had been completed, this is how it would have stood.

As you cross the moat of Angkor Wat on the great western stone bridge, the size of the structure begins to dawn on you. When you pass through the western gate of the outer quadrangle and set foot on the causeway leading across the campus to the ziggurat, the majesty of the conception takes your breath away. But there is no anticlimax. When you enter the Wat itself and scale its three successive platforms, till your eyes are level with the divine figures ensconced in the four sides of the central apex, your wonder and delight increase at every step. The workmanship is classical in its simplicity and precision. This twelfth-century masterpiece of architecture on Cambodian soil is a response to an inspiration from India, but the Khmer artist has transformed what he has borrowed into something original of his own. The exquisite forms that Man's genius has conjured out of the stone and the warm purple glow of the stone itself are set off by the radiant blue of the sky. One could spend the rest of one's life sitting here and drinking in the beauty of the scene. Could it really all have been built within the reign

of a single king? They say that each king of medieval
Cambodia aspired to build himself an Angkor, just as each
Pharaoh of Egypt in the days of the Old Kingdom aspired to
build himself a pyramid. I have not yet set eyes on the
Pyramids at Gizeh, and, for an Englishman, Egypt may
henceforth be a forbidden land. But I do not repine. See
Angkor and die. See Angkor and Borobudur in the course of
one journey, as has been my good fortune, and you will have
had a foretaste of the Beatific Vision.

28. A Glimpse of Thailand

Do you come from Boston, Massachusetts, or Boston,
England? Are you familiar with the Lincolnshire fens? Have
you visited the English or the Continental Holland, or the
waterlaced hinterland of Venice? Keep the dykes and canals;
change the turnip-fields and pastures into a green-gold sea of
ripening rice; magnify this landscape several hundredfold,
and you will be viewing Thailand with your mind's eye.

When one views it from the plane bearing down on
Bangkok from Hongkong, one sees with one's physical eye
that Man has brought this immense delta under effective
human control. The canals into which the waters of Thailand have been guided run, as far as the eye can see, in
straight parallel lines. The canal banks are lined, on either
side, with a continuous ribbon of houses, perched over the
water on stilts and canopied by trees; and, behind this belt of
dark green foliage and grey roofs, the yellow rice-fields
extend, in oblong strips, at right-angles to the waterway,
till they meet, back to back, the fields belonging to the
villages strung along the next canal. The effect is like that of
the terraces and backyards of a Western city on an enorm-
ously enlarged scale.

As we came down, we could espy, here and there, a long
string of barges being towed by a motor launch, and next
morning, when we stepped on board one of these launches

and began to thread our way through the backwaters opening off the River Menam, we realized that Venice is the miniature Bangkok of Europe. The waterway is the thoroughfare, and a skiff will carry the Thai housewife to a shop-front that could not be reached on foot, not to speak of wheels. These water-borne shops overhanging the brink of the canal are numerous, and they are well-stocked with imported goods besides the produce of the country. One gains an impression of general well-being which is confirmed by subsequent observations. After all, Thailand produces about twice as much rice as she needs for home consumption. So everybody in this fortunate country has enough to eat, and can also buy his share of the foreign commodities that flow into Thailand in exchange for the exportable surplus of the rice-crop.

The orderliness that reveals itself in the lay-out of canals and paddy fields in the countryside seems to pervade Siamese life. Bangkok, for instance, is an ultra-modern city of broad avenues and streamlined office blocks. Convert the bright-roofed temples into baroque churches, or imagine that the pagodas are cupolas, and you might fancy that you were in the capital city of one of the better-managed tropical Latin American republics.

The government of Thailand is a composite oligarchy. Part of the governing group consists of the royal family and its collateral branches; the rest is composed of able parvenus who have thrust their way into power within the last twenty years. The new men control the army and the police, and presumably they could monopolize political power and its perquisites if they chose. But the cliques within the oligarchy take care not to let their rivalries rankle into anarchic discord, and in consequence the oligarchy's position seems at present to be unassailable. No doubt they allot themselves a handsome profit on their services, and no doubt, too, they deal in summary ways with anyone who is rash enough to challenge their authority. But these sinister casualties seem to be confined to the narrow circle whose hands are near the levers of power. The rest of the population, including government officials, can do their work and enjoy their leisure unmolested so long as they do not venture to take an independent line in politics. The large new parliament house, built in the Palladian style, is within sight of the police headquarters, and the representatives of the people are carefully selected and supervised. But for the mass of the people this Tudor method of government provides in twentieth-century Thailand the same substantial benefits that it provided in sixteenth-century England. One of these boons is effective public security, which is the indispensable condition for all material prosperity and progress. Another is political independence.

Thailand is unique among South-East Asian countries in never having experienced even a transitory period of foreign occupation, except for the presence of Japanese troops in the country during the Second World War. Thailand owes this immunity partly to luck. She was able to play the rôle of buffer state between the British dominions in India and Burma and the French dominions in Indochina. But her uninterrupted independence has been mainly the reward of her own prudence, efficiency, and foresight. The Royal Government began to send students abroad to Western countries as far back as a century ago—as early, that is to say, as this practice was started in Japan by the makers of the Meiji Restoration. She has also employed Western experts to help her in training her people at home and in modernizing her life; but in her choice of nationalities she has been judicious. She readily admitted British teak-planters and French archaeologists, but, when it was a question of hiring Western generals and admirals, she showed a preference for Danes. Thanks to these wise and timely measures, Thailand has always succeeded in coping with the increasingly strenuous conditions of the modern world. Above all, she has built up a sufficient personnel of trained and experienced technicians, professional men, and administrators. There is an imposing number of Thais who have had their schooling, as well as their university education, in the West; and some of these can exchange Oxford v. Cambridge banter with one

another in impeccable unitedkingdomese. They are fully a
match for their Western schoolfellows and college mates.
Personal relations are easy and unconstrained, in contrast to
the touch of stiffness and embarrassment which sometimes
assails even the most accomplished Japanese in their social
relations with their Western opposite numbers.

One can write the word Thailand on the map without
having to add a question mark. She is there, and she is going
to stay there. Why not? She has no common frontier with
either India or China; and the Thais know how to assimilate
the Chinese immigrant in their midst. Chinese and Thais are,
after all, close kinsmen speaking languages of the same
family. Thailand can face the future with well-justified
confidence.

29. A Glimpse of Burma

'Denmark and Eire? Visit both? Surely this would be a
wasteful duplication of experiences in a crowded itinerary
through Europe. I really cannot see how there can be any
significant difference between these two little countries.
Both of them are northerly and rainy. They lie in the same
latitude. Both raise a notable surplus of dairy products for
export. Both are unaggressive. Both are Christian. Why
waste my time on visiting more than one of the two? Why
not toss up?' This imaginary rejoinder of an inadequately-
informed Tibetan tourist to his Japanese travel-agent
indicates how gravely mistaken a Western traveller would be
if he decided to toss up between Thailand and Burma.
Luckily, I did not make this easy but elementary mistake.
I found time—though all too short a time—for getting a
glimpse of both. In consequence, I can duly register their
points of likeness. Both are Buddhist countries of the Theravadin school. Both are unaggressive. Both have a relatively
low population density for Eastern Asian countries. Both are
exporters of rice. Both lie in the tropics. But, when one has

catalogued these common traits, one will despair of enumer-
ating all the differences and contrasts.

How great, for example, are the differences concealed
under the Theravadin Buddhist monk's uniform yellow toga.
In Thailand this noble raiment clothes a clergyman of an
established church. The Thai monk receives respect and
honour so long as he knows and keeps his place and obeys
the civil authorities. In Thailand the Government has the
Sangha (monastic fraternity) under control. In Burma the
status and temper of the monks remind an historian of
fifth-century Christian Egypt. The fraternity includes as
many genuine ascetics, philosophers, and saints as any
similar body anywhere at any time. But it also includes
'turbulent priests' like those who were the terror of Byzantine
governors-general at Alexandria. A mob of monks may
suddenly fling off the yellow toga and start fighting with
staves, swords, revolvers, or even hand-grenades. And Burman monks who misbehave themselves in these or other less
flagrant ways—by making money, for instance, or by
frequenting the cinema—are not easy to call to order. Like
their lay fellow-citizens, the Burman monks—normally so
well disciplined and severe—may abruptly turn violent and
vindictive. To de-frock a delinquent monk is quite a dangerous operation for his spiritual superiors. They find it safer to
boycott him in the hope that he may eventually de-frock
himself and take his departure quietly.

This picture might suggest that the Burman monks are
not such worthy followers of their Master as their Thai
brethren. But any such conclusion would be misleading. In
Thailand Buddhism is respectable; in Burma it is alive.
In Burma today, as in Byzantine Egypt, the monastic life is
paradoxical. It is both scandalous and edifying—a stumbling-
block and at the same time a source of inspiration. While
some monks are doing no credit to their cloth, others are
reviving the Theravada (they do not accept the nickname
Hinayana—'Little Vehicle'—which has been given to
Southern Buddhism by the rival northern school that claims
to be the 'Great vehicle' or Mahayana). These Burman

Buddhist revivalists believe that the authentic philosophy of the Buddha Siddhartha Gautama is a cure for the spiritual crisis of the present-day world. Their first step, taken two years ago, was to convene an oecumenical council of monks representing the five Theravadin Buddhist countries: Burma, Thailand, Cambodia, Laos, and Ceylon. The assembled Fathers achieved a huge piece of co-operative intellectual work: they made a new recension of the Tripitaka, the Pali scriptures of the Southern Buddhist Church. The text fills forty-two volumes. I watched these being printed and bound at the printing-press that is one of the Council's legacies. These volumes are finding their way over the World, and they are being followed by missionaries. Japan, where the Mahayana is just now at a rather low ebb, is one mission-field on which the Southern Buddhist revivalists have their eye.

This zeal for the Buddha's philosophy is not confined to the monks; there are zealous laymen too, including lawyers, magistrates, and business men who have had a modern secular education in Britain as well as at home. But this Ancient Indian school of philosophy, like the schools of Ancient Greece, is only for an élite. To qualify for embarking on this arduous spiritual endeavour, one must have considerable intellectual ability and training besides moral earnestness and self-discipline. Simpler 'persons' (Buddhists do not admit the existence of 'selves' or 'souls') express their piety in outward acts which the Buddha might have found spiritually valueless or even detrimental. For example, thousands of willing hands acquired merit by heaping up the vast artificial cave in which the Rangoon oecumenical council held its sessions (a cave is the traditional setting for an assembly of this kind). Other voluntary groups spontaneously combine to build a new pagoda or a new statue of the Buddha—dedicated, perhaps, to world peace or to the release of all sentient beings from the sorrowful wheel of suffering. The poorest can build a little pagoda of sand held together by a bamboo frame, or can offer a candle or a bundle of joss sticks or a bunch of flowers. Religion, at all its levels, from sublime contemplation to commonplace superstition, is the field in which Burmans of all social and intellectual classes are enthusiastic, energetic, and effective. And they devote themselves to religion, undismayed, while the transitory phenomenal world runs true to form by falling about the ears of its transitory denizens.

In the past, Burma has been as prosperous as Thailand, and she is still quite as rich potentially. Besides producing a large exportable surplus of rice, she can grow better teak and she possesses mineral oil deposits that the Thais might envy. Yet, today, Burma is, from the material point of view, in a poor way. Her bane is the breakdown of public security. Even on the railways and the main roads, traffic cannot now venture to travel by night; and whole areas, even within close range of the capital, are out of the Government's control. In consequence, Burma's economic life has been lamed and her currency has been depreciating. But the darkness of her immediate material prospects does not extinguish the spiritual light that is radiating from Burman minds. However rough her own road may be, Burma means to give something precious to the World.

30. The Old Monk

'Now I will take you to see the old monk,' said the Father Superior. We had come to the end of a colloquy in which I had been asking crude questions and had been receiving enlightening answers. We had been sitting in a monastic hall—almost Japanese in its severe simplicity—with a view of the pagoda-studded ridge and a glimpse of the mighty river at its foot. We went down together into the lane and drove through a maze of nunneries and monasteries till we came to the building where the old man was awaiting his release from the last threads of attachment to this unsatisfactory world. He was sitting cross-legged on a chair, with a rug and some medicine bottles within reach. The

Superior made obeisance to him, and the reverence and affection that radiated from his gesture and his countenance were beautiful to see. The Superior was an eminent philosopher, spiritual director, and administrator, with 300 monks and 600 nuns under his charge. But his nobility shone out clearest in his regard for his senior, and the old man received his act of veneration with the same unselfconscious sincerity with which the act itself was performed.

The old monk was full of reminiscences: his mind ran on his studies in Sanskrit. But what changes he had witnessed in the fortunes of his country during the eighty-four years of his present life up to date. Since he first entered the monastery as a child of seven, he has spent no more than eight months, in all, in his natural family; his spiritual family—the monastic Sangha—has claimed all the rest of that long tale of years. Born in the reign of King Mindon—the last king but one of Upper Burma, and the founder of Mandalay—this monk had abandoned the world seven years before the British occupation of his country. He had entered the novitiate in the year in which an invading British army deposed King Thebaw and extinguished the country's independence. He had been an adult monk now for sixty-four years, and already he had lived to see the British occupation replaced by a Japanese one, and the subsequent British re-occupation swiftly succeeded by the restoration of independence to the whole of Burma. The phenomenal world is nothing but a fleeting series of ephemeral states. This is the teaching of the Buddha, and its truth has been illustrated as convincingly by the political history of Burma within the lifetime of this old monk as it was by the political history of India within the lifetime of his Master.

The Buddha lived to see his native city, Kapilavastu, razed to the ground and his kinsmen, the Sakyas, exterminated. What may not the old monk live to see, if he tarries in this cloud of illusion for another five or ten years? I had travelled to Sagaing at the heels of the present Prime Minister of Burma and his formidable visitor, Chou En-Lai. They had been paying a visit together to the debatable districts on the Sino-Burmese frontier. The ruler of 600 million human beings had been using disarming words in his public pronouncements on Burmese soil, but he had not renounced China's claim to the three Kachin villages that are in dispute between China and the Kachin state of the Union of Burma (Burma today is a federal republic). From time to time in past ages, China has imposed her suzerainty on Upper Burma, and, in the time of the Mongol Empire, Burma was under a serious threat of being conquered from the north. There was a day in the thirteenth century when a Christian monk, standing in the city-centre of the Mongol capital, Qaraqorum, saw one army riding out through the western gate and another through the southern gate. Where were those two armies heading for, he asked. One for Hungary and the other for Burma, was the answer.

Present-day Burma is an under-populated country. Having followed in Chou En-Lai's tracks from Rangoon to Mandalay, I pursued him one stage farther, from the valley of the Irawadi up on to the rim of the Shan plateau. As soon as the road left the rice-fields, habitation came to an end, though some rare patches of pineapple and banana plantations showed that the fallow upland soils were hardly less fertile than the alluvium of the lowlands. Any population-vacuum next door to China simply cries out to be filled. I wondered what thoughts might have been revolving in Chou En-Lai's mind as he travelled through that country ahead of me.

My own goal was not the distant frontier, but the upland city of Maymyo. In the short age of British rule in Burma, the Government used to migrate to Maymyo from Rangoon for the hot season, and the ghost of the fleeting presence of these conquerors from overseas still lingers at Maymyo in the street names and in the domestic architecture. Neo-Tudor pseudo-timbered villas with Frenchified turrets were the prevailing fashion, and the streets were, and still are, called by such names as 'The Mall'. I could picture the Lieutenant-Governor's wife and the Chief Secretary's wife holding state in the clothes that I can remember my mother wearing when I was very small. The present tenants of this fantastic phantom London suburb are the Union of Burma's army and civil service; but, in this fleeting world, the inevitable question is: Who will be the next ephemeral occupant?

In the flux of human affairs, is anything even relatively permanent? Perhaps the grand parallel ranges of the Shan country, which I saw, in a bird's-eye view, on my return journey to Rangoon by air, may outlive the human race. And certainly the Irawadi River will outlive the bridge by which I crossed it en route from Mandalay to Sagaing. The bridge is closed at nightfall nowadays for fear of saboteurs. But the river, at the point where it is now spanned by these meccano girders from a child's toy-cupboard, is already a giant, though it still has more than four hundred miles more to run before it loses its identity in the Ocean. What further transformations of the unstable human scene are going to be witnessed by the river and the mountains and the monk? This was what I found myself asking as I was driving from Rangoon airport into the city through an alley of elephantine croquet hoops. They were the triumphal arches that had greeted Chou En-Lai on his return from the ominous frontier. I was following at his heels once again, and receiving a civic welcome that had not been intended for me.

31. Animal Rights

The first thing in India that strikes a foreign visitor's eye is the pleasant fact that Indian birds and beasts are not in the least afraid of Indian human beings. Age-long experience has given them a well-justified confidence that their human co-inhabitants of the subcontinent will not slaughter them; but they are not grateful to Mankind for their immunity from the risk of being slain by human hands. They do not know that they owe this to a tabu which Indian Man has voluntarily imposed upon himself. Indian birds and beasts evidently imagine that they enjoy god-given animal rights, and that Man is constrained, willy nilly, to respect these rights as part of the divine ordering of the Universe. No doubt, if Indian birds and beasts were to visit the non-Indian regions of the Earth, they would get a shock which would open their eyes to both the advantages and the draw-backs of Indian Man's code of behaviour. Outside India, Man plays Shiva with the birds and beasts and creeping things. He butchers them, but he also sometimes fattens them for the slaughter. Inside India, Man may not and will not do any positive harm to his non-human fellow-creatures, but he is not bound to do any active good to them either. 'Thou shalt not kill, but needs't not strive officiously to keep alive' is Indian Man's rule of conduct. He will not kill a cow, but he may callously allow this venerated fellow-creature to starve in the streets of a city to a point at which the poor thing licks the paving-stones and nibbles at the lamp-posts in its desperate search for sustenance. In the West the cow would not receive unasked-for veneration, and would not have to pay the Indian penalty for being treated as quasi-divine. In the West a starving cow would either be fed or be put out of its misery.

Yet even a starving Indian cow takes, and gets away with taking, liberties that a Western cow would never dare attempt. The Indian cow can raid, with impunity, the standing crop in a farmer's field or the vegetables on the counter of a greengrocer's shop. Birds are still bolder. The day before yesterday my wife and I were eating a picnic lunch under the shade of a tree outside one of the caves at Ellora when a hawk swooped down and snatched a slice of cold mutton off my plate. Our driver made play with a stick, but the hawks knew quite well that he would never hit to kill, so they ignored his impertinence and dive-bombed us thick and fast. In one's hotel the sparrows live on the electric-light brackets and flutter down on to the table to share one's meals. At tea-time a crow alighted, within three yards of me, on the parapet of the balcony and looked at me with a demanding mien. I threw him a crumb, and instantly

Brahma created six more crows along that parapet. So the crow-tribe got from me, not just one crumb, but the whole of my slice of cake.

But the road is the place where animal rights are most jealously asserted and most scrupulously respected. One expects one's driver to hoot and halt for a buffalo or a goat, but, when he shows the same consideration for dogs, monkeys, and crows, one sits up and takes notice. A buffalo was reposing in the shadow of the Ellora gate of the walled city of Daulatabad. She filled the whole roadway, and our driver shyly requested the lady's human attendant to shift her. The man complied, but he was indignant. To enter into what he felt, you must imagine the Lord Chamberlain's feelings if he were asked by a rat to shift the Queen from her throne to make room for a donkey to pass.

Subcontinental dogs (this term includes Ceylonese dogs as well) love to bask on the road's sunbaked surface. The centre-point of a cross-roads is their favourite location. When the driver hoots and stops there is an awkward pause; and then the privileged creature slowly rises to his feet and sidles off with an eloquent shrug of his shoulders. 'Haven't you learnt by this time,' his aggrieved posture protests in dumb show, 'that God created this road for our use and not for yours? If I thought that you were on some really urgent errand—going to hospital or summoning the fire-brigade—I might pardon your trespass, but, from the look of you, you are bent merely on pleasure or on business. So I ask you to ask yourself: "Was your journey really necessary?" '

Indian human beings, too, possess animal rights, of course; but, in this animal raj, humans are definitely second-class citizens. In American parlance, they are 'under-privileged'. In the animal hierarchy, humans rank as non-Brahmins, but they do not enjoy the benefit of being a scheduled caste. No allowances are made for them.

Suppose that this wayfaring Southern Brahmin were so envious of that basking dog's state of bliss that he ventured to lie down on the road by the dog's side. He would not have a dog's chance; he would merely have a Southern Brahmin's;

and, if the driver at the wheel of the next passing car happened to be a non-Brahmin, the basking Brahmin's expectation of life might be short. His best chance of survival would be to nestle up so close to the dog that the driver would be forced to choose between running over both baskers or neither. In that situation the basking Brahmin would escape death—leaving his non-Brahmin adversary vexed at having been compelled to forgo an opportunity of reducing the number of living Brahmins by one.

How are we to appraise this Indian ethical code? It shines by comparison with the official Christian doctrine that God has created birds and beasts for Man to do what he likes with them. But the Indian tabu on taking non-human life has its seamy side too. The sacrosanctity of Indian cows, for example, is a senseless burden on their human devotees. The over-stocking of the country with under-nourished cows and destructive goats is one of the greatest obstacles, in India, to the improvement of the rural economy. And life is also a curse for the animals themselves; for the cow's divine right is merely a right to live. It is not a right to enjoy a decent livelihood. And it is no fun being a demigoddess if you do not know where to turn for your next meal. If I were destined to be re-born as a cow and were given a choice between an Indian and a Western birthplace, I believe I should opt for the West. In India I could be sure that I should never be put to death, but I could not count on anything beyond that. In the West my life might be cut short by tyrannical human hands, but it would probably be a happier life while it lasted. There is no provision for the pursuit of happiness in the Indian animals' bill of rights.

32. The New Map of India

All the world knows that the map of the Indian sub-continent suddenly changed colour in 1947. In that year the familiar uniform red of the British Indian Empire faded out and was replaced by a complex new tricolour design. Three sovereign independent states—the Indian Union, Pakistan, and Burma —made their appearance as local successors of the red raj that had been so conspicuous a patch on the Earth's surface for the previous hundred years. This much is common knowledge; but the revolutionary consequences of what happened in 1947 are perhaps not so well known outside the subcontinent. I, at any rate, had not realized them before I came across them on the spot.

The difference between the old map and the new map can be put in this way: the old map was not so irrational as it looked; the new maps of the Indian Union, Pakistan, and Burma are not so rational as they seem.

The old map of the British Indian Empire was, it is true, a museum piece. It was a fossilized record of the last phase in the scramble for power during the interregnum between the decay of the Mughal raj and the establishment of the British. The boundaries between British-administered territories and autonomous Indian states were fortuitous products of diplomacy and war. They were exceedingly complicated, and the administrative map that they produced cut across all natural lines of division. The administrative units corresponded neither to linguistic areas nor to economic regions. Speakers of the same language were partitioned among half-a-dozen different administrations, and, conversely, a presidency or principality would comprise fragments of half-a-dozen linguistic areas. The internal boundaries cut across the railways and the roads. In short, these internal boundaries of the old British India would have strangled the subcontinent to death if they had been taken as seriously as the new lines that have now replaced them. Happily, however, for the India of yesterday, the old internal boundaries were never allowed to break up the subcontinent's essential unity, and the overriding forces making for unity were in those days very strong. The Hindu and Muslim religions and cultures overrode all differences of language and race, and the British raj contributed a number of modern unifying forces: a common army and common civil service, a lingua franca in the shape of the English language, and a unitary network of means of communication. The British raj did not give the inhabitants of the subcontinent the boon of national independence, but it did preserve them from the evils that have been the price of national independence in Eastern Europe and Western Asia. Since 1947 the history of the Indian subcontinent has been taking an East-European turn. The question today is: How far along that tragic road will India and Pakistan be driven to travel?

The partition of the British Indian Empire into the Indian Union and Pakistan has produced a new mosaic of international frontiers that are quite as irrational as the old internal boundaries of the British raj, but are much more detrimental than those ever were, because the new frontiers, unlike the old boundaries, have been erected into impassable barriers. The two regions that have suffered the most cruelly are the Panjab and Bengal. Here, two language areas have been partitioned by new lines that cannot be crossed, and these lines also play havoc with economics. Eastern Bengal has been cut off from Calcutta, which is its natural metropolis, and the Hindu minority, which used to manage Eastern Bengal's business life, are now refugees on the western side of the line. As for the Panjab, its prosperity depends on the maintenance of a unitary system of water-control, and the partition of the province has made this now impossible.

In compensation for the irrationality of her new frontiers, the Indian Union has been rationalizing her internal boundaries. Within these last ten years, the administrative map of the South has been streamlined to correspond with the local linguistic areas. This revolution was started by a demand from the Telugu-speaking population in the north-east corner of the former Presidency of Madras. They asked for a separate Andhra state of their own; and, when once this first demand had been conceded, it was inevitable that the whole of the South should be re-grouped into four states corresponding to the areas of the four Dravidian languages. This re-drawing of the administrative map is rational, but it is also a dangerous game, as is shown by Europe's tragic experience. Linguistic nationalism is a divisive and explosive force, and the wiser heads in India seem to be dubious about the consequences of this rational administrative reform. They fear that the local consciousness of being a Tamil, an Andhra, a Keralian, or a Kanarese may gravely weaken that overall consciousness of being an Indian that has been fostered in the past by the combined effect of a common Hindu culture and a unifying British raj. The modern history of Eastern Europe certainly gives ground for these Indian anxieties. Is a Telugu-speaking Indian going to become a semi-foreigner in Madras, and a Tamil-speaking Indian a semi-foreigner in Bangalore?

The crux of the new process of map-making has been the city of Bombay. Since Bombay is the economic capital of India—India's Manchester and Liverpool rolled into one—the city's destiny is a matter of supreme importance. But how is one to dispose of a great city in which labour is Maharashtrian while capital is Gujerati, Parsee, and Sindi? Geographically Bombay is part and parcel of Maharashtra, but, if the city had been merged in a separate Marathi-speaking state, as Madras has been merged in a Tamil-speaking one, this might have boded ill for the non-Maharashtrian minority to which Bombay owes its economic prosperity. A Gujerati proposal to turn Bombay into an autonomous city-state naturally aroused furious Maharashtrian opposition. The problem has been solved by making a single mammoth state out of Bombay city, Maharashtra, and Gujerat combined. This is perhaps the only solution that is here possible, but it is one that displeases Maharashtrians and Gujeratis alike; and this stormy episode of Indian administrative history illustrates the limitations of the policy of recasting administrative areas on linguistic lines.

The liquidation of the British raj in India, like the previous liquidation of the Mughal raj, has been followed by a scramble for power, but the winning quality today is neither the Maratha's valour nor the Bengali's penmanship, which made the fortunes of these two peoples in the eighteenth century. The twentieth-century winner is the Gujerati with his business sense. The Gujerati industrialist is, in fact, the British sahib's principal heir; and Bengal, with her wings broken by partition, may resign herself to being eclipsed. But what about the Maharashtrian, with his masterful character and his unforgotten past political greatness? Shades of Shivaji, Ghokale and Tilak! Are their kinsmen to resign themselves to becoming Gujerat's helots? Today, the Maharashtrian is carrying a chip on his shoulder. I augur that more will be heard of him again before long.

33. Grappling with a Sub-continent

For an historian who is travelling round the World via South America and Southern Asia, India is the most important and interesting country on his route. She is important, to begin with, because of the sheer size of her population. No other single country, except China, carries so many of Mankind's eggs in one national basket. The people of India are so large a contingent of the whole human race that their destiny is a matter of general human concern.

India is also important because she is one of three great countries—the other two being China and Russia—that contain, between them, the bulk of the World's peasantry. When the peasants of Pakistan, Indonesia, Mexico, and Eastern Europe are reckoned in, the World's peasantry still amounts today to something between two-thirds and three-quarters of the World's total population. This means that the peasantry's future is going to be decisive for Mankind's, and the crucial question for the peasantry is how they are to come to terms with the modern way of life that has suddenly been conjured into existence by the Industrial Revolution. In Russia, China, and India alike, energetic attempts to modernize the peasantry are being made in our time; but the experiment in India is uniquely important and interesting, because, in India alone of the three titanic peasant countries, the campaign is being conducted on liberal lines. In the two Communist peasant countries, the peasant is being taken by the scruff of the neck and is being forcibly put through the modernization process. It remains to be seen whether the effects of this dragooning will be permanent, but it is certain that the price has been the loss of freedom, and this is too high a price to pay even for indispensable economic progress. India, on the other hand, has chosen the harder and slower way of trying to persuade the peasant's conservative mind to opt for modernization voluntarily as a result of being rationally convinced of its advantages. It is obviously a matter of immense importance for 'the Free World' that this courageous and imaginative Indian experiment should succeed.

India is also an historian's cynosure for a dozen other good reasons. There is her present-day experiment of re-drawing her internal boundaries on linguistic lines. Will India succeed in carrying this experiment out without bringing on herself Eastern Europe's tragic fate? And will she succeed in her international policy of trying to persuade Russia and America to resign themselves to co-existence? As this is the only practical alternative to an atomic third world war, it is a major concern of the human race that the Indian policy of peace-making should not fail. And anyway, whether it fails or succeeds, it is a matter of great interest for the contemporary historian to see something of it at first hand.

But, of course, the historian's interest is not confined to contemporary events. The whole of past history is equally his field; and major events in Mankind's history, since the dawn of civilization, have taken place on Indian soil. India occupies a central position in the festoon of civilizations that is slung across the Old World from Japan at one top corner to the British Isles at the other. So the strategic and political and economic geography of the sub-continent—which, for these purposes, includes Pakistan—is meat and drink to the historian. He wants to see, with his own eyes, the lie of the land and the look of the landscape.

India reveals herself on her roads. An Indian road is never empty and never dull. There is a constant gentle flow of slowly moving traffic: pedestrians and bullock-carts; flocks of sheep and goats and troops of monkeys; country buses (a revolutionary force), no longer pulled by bullock-power but driven by internal combustion engines; an occasional lorry and a still less frequent elephant. Three or four millennia are ambling along side by side; and they do not even keep moving; they camp for the night by the wayside, with the bullocks unyoked and their drivers sleeping snugly under the wheels. In Southern India the cart-wheels are as big as the driving wheels of a locomotive; in Hindustan they are small, with clumsily thick rims; in Upper Sind they are solid, with four holes scooped out of them to lighten their weight; and the turning wooden axle screeches and whines with a music familiar to travellers in Turkey. In Lower Sind, on the other hand, spokes reappear, and the wheels are small and elegant. The bullock-cart is a fascinating object of study—and an important one too; for this must still be by far the commonest form of wheeled vehicle in the World. The total number of the World's motor-cars and rolling-stock must be trivial by comparison. So, on the Indian road, you meet the World's age-old peasantry following its age-old way of life, and the historian never tires of the spectacle. Re-read Kipling's description, in

Kim, of life on the Grand Trunk Road, and you will know why.

But, alas, for the Western wayfarer, all Indian roads lead, in a trice, not to the seven and a half lacs of villages in which the people of India live, but back into the Western World on Indian ground. Travelling through the countryside is an indulgence that is doled out to the inquiring visitor parsimoniously. After a day or two of seeing India, he is politely but firmly steered back into a British-made cantonment or factory: Rawal Pindi or Bangalore; Calcutta, Madras, or Bombay. In Calcutta you are still not quite out of India; for, though Calcutta looks like Pimlico if you keep your line of vision tilted to the second storey, one glance at street level brings India back incarnate in her cows. But in Bombay the municipality has managed to banish the cows to the outskirts, and you find yourself interned in one of the standardized super-cities of the modern world. Bombay is full of interesting people; much of the World's business is transacted there; but you might as well be in Liverpool or in New York. Through the windows of your too comfortable hotel, you look longingly, across the estranging sea, at the mistveiled outlines of the Western Ghats. Over the top lies Maharashtra; but this authentic India is as remote as if a whole ocean lay between it and Bombay Island.

Next time I visit India, I shall not make any engagements or commit myself to a terminal date. I shall buy a bullock-cart (Andhra type) and a pair of patient-eyed white oxen; and then I shall set off on a journey without end. If ever I return, I shall come back, this time, with a cargo of real knowledge piled high between my slowly turning wheels.

34. The Awakening of the Indian Peasantry

Is 'awaken' a transitive or an intransitive verb? I have never been able to decide, and I do not want to be told the answer now; for an ambivalent meaning of the word exactly fits my present subject. The Indian peasantry are certainly being waked up today by a dedicated minority of their urban fellow-countrymen, but no amount of nudging or prodding would avail to arouse Rip van Winkle from his long slumber if something were not astir inside the sleeper. And, even if his would-be benefactors knew that they could wake him up against his will by sticking pins into him, they are too humane and wise and scrupulous to administer this Russian treatment. Their aim is to help the Indian peasant to help himself; and they will put up with frustrations and setbacks rather than coerce him. This is why the present Indian community development work is both admirable and intensely interesting.

How long has the peasant been asleep? Almost as long as the time that has elapsed, up to date, since agriculture was invented. Perhaps as many as eight thousand harvests have been reaped in the World so far; so not much less than eight thousand years may have passed over the sleeping peasant's head.

What accounts for this prolonged state of coma? The peasant has been stupefied by the weight of the burdens placed on his shoulders. Cities and wars, pyramids and cathedrals, arts and crafts, kings and priests, soldiers and Brahmins—all these have climbed on to the peasant's back and have lived, as parasites, on his labours. They have stripped him of his surplus production, leaving him to live at starvation level, while these exotic institutions and privileged minorities have battened on the fruits of his work.

Civilization, with its two congenital diseases, war and slavery, has been built up at the peasant's expense; and, till the other day, the peasant has taken it for granted that this is his unalterable fate. Look into his countenance, and you will see there the same suffering, and the same patient endurance of it, that you find in the beautiful eyes of the mild oxen who pull the peasant's plough and draw his cart until they drop in their tracks from sheer exhaustion. This is how the ox's bucolic master, and his womenfolk and his children, have lived and died since civilization began.

The peasant's fatalism has, of course, been intuitive. It has not been founded on a reasoned interpretation of economic facts. Yet the facts warranted it down to the outbreak of the eighteenth-century agrarian and industrial revolution; for, till then, Mankind's surplus production was so small that, if there was to be such a thing as civilization at all, it was bound to be the monopoly of a minority enjoying it at the peasant majority's cost. Today, for the first time in history, there is a possibility of amenities for all. All over the World today, the peasantry are awakening to this revolutionary change in their age-old situation. In India today, it is the policy of the powers that be to help the peasant to attain the better life that is now at last within his reach.

When we are talking of human beings, 'better' means 'better spiritually'. But in human life the distinction between soul and body is an artificial dichotomy. Man cannot develop his spiritual faculties if the material conditions of his existence are depressed to an animal level. Where the level is as low as this, spiritual and material betterment must go together; and both are catered for in the present community development work in India.

Any attempt to improve the condition of the teeming Indian peasantry has to be on a gigantic scale, and the whole mass cannot be leavened in a single operation. The work has been started in blocks of villages distributed all over the sub-continent. It is hoped that, in a few years, the network of the organization will cover all the villages that there are.

At the headquarters of each block there is a little team of experts—a medical officer, an agricultural adviser, a civil engineer—but the key men and women on the professional staff are the workers in the villages who are in direct touch with the people. These village workers have to know something about road-building, well-digging, public health, and crops, and they have also to be diplomatists, because it lies with them to get the villagers moving under their own steam. The work achieves success when leaders arise in the villages who take up the work themselves and persuade their neighbours to follow them.

The officers of the community development organization set great store by winning over the village women. If the women are not persuaded of the value of the work, they will effectively prevent the men from moving. But, if once the women are convinced, the men's concurrence is assured. Women are, of course, conservative-minded, but they are practical-minded too; and prejudice will not inhibit them from adopting sanitary arrangements, or even 'family planning', if it has been demonstrated, to their satisfaction, that these innovations benefit their children.

What are the stages in the development process? The crowning achievement is a schoolhouse built with substantial contributions, in labour and money, from the villagers themselves. But first things must come first, and, for the improvement of life in an Indian village, the first necessities are wells and drains. In an unregenerate Indian village the lanes ooze with a mixture of cow-dung and human sewage, and this source of a hundred debilitating infections seeps into the village well, if there is one. So the first step is to dig a cement-lined well with a high rim to shield it from contamination at ground-level. The second step is to convert the poisonous lane into a concrete path with a concrete drain running alongside of it. These elementary improvements work wonders, not only for public health, but also for personal self-respect. Such work may sound prosaic, but the spirit behind it is imaginative and humane, and the practical idealism of this great Indian enterprise may be going to bring about one of the most beneficent revolutions in the peasantry's life that have been known, so far, to history.

35. Indian Rivers

India casts a spell over visitors from all quarters of the Earth. The Chinese Buddhist pilgrims who made their way to Gandhara and Bihar in the fifth and seventh centuries of the Christian Era felt India's charm just as strongly as the present-day secular Western inquirer. There are few countries in which the foreign traveller is so much frustrated and exasperated; there are fewer that he so keenly regrets to leave and so eagerly looks forward to visiting again. Long after one has seen the last of this fascinating sub-continent, the music of its life goes on singing in one's ears. It is a strange orchestration, in which a harmony is produced by a mixture of strains that would sound discordant in any other country. The creaking of bullock-cart axles comes into it, and the cawing of crows; but the dominant strain is the inaudible voice of the rivers, which speaks to the eye and transmutes itself into poetry in the enchanted mind.

I have not seen the rivers of India in their monsoon spate. Then, no doubt, they roar and rage like Shiva's bull lashed into fury. I can see them in this mood with my mind's eye, because, in imagination, I can fill with foaming water the vast sand-beds or shingle-fields through which, in other seasons, each river roams like a beneficent python (beneficent because even the most tenuous trickle of running water is a gift of the gods in so thirsty a land).

In England, where it rains all the year round, and where mountains are rare and diminutive, the typical river flows flat and slow between banks, with no third element besides the water and the securely dry land that confines it on either side. In India, in all seasons except the monsoon, the most characteristic feature of a river is neither the watercourse nor the shores, but the vast sandy or shingly no-man's-land that spreads itself out between the embankments. When you arrive at the entrance to a bridge over an Indian river, you do not expect to see water below your wheels; you expect to see sand or shingle that may be submerged for a few days or weeks each year; and, as you pass rapidly over the winding shallow water-channels, you marvel at the god's—or goddess's—forbearance. The divinity is content with so little when, if it chose, it could take so much. How meekly the rivers of the Panjab, and Father Indus himself at the Sukkur Barrage in Sind, submit to Man's impertinent diversion of their waters into Man-made canals, to irrigate the land at Man's will, not at the river's. But beware of taking even the most insignificant Indian river for granted. If you do not study his ways and humour his caprices and pay him deference and, in short, take him seriously, one day he will rise in his wrath and teach you a lesson—breaching his Man-made embankments, sweeping the barrages away, and choking those laboriously-dug canals with silt brought down from hundreds of miles off.

Rivers of India, you haunt my memory. Holy Ganges, do you remember, I saw you first, as is, indeed, meet and right. I had a tantalizing glimpse of you from the air above Patna, where you had already collected your northern affluents, and then I embarked on your waters, up stream, past the ghats of Benares. Even here, you had doubled your volume by swallowing the Jumna, yet still you were not quite great enough (forgive my blasphemy) either to drown all your sands or to purify the refuse that your human devotees cast into you.

Son River, when I think of you, I remember the vast sand desert that you have inflicted on the plains of Bihar. Our leisurely train, en route from Mogulserai to Gaya, took ten minutes to traverse that yellow waste; but, when it came to your living waters, its sluggish wheels crossed them in a flash. Brahmaputra, with your innumerable backwaters and attendant streams, how many sails did I count on your surface as we circled low in the air over Eastern Pakistan? You looked like a beneficent purveyor of waterborne traffic, but the villages, crowded together on every slight elevation of Bengal's marshy ground, told a tale of devastating floods in the season of the melting of the snows.

Godavery and Kistna, I first saw you both on the same evening—glistening silver grey in the failing light, miles-wide within hail of the sea. And then I saw each of you again —you, Kistna, at Nagarjunakonda, where you were spouting your waters between limestone reefs and were remembering that, once upon a time, you had shielded Vijayanagar from Dar-al-Islam, even though today the impious civil engineers are bitting and bridling you with a dam. And you, Godavery, I saw you, for the second time, far, far up your long-drawn-out course. On your bank stood Paithan, the capital city of the ancient Andhras; and, sitting under a tree, I watched bullock-carts and cattle, and donkeys and pedestrians, fording your imposing stream (the goats, alone among the wayfarers, could not cross). So I rolled up my trousers and forded you among the rest, and was not wetted above the thigh.

Sutlej and Beas, I saw your watersmeet as our plane streaked over you towards Amritsar, and I remembered two historic occasions that had both been big with consequences. Do you, Lord Beas, remember the day when Alexander's Macedonians refused to gain your left bank? And you, Lord Sutlej, the day when the Sikhs insisted on gaining yours?

And now you, Father Indus, last but not least of the rivers of the sub-continent to be crossed by a traveller circum-ambulating the globe from east to west. I met you first at Attock, where you suddenly contract your sprawling shingle-bed into a deep and swirling channel between imprisoning bluffs. Here, just below the British-built bridge, the in-domitable Jalal-ad-Din Khwarizmi shook his fist at his Mongol pursuers as he pushed his horse over the rock's brow into your foaming waters. And there, a mile or so

above, I paused to listen to the sweet sound of your watersmeet with the River of Kabul. In the dry season you
courteously allow your respectable tributary to contribute
more than you do to the common stock. That day, I believe
I could have crossed your shingle-bed on foot; but the
breadth of it told me how you behave when you bring down
the snows of the Himalayas. And then I bade you farewell
on your lowest reach, near Tatta. The caravels, with their
rudders, were unloading firewood, and the buffaloes were
returning from their day-long wallow in your waters. O
peaceful and peacegiving scene, may I live to behold you
again.

36. Indian Temples

No 'Works of Man' ever have played or can play so important a part in India's history as her god-given rivers.
If the sub-continent were not watered by rivers, it could not
support life. So the rivers have been enshrined in Indian
myth and ritual, and they have never been more important
than they are in this secular-minded age, when they are being
tapped scientifically for irrigation. A time may come when
every river in India will have been drained dry to feed
India's rapidly growing network of irrigation canals, and
when the storage capacity of India's reservoirs will have
become vast enough to hold the whole volume of the monsoon rain. But, if that time does come, the empty beds of
Nature's superseded waterways will bear witness to the
rivers' enduring value for the country.

By comparison with the rivers of India, her temples are a
recent and minor innovation in her life. This may sound
surprising in a sub-continent where religion has always
loomed so large; yet history bears out this apparently
paradoxical statement. In the earliest centres of Man's
civilization, 'Iraq and Egypt, the temples were the veritable
seeds of the cities. The god in the temple was the owner of the

irrigated land; his servitors became the administrators of the
country; and their headquarters became the nuclei of urban
settlement. There are cities in the south of India today in
which the temple occupies the same central and dominating
position. At Chidambaram, for instance, the city lies four-
square round the four-square temple enclosure with its
quartet of tower-crowned gates; and at Madura, I am told,
the relation between city and temple is the same. As I
circumambulated the temple of Chidambaram, and gazed
at the god's gigantic processional cars laid up, outside
the temenos, to await the annual festival, I fancied myself in
ancient Ur or Babylon. Perhaps the Babylonians may have
influenced the religious architecture of Southern India
(their Sumerian predecessors are known to have been in
touch with the ancient civilization of Mohenjo-daro and
Harappa in the Indus valley). The temple towers of Southern
India are certainly reminiscent of Babylonian ziggurats.
Yet, if we ventured to credit them with a Babylonian
origin, we should be in danger of falling foul of the experts
in Indian archaeology.

Not the Babylonian ziggurat but the Buddhist stupa is the
prototype of the Indian temple according to current archaeological doctrine. Archaeological theories have a disconcerting
way of boxing the compass; but at least it seems to be securely
established that, in India, Buddhism was the mother of
ecclesiastical architecture. The Aryan barbarians who
destroyed the ancient Indus culture probably worshipped
their gods under the open sky. It was the Buddhists who
designed the first substantial religious buildings on Indian
soil: reliquaries, called stupas, to hold relics of the Buddha;
and monasteries, called viharas, to house the monks who were
seeking a happy issue out of this life in accordance with the
Buddha's precepts. The primitive stupa was a round barrow
of earth surmounted by a pole that was garnished with a
series of umbrella-shaped disks. When this structure was
translated into stone, Indian ecclesiastical architecture was
born.

The Buddhists acquired a habit of carving stupas and

viharas out of the living rock inside caves driven into a mountain-side. You can see some of these at Karli, on the rim of the Maharashtrian plateau, on the road up the ghat to Poona from Bombay. And at Ellora you can see how the Buddhist cave was taken over by the Jains and the Hindus; for, at Ellora, caves hewn by followers of all three religions are ranged, in a titanic row, side by side.

I need not describe the mighty Hindu temple at Ellora that has been created, not by laying stone on stone, but by cutting away the living rock till the pattern, conceived in the architect's mind, has been laid bare in a single solid block. This marvellous achievement of human genius and industry is familiar. But there is more beauty in the earlier, smaller, and simpler rock-hewn temples at Mahabalipuram, on the Coromandel Coast between Madras and Pondichéry. In fact, the history of the Hindu temple is a story of increasing elaboration. Mahabalipuram, hewn in about the seventh century of the Christian Era, is almost Greek in the restraint of its conception and in the gracefulness of its lines. But, as century follows century, and the rock-carved temple increases in stature and eventually turns into a pile of intricately carved stones, the beauty ebbs away. In the latest and biggest examples, which date from the age when the Empire of Vijayanagar was providing a citadel for Hinduism in the South against the assaults of Islam, the decoration quite overwhelms the design.

The Hindu temple may be a failure as a work of art, but it is a magnificently successful expression of the feelings of a religion that glories in the prodigality of Nature, the great mother of both life and death. From Chidambaram they took us to Gangaicholapuram. Night had fallen before we arrived, and the great tower soared aloft into the black sky, with the figures of the gods lit up for an instant here and there by the wavering light of our electric torches. As we groped our way along a pillared corridor towards the holy of holies, the strident temple music struck up, and the priest performed his ministrations to the god resident in the principal idol. For a moment, under the spell of the darkness and the din, the

Western visitor could participate in the ecstasy of the Hindu worshippers. The next moment, the second Commandment in the Decalogue had re-established its sway over his Judaic conscience. But that moment of communion with Hinduism was illuminating. It taught the inquirer something about the part that the Hindu temple plays in Indian life.

37. Indian Forts

While India's rivers and temples are still vital today, her forts are obsolete. In the bombing-age, an eyrie is a less eligible defensive position than a rabbit-hole. So the study of forts can be left out of the curriculum of a present-day military cadet. But the famous forts of the World cannot be ignored by the historian; for, till yesterday, the forts have been making history all through the five thousand years that have run since civilization began.

In flat England the fortress perched on a crag is not a familiar feature of the landscape. Most English castles stand on some gentle rise of the ground that would not even be considered as a possible site for a fort in countries where Nature has generously provided the human fort-builder with peaks and precipices. There are, of course, some good sites in Scotland which have been turned to account long ago. But I had scaled the Castelli Romani and Acrocorinthus and Afiun Qara Hisar before I set eyes on Edinburgh Castle, and I have not seen Stirling Castle yet. For me the fort (arx, rocca, kastro, qal'ah) has always been associated with the Mediterranean. Where there are forts I feel at home, so my heart leapt up when I found even bigger and better forts in India.

When I first walked about in Greece, I made it a rule to take in my stride, in the course of my journey, any fort whose altitude was marked on the map as being lower than 1,000 metres above sea-level. If the figure was, say, 973, I would run up and down again, in passing, with rucksack and

raincoat on my back. I thought nothing of it, and I made it
my permanent working rule. It is indeed an excellent rule
for a wayfaring historian, because the summit of a fort is
likely to command a wide view, and the lie of the land is the
one thing that an historian must see with his own eyes,
because this is something that neither photographs nor
contour-maps can convey. When I found myself in India
this year, and saw her magnificent forts rise, one after
another, above the sky-line, I followed my life-long rule as a
matter of course, but India soon taught me how inadequate
Man's physical equipment is for carrying out all his intellectual agenda. When I contracted my habit of scaling
forts in Greece I was 23, and now I am 67, and am exerting
myself in a tropical climate. If I could have recaptured those
expended forty-four years, I could have reached the summit
of Daulatabad, instead of prudently turning back at the
moat, just where the interesting part of the ascent began.
But it would be senseless to kill oneself in the pursuit of
knowledge that one will only be able to use if one manages
to stay alive. So prudence has the last word, though it is a
hard word for the elderly but still eager inquirer to swallow.

Even so, my life-long passion for scaling heights has not
gone completely unsatisfied on the Indian sub-continent. At
Golconda I did climb 'the lovers' staircase' to all but the
topmost roof of the palace that crowns the citadel. At
Tughlaqabad I reached the very top, and looked far and
wide over the grim landscape in which the distant domes of
New Delhi and Shahjahanabad rear themselves up so in-
congruously. And, though I regretfully forbore to climb the
Kutb Minar, I did gain as wide a view by taking the
elevator to the top floor of the brand-new Ashoka Hotel.
This, of course, was cheating, but it was perhaps legitimate
sharp practice at my age; and at Gwalior the tide of modern
progress swept me to the summit without giving me a choice.
Murray's guide-book had informed me that the loan of an
elephant was the only alternative to making the ascent on
foot. But nowadays nobody thinks of climbing the historic
ramp that zigzags up through five successive gates. A nicely

graded road now wafts your car to the top in a trice—too fast for you to have time to scan the huge Jain statues carved in the rock, unless you have the good fortune to be slowed down to a civilized pace by finding yourself at the tail of an unhurriedly ascending bullock-cart.

When one sees Gwalior, one finds it hard to believe that Nature did not deliberately site and shape this fort for Man's convenience. Here is an acropolis that dwarfs the one at Athens and that has needed no artificial building-up. The cliffs are a fortification in themselves, and this natural fastness is so placed that it commands the most important of the routes between the Deccan and the Ganges Valley. At Golconda and Tughlaqabad, Nature did just enough of the work to incite Man to crown the crags with walls and battlements. But here, as in Greece, there is no sharp line between what Nature has begun and what Man has completed. The masonry seems to grow out of the living rock on which it is founded. Soon, no doubt, Tughlaqabad will be enveloped by the box-shaped tenement houses of New Delhi. Already these have lapped round tomb after tomb that, for centuries, has stood in stately solitude; and this army of white cubes is still on the march. Yet, even when Muhammad Tughlaq's desolate city has been invested, its black walls will still hold their own. Tughlaqabad is too rugged and too vast for even New Delhi to capture.

38. Six Days in Ceylon

Six days for seeing a country? Well, it depends which country it is. On my first visit to Southern Asia, many years ago, I had six days, between boats, for reconnoitring the Indian sub-continent. I went in at Karachi and came out at Bombay, with glimpses of Sind, Jodhpur, and Ahmedabad in between. Those glimpses were of priceless value, but, as I discovered this time, I had really seen next to nothing of that vast expanse. Even the two months at my disposal on my present journey turned out to be an utterly inadequate allowance for acquainting myself with so large a slice of the land-surface of the globe. But switch over from India to Ceylon, and your six days become a period in which substantial results can be achieved; for in Ceylon you are pitting yourself, not against infinite space, but only against an island of manageable dimensions.

Your task in Ceylon will also be lightened if your interest is concentrated on the island's dry side, which is the side where the history of Ceylon was made for 2,000 years and is being made again in the present chapter of the story. There is a rain-soaked south-west corner of Ceylon which the historian can ignore, since it was of little account in the island's life till the recent advent of tea-plantations and hill-stations. At the highest and most fashionable hill-station (I forget its name), a homesick Scotswoman can lodge (so I am told) in a semi-detached villa with red-brick walls and blue-slate roof, and there she can indulge in her native sport of being chilled to the bone by Scotch mists that are guaranteed to penetrate three layers of British-woven woollen clothing. This is hearsay; for I did not think it necessary to visit those parts. After all, I can enjoy much the same amenities at home in London without waste of time or expenditure of effort.

What drew me to Ceylon was a pair of notable books: Leonard Woolf's *The Village in the Jungle* and John Still's *Jungle Tide*. Both writers were civil servants; both were posted on the dry side of the island; and both were describing what they had seen, over a number of years, in the course of their own daily work. Ever since I read those two books, I have longed to see the country that is the scene of them. Now, at last, my cherished desire has been fulfilled, and the reality has surpassed my great expectations.

I was nearly foiled at the start; for, when we landed in the Tamil town of Jaffna, at the northern tip of the island, we found ourselves in danger of being immobilized by one of those communal conflicts which, in these days, are apt to make havoc of the inquiring traveller's best laid plans. In

Ceylon the majority of the population consists of Buddhist Sinhalese; but very many of the desirable jobs in the island have gone, in the past, to the Hindu Tamil and the Christian 'Burgher' minorities, which have been more enterprising than their Sinhalese neighbours in equipping themselves for life in the modern world. The Sinhalese have a chip on their shoulder, and, having discovered how to exercise the power that automatically accrues to the majority of the electorate in a parliamentary democracy, they are feeling tempted to abuse it. A Sinhalese ministry had just decreed that the number-plates of all cars in Ceylon must bear a sign in the Sinhalese alphabet; the Tamil minority had threatened to retort by lying down in front of any car that complied with the regulation. Our choice seemed to lie between being arrested for breaking the law and being stopped in our tracks by a row of prostrate Tamil bodies. We escaped the dilemma by slipping away in the night from Jaffna to Elephant Pass, half-way out of the Tamil country.

The jungle on the dry side of Ceylon is like the jungle in Yucatan. Its greenery is so fresh that one can hardly believe in the drought, and it is so full of wild animals and birds that one wonders how far they have to trek for a drink. They must all qualify as bona-fide travellers. Grey monkeys, with black faces and S-shaped tails held stiffly erect, peer out at the passer-by between the leaves and then swing their way up to safety in the boughs.

You do not understand this country till you come to the bunds: the long dams built by the ancients at the mouths of valleys fanning out from the horseshoe-shaped central highlands. Below each bund there was once a spreading oasis of paddy fields, till war and anarchy brought these magnificent engineering works to ruin and temporarily shifted the focus of agriculture and population to the rain-watered south-west. Today the tide is flowing back again. The bunds are being repaired, the reservoirs are re-filling; the paddy fields are being re-cultivated; and peasants are re-colonizing what was recently a wild beasts' land. The recentness of this work of restoration is proclaimed by the weird forests of dead trees—trees killed by the rising water, but not yet rotted away—which still infest the reconditioned reservoirs.

If you wish to have a bird's-eye view of this panorama, climb to the top of Sigiriya—the crag that, 1,500 years ago, was transformed into a palace-fastness by a king who, according to one account, had committed a crime which made him live in fear of assassination. The climb is a stiff one, even if you are not attacked by bees on the cliff face, but the physical exertion is worth while; for, on that astonishing summit, you find yourself transported back in time to the days when the dry side of Ceylon was at its zenith.

39. Sravana Belagola

As our wheels swerved off the tarmac on to an unmetalled side-track, my spirits rose. The worse the going, the better the chances of getting into touch with the country. One does not, after all, do this travelling in quest of comfort. If comfort were one's object, one would be wiser to stay at home. One travels to gain knowledge at a cost, and, for the past two days, this objective had been eluding me.

When you bowl along the excellent road from Bangalore to Mysore, you find yourself traversing the South Indian plateau without ever beginning to become intimate with it. Only that precious hour salvaged for a hasty visit to Seringapatam had brought us into communion with India, present and past. As we stood on the breach near the head of the triply fortified island, time seemed to ebb back from 1957 to 1799. Nothing more had happened on this spot since the storming of the stronghold. Up-stream, the waters of the Cauvery River shone blue as they threaded their way through the ice-pack of reefs gleaming white like giant crocodiles' teeth. On the day when Tipoo Sahib lost his kingdom and his life, the reefs must have been gleaming and the waters sounding just as dazzlingly and as musically as now. And then, as now, that little hermitage, perched on a rock in the river-bed, just above the point where the waters divide, must have been radiating its spirit of serenity—even though, on that day, the shot from the besieger's batteries was skimming low over its frail roof. That hour had been an illuminating one, but we had quickly been re-captured by the modern world, which is uniform from China to Peru. Well, now at last we are off the tarmac; perhaps we are going to break our way out into reality.

As we jolted along the 'dirt road', just fast enough to keep clear of the dust raised by our wheels, the surface of the plateau came to life. It washed round us like a choppy sea turned to stone, with crops of hardy cereals sprouting green in the troughs between the boulder-waves. On and on it rolled, till a vertical object rose above the horizon, and then a smaller vertical object on top of that. Sravana Belagola! The titanic white statue carved out of a mountain top. We are within sight of the goal of today's detour.

That heroic human figure into which the living rock has been carved portrays one of the Jain Tirthankaras—the saints of an Indian religion that was founded about 2,500 years ago in the same generation as Buddhism, but whose fate has been strangely different from its more familiar sister's. Buddhism's fortunes have been the same as Christianity's. After converting half the World, it has lost its hold on the country that brought it to birth and that is, in consequence, its holy land. The only Buddhists in India today are a handful of foreign Buddhist devotees who cluster round the scenes of the Buddha's Ministry in Bihar, and some members of the 'scheduled' castes who have recently proclaimed themselves Buddhists as a protest against the raw deal that has been dealt to them by Hinduism. By contrast, the Jain religion has never ceased to have adherents in India, but has never made converts outside the limits of the sub-continent.

Sravana Belagola is a living Jain holy city. Two austerely naked mountains here rise perpendicularly out of the plateau's undulating surface. In the hollow between them

lies a tank surrounded by solidly-built stone houses with
finely carved lintels and doors. From the summit of the
higher of the two mountains the stark figure of the Tirthankara soars into the burning sky. The lower mountain is
crowned with temples and pierced with sacred caves. I
climbed both mountains in the midday heat, with the sun-
drenched rock scorching the naked soles of my feet (every
inch of both mountains is holy ground which one has to
tread unshod). The climbs are hard and painful, but they
are rewarding; for they do give the foreign inquirer some
sense of the spirit of the religion that has impressed itself so
powerfully on these two huge masses of stone.

We did not leave without paying our respects to the Jain
bishop of the place, a little old man in a yellow robe who is
the only surviving representative of his order in this region.
His wrinkled face lights up with a benignant smile, and the
austerity of his way of life stands out against the splendour
of the richly carved stone palace within which he happens to
be camping on his journey through this life.

The atmosphere of Sravana Belagola is distinctive but
elusive. It is utterly Indian; yet it is also utterly un-Hindu.
Here, too, as inside the ramparts of Seringapatam, time ebbs
back into the past; but, in this Jain holy city, the extent of the
ebb is enormous. The recoiling wave sweeps the passing
visitor back into an age at least twelve centuries out of date
—into India as she must have been before Shankaracharya's
brief passage through the World set Hinduism on its present
course. The Jain Church is a living remnant of this ancient
India which time's flow has all but submerged. First
Shankara's militant Hinduism and then Mahmud's militant
Islam have deluged the sub-continent. Only here and there a
Jain community still holds its head above the surface of the
flood, as the statue carved out of the mountain top stands up
out of the sea-like plateau. That towering figure, noble in
mien and stiff in posture, reminds a classically educated
Western visitor of some statue carved in Greece in the
sixth century B.C.—the archaic age in which the Jain
Church was founded in India by Mahavira. Has India lost

or gained by becoming what Shankaracharya has made of her? Put the question to the Tirthankara. His stone lips will go on smiling and his stone eyes go on gazing into space. The sage has, long since, risen above all the chances and changes of history; so our question will receive no answer from that severely serene countenance. Hindu India must find the answer for herself.

40. Amritsar and Lahore

Minnesotan reader, imagine, if you can, that the perversity of human nature has split your splendid state in two by driving an international frontier in between Minneapolis and St. Paul. Imagine that every Catholic in the United States, north-west of that outrageous line, has had to flee for his life, leaving home, job, and possessions behind him, and cross the line to live the wretched life of a 'displaced person' on the safe side of it. Imagine that every Protestant south-east of the line has had to make the same tragic migration in the opposite direction. And then imagine that the road traffic across the new frontier has been entirely cut off (there is a no-man's-land, two miles broad, that is forbidden ground for cars travelling in either direction). Railroad traffic still survives, but it has been reduced to a single train a day. The armed guards on board it change as the fearsome border is crossed. Imagine all this, and you will have pictured to yourself what has happened in real life to that unfortunate country the Panjab and its historic twin cities, Amritsar and Lahore.

Amritsar is a creation of the Sikh religion. The Golden Temple was planted in the wilds, and a secular city grew up around it. But, till the deadly partition in 1947, a Sikh who lived in Amritsar never dreamed that he might be debarred from carrying on his profession in Lahore, while a Muslim who lived in Lahore never dreamed that he might be debarred from owning and cultivating a field in the district of Amritsar. Lahore was the Sikhs' and Muslims' common capital; the broad Panjab countryside was the common source of their livelihood.

Why has the rankling memory of an ancient feud impelled these once intermingled communities to sort themselves out at such a dreadful cost to both of them? The fate that they have brought on themselves seems ironic to the foreign inquirer who feels sympathy for both alike; for, as it appears to the outsider, the Sikh faith and Islam have a close affinity with one another. The atmosphere of Amritsar strikes a Western observer as being decidedly Islamic and, indeed, almost Protestant. Hindu worship is a casual disorderly affair; Sikh worship is as precise and as highly disciplined as the proceedings in a mosque or in a Calvinist church. The Granth Sahib, which is the Sikh Khalsa's holy scripture, is an anthology in which selections from the works of Kabir and other Muslim mystics find a place beside the works of Guru Nanak, the father of the Sikh faith. And the veneration paid to the Granth Sahib goes beyond the furthest extremes of Protestant Christian bibliolatry. Why could not Sikhs and Muslims—and, for that matter, Hindus as well—go on living side by side in an unpartitioned Panjab? The perversity of human nature is the greatest of the mysteries of human life.

We took that international train and arrived at Lahore, without incident, in advance of the scheduled time. How strange to see Ranjit Singh's tomb shouldering its way between fort and mosque. It was certainly a provocative act to plant the Sikh war-lord's sepulchre at the most sensitive spot in the Muslim quarters of Lahore. But, then, who built that magnificently austere imperial masjid, whose courtyard is bigger than that of any other mosque in the sub-continent? The builder was Aurangzeb. And who committed the provocative act of razing the principal Hindu temple in Benares and planting a mosque in its place? Aurangzeb again. Who else could it be? And so the tale of wrong and counter-wrong stretches back through a long chain of generations.

As a result of partition, Lahore has gained in political importance. It is no longer the capital of a unitary Panjab, but it has now become the capital of a unitary Western Pakistan. Yet it is no longer what it was when Kim clambered over the famous cannon (which still stands in its place) in a city that was then still a common home for the followers of three faiths. Amritsar has a surer future, for it will remain the religious centre of the Sikhs so long as the Khalsa endures; and the Sikhs, in losing the Panjab, have gained the World. Today they are established all over India (above the wheel of every second bus and taxi, you spy that unmistakable bearded and turbaned head). And they have not kept within India's frontiers. They have made their way eastwards through Burma and Singapore and Hongkong to the Pacific slope of Canada. They are the burliest men on the face of the planet—tough and capable and slightly grim. If human life survives the present chapter of Man's history, the Sikhs, for sure, will still be on the map.

41. Gandhara

When the Greeks, led by Alexander, overthrew and overran the Persian Empire, they made good their hold on their sudden vast conquests by planting settlements of their own people at key points. For most of these Greek colonists, this meant a permanent exile in unfamiliar and uncongenial landscapes and climates: the torrid canyon of Upper Egypt, the bleak highlands of Anatolia and Iran, the plains of 'Iraq and the Panjab, with their extreme seasonal variations of temperature, or the desert through which the River Euphrates wends its way on its long journey from the Armenian mountains to the Babylonian black earth. The hardihood and endurance of those Greek pioneers is impressive. Their community at Dura-Europus, on a bluff overhanging the Euphrates on the desert section of its course, maintained itself for five or six hundred years. I have not set eyes on

Dura yet, but I have a vivid visual memory of the little
Greek theatre that still stands today among the vast rubble
mounds of Babylon.

These Greeks holding their own in an alien environment
were heroes; but, naturally, they rejoiced when they
stumbled on some patch of Asian country in which they felt
at home. One such replica of their native Greece was the well-
wooded and well-watered hill-country east of the River
Jordan. The Greeks pounced on it and turned it into a
decapolis: a cluster of no less than ten Greek city-states, of
which the best preserved today is Gerasa, and the most
famous is Gadara, home of the Gadarene swine and the
elegiac poet Meleager. A second Greece-in-Asia was
Gandhara: the basin of the Kabul River, which is the
principal right-bank tributary of the Indus. Here, almost
at the easternmost verge of the Greeks' new dominions, was a
land of Grecian mountains, springs, streams, greenswards,
and vineyards. This must be the legendary Nysa, the birthplace of the god Dionysus. The Greeks took to this unexpected Indian paradise as kindly as they took to the nearer
Transjordanian hills. It is a long way to Gandhara from the
shores of the Aegean. Yet Greek rule lasted there for three
hundred years, and Greek cultural influence for another
four or five hundred years after that.

It is no wonder that the Greeks held on to Gandhara
when once they had discovered it; for, unlike the Transjordanian decapolis, Gandhara combined the Greek colonists' two desiderata. It was not only a congenial new home for
them; it was also a strategic position of first-class importance.
The Kabul valley is a meeting-point of routes running in
from, and out to, the Indian sub-continent, the Central
Asian oases, and, far away across the Iranian plateau and the
Babylonian plains, the shores of the Mediterranean Sea.
In offering the Greeks this double attraction, Gandhara was
unique among the countries of Western Asia. It is no accident
that, twenty-two centuries after Alexander's day, this country
fascinated the British, as it had fascinated their Greek
precursors.

Like my fellow-countrymen a hundred and twenty years ago, and like Chandragupta, Alexander's Indian contemporary and emulator, I approached Gandhara from the Indian side. The five rivers of the Panjab are knit together, nowadays, by a network of canals, and from Sutlej to Jhelum there is a continuous carpet of fields. But, above the Jhelum's western bank hangs the Salt Range, bare as the moon; and, when you have threaded your way between this barrier and the southern foothills of the Himalayas, you find yourself in a rocky wilderness, tenanted only by the cantonment-city of Rawal Pindi. You must press on, from Pindi north-westward, along Sher Shah's Grand Trunk Road, into a pass in a farther range of hills which is commanded by a con-spicuous monument to John Nicholson, and then you will find yourself in another world, laved by flowing waters and spangled with wildflowers. Here lie the imposing sites of the three successive cities of Taxila: the first Indian and Persian, the second Greek, the third Kushan. You may or may not yet have crossed the official frontier of Gandhara; the historians dispute as to whether Taxila was included in it. But you are already in Gandhara if landscape and climate are the test.

The Greeks' Gandhara, like Caesar's Gaul, was divided into three parts: the basin of Taxila, east of the Indus; the lower basin of the Kabul River, east of the Khyber Pass; and the upper Kabul basin, where the river flows through open country above its point of entry into the Warsak Gorge.

We peered up the gorge from the point where the river emerges from it, and then we headed for the Khyber Pass; and, in an hour or two, I found myself at the famous pass's western foot, looking over into Afghanistan. As I edged towards the line of whitewashed stones that marks the frontier, craning my neck to catch a glimpse of the snow-covered Hindu Kush towering over Kafiristan, a soldier in the Afghan control post shouted to me gruffly to keep my distance. At the same moment, he courteously lowered the chain across the road to permit a camel to pass, and the creature crossed unchallenged, head in air, lifting its feet above the chain with a disdainful gesture. This was, of course, quite in order. I had no Afghan visa, while the camel, no doubt, had produced three passport photographs (full-face and profile; $2 \times 1\frac{1}{2}$ ins.) and had filled in a form disclosing the names and birthplaces of his father and his grandfather. In fact, he had complied with the regulations, and I had not; so I had no ground for complaint. All the same, I felt aggrieved and, even more sharply, envious. One day, I swore to myself, I will follow in that camel's footsteps, and will spurn the lowered chain as proudly as he did. Yes, I, too, am going to set foot in Upper Gandhara before I die.

42. The Dissolving Frontier

What a characteristic scene of modern life in this age of technology. The mouth of a gorge is to be blocked with a dam. A diversionary tunnel has already been driven through the mountain-side to carry the river's waters while the dam's foundations are being laid. The workshops sprawl over the plain; the workers' housing estates climb the mountains' flanks and perch on their spurs on either side of the narrow valley. Who are these labourers who swarm like ants, shovelling, blasting, carting, driving? I have put the question to the Canadian controller of labour, and he tells me that they are the local tribesmen: Mohmands from the hills north of the river, Afridis from the hills south of it. The project is in Canadian hands, but this wilderness is not the Laurentian Shield or the Rockies. We are at the mouth of the Warsak Gorge, through which the Kabul River forces its way en route from the plain of Jelalabad to the plain of Peshawar; and my Canadian mentor is at home in two worlds. When he turns to say something to one of his men, his speech changes from English into Urdu. He is the son of a Canadian missionary in the U.P., and Hindustani, the lingua franca that is the parent of both Urdu and Hindi, is his second mother-tongue.

The Warsak Dam is Canada's gift to Pakistan under the Colombo Plan, and the project is admirably designed for solving the problem of the frontier that the Pakistanis inherited from the British, and the British, a hundred years back, from the Sikhs. The mountains are bare and barren; the patches of cultivable ground in the torrent-beds are small and rare; the highlanders are numerous and hungry. They must either starve or make their living off the eastern plains into which their valleys open. They will not starve without fighting; so, for the rulers of the plains, the alternative to being at war with the highlanders is to provide them with some alternative occupation.

During the British century of the frontier's history, which ended in 1947 with the transfer of power to the newly constituted government of Pakistan, a state of war had been the rule. There had been a vicious circle of raids, punitive expeditions, reprisals, and then more punitive expeditions on a larger scale. History kept on repeating itself, but with an increasing tendency for the burden of frontier defence to grow heavier out of proportion to the effort exerted by the tribesmen. A few thousand highlanders, armed with modern rifles—weapons bought or stolen from across the line, or manufactured at home by cleverly copying Western models —were able to keep in play large forces of regular troops, equipped with elaborate and expensive apparatus and served by a host of non-combatants on the lines of communication. The balance was shifting in the barbarian's favour, and this at an accelerating pace; and the history of the frontiers of the Roman and the Chinese empires bore witness to one of the ways in which the story might end. The growing financial burden might eventually break the back of the defence, and then the barbarians might burst through into the plains, like one of their own mountain torrents in spate.

This had not, however, been the way that the story had ended always and everywhere. The Scottish highlanders,

for example, who had pushed their way as far as Derby in
1745, had not, after all, overrun Britain. Instead, they had
been converted from pugnacious barbarians into respectable
and industrious citizens by being enticed into the new mills
of Glasgow and the new homesteads of Upper Canada. That
ending to the story of frontier warfare was a happy one; and
today, two hundred years later, the Government of Pakistan
is trying to make the story of the Pathan frontier come to an
end in this happy Scottish way. Perhaps it would have ended
like that if the British dispensation had continued; for that
British century had already brought the modern world to the
threshold of the Pathan highlander's hovel. Anyway, the
transformation scene is in progress now; and the Pakistani
heirs of the British raj deserve credit for the imaginativeness
and the boldness of their approach to the frontier problem.
I met the political officer who had taken the decision to
withdraw the troops from the cantonment at Razmak in the
heart of Waziristan. 'We leave the place to you,' he had said
to the Wazirs. 'You can do what you like with it.' The tribesmen were so taken aback that, instead of razing the evacuated
cantonment to the ground, they took care of it as a valuable
piece of public property.

Those well-housed Afridi and Mohmand workers on the
Warsak Dam will not go back to their hovels in the hills.
When the Warsak project is complete, they will take up
holdings on the hitherto barren tracts of the plain that the
Warsak reservoir is going to irrigate. And the power that the
reservoir will generate will give them electricity in the home.

I visited the famous arms factory in the strip of un-
administered territory between Peshawar and the Kohat
Pass. The gun-smiths there are still turning their lathes by
foot-driven wheels; but their workshop is now lighted by
electricity laid on from the Peshawar power-station, so the
future retort to a shooting incident will be, not a punitive
expedition, but one of those 'forms', threatening to cut off
the current, that are served on a user when he is late in
paying his quarterly bill to the electricity board. In falling
for electric light and hospitals and schools, the tribesman is,

indeed, placing himself at civilization's mercy. Soon those lathes will be operated by electric power instead of by foot-work, and the craftsmen will be turning out bicycles and motor-buses instead of the rifles, revolvers, knives, and battle-axes that are their present stock in trade. Their children will go to the University of Peshawar (a hostel, with free board, lodging, and tuition, has already been built for them there). Their grandsons will become garage-hands; their grand-daughters, shorthand typists. A prosaic ending to a romantic story? Well, if the story does end like this, it is not to be regretted; for the superficially romantic story of the frontier turns out to have been nasty and brutish when one scrutin-izes it.

43. Mohenjo-daro and Harappa

How will the present generation's record read in retrospect (assuming that we leave successors to keep the record, and do not wipe ourselves out)? Our age will be remembered, I fancy, for its paradoxical combination of signal failures with signal successes. We have failed dismally to dwell together in peace and unity; we have succeeded brilliantly in disinterring the forgotten achievements of our predecessors. In our life-time at least three new civilizations that had lain in oblivion for several thousand years have been brought back to light by the archaeologist's spade: the Minoan civilization on the Aegean island of Crete; the Shang civilization in the Yellow River basin in Northern China; and the Indus civilization in Western Pakistan. Having long ago seen Minoan Cnossos and Phaestus, I had set my heart on visiting Mohenjo-daro and Harappa, which are the two principal sites of the Indus civilization that have been excavated so far; and now, on my present journey round the World, I have fulfilled this cherished desire at last.

Both sites are mounds that stand up dramatically out of the boundless plain. Their height and extent bear witness to the scale of urban life in the Indus Valley when this civilization throve there in the third and second millennia B.C. It was a competent, business-like civilization. The size and texture of its bricks is the first feature of it that strikes the visitor's eye. It might tax the skill of the most up-to-date modern brick-works to match these bricks that were baked four thousand years ago. They would last for ever if they were not being corroded by the salt that works into them from the sub-soil. The next thing that one notices is the matter-of-fact nature of the uses to which these magnificent bricks were put. The two cities were laid out on a rect-angular plan, with straight streets, of varying widths, crossing one another at right angles. Sewers, baths, and granaries, not temples or palaces, were the first items on the builders' agenda. The baths were made effectively water-tight. The granaries were conveniently located on quays by the river-side. But the town-planners did not foresee the tricks that the rivers were going to play on them in the course of ages. The Indus has sidled away from the quays of Mohenjo-daro, and the Ravi from the quays of Harappa. No matter! The two cities had been laid waste by fire and sword before the rivers deserted their desolate emplace-ments.

Who built these great cities and lived in them? The origin of their inhabitants is a mystery. The cities seem not to have grown up gradually, like Ur or Paris, but to have been laid out deliberately on a plan, like Washington or New Delhi or Canberra, and the material remains of their culture show little sign of being related to the more primitive ancient cultures of Baluchistan. This suggests that the fathers of the Indus civilization had not only come from somewhere outside the sub-continent, but had come from far afield. After they had established themselves in the Indus Valley they were in touch with the Sumerian civilization in the lower valley of the Tigris and the Euphrates. Seals inscribed in the Indus civilization's script have been found on Sumer-ian sites. This script has baffled attempts to decipher it so far; but it is manifest that it is not derived from the Sumerian

people's cuneiform characters. So 'Iraq cannot have been the
Indus civilization's starting-point. Was it brought in from
Iran, or perhaps from distant Anatolia? Mohenjo-daro was
evidently its focal point; and this is just the place where the
west bank of the Indus would be reached by invaders
entering the sub-continent through the Bolan Pass. And how
far east did this civilization spread into India before it was
submerged by a later wave of invaders from the north-west?
One new Indus-culture site has recently been found in
East Panjab, and another in Kathiawar. When the great
mounds at Thanésar and at Máthura are eventually opened
up, will the Indus civilization reveal its presence in their
lower strata?

The Aryan barbarians, who may have been the Indus
civilization's destroyers and were certainly its successors,
eventually succumbed, as we know, to the race and culture of
the older occupants of the sub-continent in spite of their
efforts to keep their intrusive race and culture unadulter-
ated. Did the bearers of the Indus civilization go the same
way in the course of their millennium on Indian ground?
The severely practical lay-out of their cities strikes the
amateur observer as being a thoroughly un-Indian trait.
Their prosaic concern for efficient drainage has perhaps
never since been emulated by the native sons of the soil
until almost within living memory, and even then the
inspiration has come to India from abroad. But look now at
this seal. Though we cannot yet read the superscription, the
image is, beyond doubt, a representation of the god Shiva,
and this magnificent humped bull can only be Shiva's
familiar, Nandi. Did the builders of Harappa and Mohenjo-
daro bring Nandi and Shiva with them from their still
unidentified place of origin? Or did they find them already
reigning in India, and fall under their spell there, as their
Aryan successors did?

What a string of unanswered questions and unsolved
problems. Some lucky stroke of an exploring pick-axe may
lighten our darkness before these lines go into print.

44. By Catapult from Karachi to Beirut

We were slung into the air at half-past four in the morning
—a bad hour at its best, and it is at its worst when one has
had to rise at half-past two. As we soared aloft, the waters of
the Hab River, the eastern boundary of Baluchistan, shone
with a silvery sheen in the moonlight. In a moment we were
over the sea, and then I must have dozed; for, when I next
became aware of the Universe, we were passing the frontier
between Pakistan and Persia, and the dawn was overtaking
us. I drank to the dregs the dismal vision of Persian Baluchistan. 'When God made Baluchistan, He laughed'; and He
must have laughed again when He made the Horn of
Arabia. Here it comes, shooting up suddenly from the water.
The Gulf of Oman is already behind us, and we are sailing
at right-angles over a range of mountains looking like a
crumpled sheet of brown paper. No sign of life on that
wrinkled patch of the Earth's skin. Twenty-eight years ago,
when I was steaming through the straits of Hormuz in the
opposite direction, cape Musandim, the tip of the Horn,
was wreathed in clouds, but that was in rainy September, and
this is arid March.

By this time the sun has lighted up the cabin window, and
the brown-paper mountains have changed into yellow sand.
Yes, God must indeed have laughed when He buried the oil
under the desert, and have laughed again when the diplomatists, sitting huddled round a small-scale map, so light-
heartedly drew their international frontiers in neat, straight
lines over a terrain which, so they believed, could never
acquire any value. The joke was that they signed and sealed
their treaties just before the oil prospectors got to work. If
the diplomatists had waited till after that, they would have
haggled over every square foot of Arabian sand as anxiously

as if it had been the Saargebiet or the Donbas; for the wealth
of Arabia Deserta has now outshone the wealth of Ormuz
and of Ind.

The sand has vanished in its turn; we are over the water
again; and I am peering backwards over my right shoulder
at the throat of the straits and the butt end of Qishm Island.
But my eyes are soon captivated by the panorama of the
mountains of Laristan and Fars. There is no doubt about
the first three tiers, but is the fourth tier rock or cloud?
If it is solid rock it must be the rim of the high plateau, and
the oases of Yazd and Kirman must lie only just behind that
giant curtain.

Now the mountains sheer off, and the sea suddenly
changes colour from blue to brown. I am catching the Twin
Rivers at their age-old work of filling the Gulf with silt
brought down from the Armenian mountains. The silt-dump
shows up through the thin film of sea-water, and I am trying
to make out whether the sea has petered out and the dry
land begun when the question is answered for me by the
emergence of a palm grove and a house—the first sign of
human life that I have seen since we were catapulted out
of Karachi airport some four or five hours ago. The palm
groves and the houses multiply, and the mud-flats are parted
by a waterway with steamers plying on it. What can this be
but the Shatt? Yes, it must be the Shatt, for this labyrinth of
fantastic apparatus, surrounded by neat housing-estates,
that is now elbowing the palm groves aside—this can only be
Abadan. The debouchure of the Karun River into the Shatt
conclusively settles that point. When I was steaming down
the Shatt those twenty-eight years ago, how wistfully I
looked up the Karun River into Persia. I look up it again
expectantly now; for this time, God willing, I am going to
visit Persia in due course.

Next Basra comes and goes; we are flying over a dismal
lake; and, to the north of it, the Shatt collects the waters of
three tributary rivers. The Shatt is surprisingly jejune, and
its feeders are mere trickles. That trickle over there must be
the Karkheh, but can these two others really be the Tigris

and Euphrates? 'What is that little creek?' an American visitor once inquired of an old friend of mine as they sat opposite one another in the train between London and Oxford. 'The Thames.'—'Not the famous Thames?'— 'Yes, the famous Thames'; and the American collapsed. So this is what the famous Tigris and Euphrates look like from the air.

My goodness, here is Najaf. I spy the Golden Dome. It is blazing like a burning-glass under the drum-fire of a Sun who is now racing towards his zenith. The dark edge of the palm groves fades out of sight as we shoot away over the gravelly desert. Flat steppe and dry ravine, steppe and ravine, ravine and steppe. The landscape is becoming monotonous, when my eyes start out of my head; for here is one ravine that is running with sky-blue water—blue water that turns into cascades of white foam where the ravine becomes precipitous. This must be the Wadi Hauran, but whoever heard of water flowing down it? But the wonder of wonders is the last. Two lines of snow-covered mountains rise one behind the other: Antilebanon and Lebanon! The brown gravel of the desert breaks out into a rash of little black volcanoes, and then it turns green. We are over the Ghutah. By Abana and Pharpar, we are over Damascus, and in twelve minutes more we have skipped across both those great white ranges and are circling down over a sea that is not the Persian Gulf but the Mediterranean. Mare Nostrum; Beirut; why, I am almost back in England. What a bathos. Can it be true that only this morning I was gazing at Baluchistan?

45. Skirting Israel

When you travel southward from Beirut, the first intimation of the neighbourhood of a danger-zone is a military in-spection-barrier across the road at the northern approaches to Sidon. This first barrier is not a serious one, and the

innocent traveller can get through without being required
to produce any special papers. From Sidon he can then drive
on, without let or hindrance, to Tyre, and there, standing
among the disinterred ruins of the ancient city, overlooking
Phoenician Tyre's 'Egyptian harbour', he will find the
frontier within full view along the southern horizon. An east-
west range of mountains dips into the sea at Cape Nakura,
and beyond that, he knows, lies the land that once was called
Galilee.

The Greeks called Cape Nakura 'the Ladder of Tyre'.
If mule and man were prepared to clamber over the mount-
ain's shoulder above its plunge down a steep place into the
sea, they could pass—just as they could, north of Beirut, at
the Dog River, where a series of conquerors, ranging from
Ramses II in the thirteenth century B.C. to the British in
1942, have carved records of their passage on the rock. At
Cape Nakura, though, the Ladder has now been removed.
Look closely at the rails on the Beirut-Nakura section of the
Calais-Cairo railway; they are rusty today from disuse.
Haifa, on the far side of the dividing cape, might as well be
a million miles away.

At Tyre we turned inland, past a gaunt shanty-town of
refugees from what is now Israel, towards our present ob-
jectives: the Jabal 'Amil and the two Crusader castles,
Toron and Beaufort, that dominate this Shi'ite Muslim
country. The Jabal 'Amil is vastly interesting to an historian,
because it was from here that, in the sixteenth century,
Shah Isma'il and his successors on the throne of Iran
recruited Shi'ite doctors of the law to instruct orthodox Sunni
Muslim Persians in the heterodox form of their faith that the
Safavi dynasty was forcing upon them. Nowadays the South
Lebanese Shi'ites make their fortunes, not as theologians in
Iran, but as shopkeepers in the United States. Their success
in business in the New World is advertised in the magnificence of the houses that some of them have built for them-
selves in their local capital, Nabatieh. As for Beaufort and
Toron, they are magnets, not only for an historian, but for
anyone with a touch of romantic feeling in him.

I was not specially concerned with Israel on this occasion, but, as I have no less zest for current events than I have for less recent history, I was not sorry that today's journey was going to take us—if we got through—within a stone's throw of the Lebanon-Israel border. My road from Tyre to my two castles dipped down, the map told me, into the south-east corner of Lebanon, and then ran northwards, edging closer and closer to the armistice-line, till, opposite the northern tip of Israel, it apparently ran almost within a stone's-throw of the perilous boundary. How enticing! Let us go and see what happens.

What did happen was no more than a series of parleys at military inspection-barriers straddling the road at shorter and shorter intervals. I had in my hand a magic document which waived these barriers aside, one after another. The Lebanese military authorities are careful and strict, as it is their duty to be; but they are also cheerful and friendly, and my 'open sesame' proved to be a potent one. So at Tibnin we duly mounted to the top of Toron Castle, with an amiable soldier detailed to show us the way, and from there our eyes, ranging over the rolling grey scaurs and green corn-fields below us, caught Beaufort, the main goal of our journey, towering up far away to the north-north-east. Descending from our first objective, now achieved, we set out again on our southward-bending road.

After we had rounded the great bend and passed through the little town of Meis Jabal, we sighted a village, with some tall buildings in it, on a commanding hill-top to our right front. 'That is Manara,' said our driver, 'that is in Israel.' As he said it, he looked at me out of the corner of his eye to watch the effect of his sensational announcement, and I did feel a slight frisson at finding myself within a few hundred yards of so commanding a position in a hostile neighbour country. A few minutes later, we came much closer than that to the Lebanon's formidable neighbour. At the exit from the village of Adeiseh, the road suddenly turned east and climbed over the watershed between the Mediter-ranean and the Great Rift Valley that runs southward from Turkey through 'Aqaba to Tanganyika. In an instant the flat bottom of the valley broke into view, with Lake Huleh, behind one's right shoulder, in the southern distance; and this glimpse of Israel was impressive. The swamps that used to cover part of this section of the valley had been transformed into a chequer-board of fields, and the fields were interspersed with big villages or small country towns. Blocks of tall apartment-houses, and plantations of trees, were conspicuous features. Up the opposite slopes lowered Syria, under a blanket of cloud that veiled the snows of Mount Hermon.

What is that white sugar-loaf, not a stone's-throw, but a foot's pace, away from the right-hand edge of the road? It must be a boundary mark, and, look, here comes another and another. Invisible eyes may be keeping track of us through field-glasses from the farther side; so I do not feel inclined to trespass, even by a toe's length. Yet here is a branch-road crossing the frontier to the right and leading to that village over there about three-quarters of a mile away. The village must be in Israel, and so it is: it is Metulleh, at Israel's northernmost tip. And now look at that side-road again. You will notice that it is half overgrown with grass. Like the Beirut-Haifa section of the Calais-Cairo railway, it has been out of commission for nine years. Once upon a time, one could travel along it out of Lebanon into Palestine. But today there is no longer a country called Palestine, and the former road into Palestine is derelict.

46. Beaufort

Where one stands and looks, from inside Lebanon, at Metulleh, inside Israel, one is on the southern lip of the Marjayyun. 'Meadow of Springs': a lovely name for a lovely place. This is a fertile upland basin, welling with the springs that are Jordan's north-western sources, and dropping these waters over its lip into the Israeli section of the Rift Valley.

And now, from the village of Khiam, on the eastern rim of the lovely Marj, I am peering round the southern foot-hills of Mount Hermon towards Baniyas—the grotto-spring named Paneion in honour of the Greek god Pan. Here the Macedonian emperor of Western Asia, Antiochus III, once defeated his Macedonian cousin, the King of Egypt, and robbed him of 'Hollow Syria'. I was standing on a spot of surpassing historical interest, and I was also on the threshold of the Holy Land. For Paneion became Caesarea Philippi. And was it not here that Peter made his declaration of belief that Jesus was the Messiah?

But now the Sun is past his zenith, and we must tear ourselves away from this entrancing tableland, wedged in between Jordan and Litani, to gain the soaring heights of Beaufort on our eastern horizon—so near to us as the shell or the rocket flies, but such a long way off by road. Passing for the second time through the town of Marjayyun, we plunge down, this time, into the Litani's gorge, and, at each descending zig and zag, Beaufort strides nearer and towers higher. Now we are directly below the mighty fortress, with no obstacle between it and us except the rushing green river backed by an unscalable precipice many hundreds of feet high. When we do at last approach Beaufort, it is from the opposite side and by a circuitous route. And here my 'open sesame' almost plays me false. So many barriers had fallen at the display of this magical piece of paper that I had come to take it for granted that it was invincible. But here, at the very last military barrier, almost within bowshot of the western foot of the great ridge on which Beaufort perches, the sergeant has doubts. 'The document doesn't mention Beaufort by name.'—'No, but it franks the bearer for all places of historical interest in the Southern Lebanon, and you will agree that this castle is one of them.'—'I am sorry I can't let you pass.'—'Now, couldn't you perhaps telephone to your colonel?'—'Well, I will give you a soldier to take you up.' So the magical paper prevailed in the end over the scrupulous sergeant's misgivings.

The view from the top of this massive castle on the crags

is one of the Wonders of the World. To the west the Shi'ite
countryside rolls away to the shining sea. To the east, as
one looks straight down between one's feet over the edge of
the precipice, the voice of the rushing River Litani fills one's
ears. Once upon a geological time the Litani was rushing to
mingle his waters with the Jordan's. But then he suddenly
changed his mind and swerved off at right-angles westward
in search of the Mediterranean. If man-made frontiers
were as old as natural ones, you might have fancied that
Litani had shied away from Israel and had turned at an
angle of ninety degrees in order to keep within the bounds of
his native land the Lebanese Republic.

And now raise your eyes from beneath your feet to above
your nose and scan the panorama to the east. Mount Hermon
is awe-inspiring, even though the clouds are hiding his snows.
And look once again at Metulleh, this time not from a level
but from above. Seen from Beaufort, Israel's northern out-
post looks like the head of a giant who has planted his feet in
the Rift Valley and is resting his chin on the rim of the Marj.
What is passing through the giant's mind? Is he perhaps
casting covetous eyes on the lovely 'Meadow of Springs'?
As for ourselves, we are content. We have come, we have
conquered the doubting sergeant's scruples, and we have
beheld what must surely be one of the World's most magnificent landscapes. That is enough for one day's work. As we
head for the coast and for Beirut, the sublime castle long
hangs suspended behind us within view. A sharp turn in the
road, and a hillock blots Beaufort out and reveals, round its
shoulder, an incongruous vista of oil storage tanks, refining
plants, and tankers riding at anchor. Here ends Aramco's
pipe-line from Sa'udi Arabia to a sea that is on the Frankish
side of Suez. The transformation scene is complete. It is
high time for the Sun to set.

47. Hauran and Jabal Druz

As our car swung into the southward exit from Damascus, I could hardly believe my good fortune. Only a day or two ago, I had been wondering whether an Englishman would be admitted into Syria after the invasion of Egypt last autumn. Yet now, here I was, on Syrian ground, starting off along one of the most famous roads in the World: the Muslim pilgrims' road, the Biblical 'King's Highway'. Beside us ran the rails of the Hijaz Railway, and my thoughts raced along the line, ahead of the car. The gorge of the River Yarmuk, where the last Roman Army of the East was destroyed by the Muslim Arab conquerors; the Greek cities of the well-watered Decapolis; the Crusader castle at Kerak; Mutah, where the Romans crushed the first Muslim raid northward within the lifetime of Muhammad himself; and then all the bridges and culverts that T. E. Lawrence blew up in the First World War: all this lay on our road if one followed it far enough. My daydream had already carried me to Medina; and the illusion was encouraged by the desolateness of the landscape through which we were now passing. The great south road from Damascus does not traverse the Ghutah—the Damascene paradise of poplars and fruit-trees fed by rills of running water. Low, bare hills were rising on either hand; and, after we had crossed the saddle between them, the tawny waste was broken by just one ribbon of green along the banks of a little river that appeared to have lost its way. Can this be the famous River Pharpar? And can we really be heading for one of the granaries of the Roman Empire? The land here is under the plough, but the soil looks too dry and barren to bear wheat.

In the course of the two hours that it took us to reach Deraa, I changed my opinion. The colour of the ground had soon changed to a porphyry-dark red. We were travelling over decomposed basalt, one of the most fertile soils in the

World; and the rolling red Hauran, clothed in brilliant green crops, spread out round us for miles like a sea gently rocked by a ground swell. If only I could set eyes on the real sea to my right—I mean, the Sea of Galilee, which so deeply moves the feelings of anyone born in Christendom. It must be less than an hour's drive away from where we are now; but it might as well be on the Moon; for its eastern shore has become a danger-zone. If Jesus were to take ship from Tiberias today, seeking to land on this side of the Lake, He would draw fire from two alerted armies.

By now we have turned our backs on Gennesaret, and are heading due east for Bosra, the capital of the Roman province of Arabia, which was the Nabataean Arab Kingdom before that. Have you ever seen a Roman theatre encased in a medieval castle? The castle-builders—they were Saladin's successors—did not do violence to the Roman masonry; they simply built round it and upon it; and, as the Ayyubid castle keep is being dismantled, storey after storey, by the present-day Syrian Department of Antiquities, tier below tier of the Roman auditorium is being brought to light intact. It must be the best-preserved Roman theatre in the World, thanks to the use made of it by medieval warlords.

That night we slept in the archaeologists' house on the top of the castle's outer ward, just behind the magnificent baroque back-scene of the theatre's stage. Stepping out of one's bedroom door at dawn, one found oneself facing the highest rows of the theatre's seats; and, when the Sun licked up the mist, the Jabal Druz rose up along the eastern horizon.

Imagine a very huge giant emptying out giant-size sackfuls of big basalt boulders, as a child might empty out paperbagfuls of monkey nuts. Make the top of the heap rise five or six thousand feet above sea level, and sprinkle the higher altitudes of the boulder dump with dwarf oaks. That is the best notion that I can give you of the Jabal Druz. Here and there, the cones of volcanoes stand up in the distance; and, as we approach the hills, the face of the country changes.

The endless wheatfields of the Hauran give way to boulder-fields with rarer and rarer patches of good red soil between them; and the people turn from Muslims into Druz. You can tell who they are by the women's clothes. Druz women are still faithful to the local fashions that the Crusaders' wives and daughters brought back with them from Syria to Europe. So the present-day Druz women by the roadside have a familiar look to Western eyes.

But how can I give you a picture of the two cities of the Roman Age that were the goals of this day's journey? One of them, Shahba, had the luck to be the home of an ambitious soldier who adroitly threaded his way to the throne of the Roman Empire—supplanting a family of grandees from the North Syrian city of Homs. Philip drew on the resources of the imperial treasury to transform his village into a splendid city, equipped with everything that a Graeco-Roman city ought to have: walls, gates, religious centre, baths, theatre, and a shrine for Philip himself. Since I started to write this article, I have seen Shahba-Philippopolis once again—and this time, unexpectedly, from the air. The square frame of the walls, with the two main streets crossing each other at right-angles, stood out as clearly as if they were fresh from the builders' hands—as, indeed, the Roman paving still is, after more than 1,700 years of wear and tear.

Shahba had some local resources for maintaining its adventitious grandeur: a curving green valley, with wheat-fields bordering the stream in the valley bottom, and vine-yards and orchards on the stoney hillsides. Kanawat, on the other hand, climbs steeply up the brow of a deep ravine, right in the Jabal. How did the people of Nabataean Canatha manage to build that Odeum and Nymphaeum, on the far side of the cascading stream, out of the produce of a basalt boulder-heap? And, when the Roman pavement has carried your feet to the summit of this steep city (now a Druz village), you are lost in amazement at the splendour of the three buildings that crown it: a huge pagan temple and two great Christian basilicas. My wind-fall flight over the Jabal the day before yesterday gave me a clue to the mystery. All over the mountain the interstices between the boulder-heaps have been cultivated up to the snow line (a few flecks of snow still survived on the 13th April on the mountain's eastern face). What wonders Man's industry can achieve. But what havoc his folly can make of his noblest works.

48. 'Aqaba

Waking up sixty-eight years old, I found myself wondering what I could still do. When I had been only sixty-seven, I had scrambled up to the Deir—a surprising baroque tomb carved out of the top of one of the crags that crowd round Petra. Indeed, I had scrambled on farther, to a point where, looking westward through a gap between two rock-waves in a cataract of jagged ridges, one could just catch a glimpse of the floor of the Wadi 'Araba—the section of the Great Rift Valley where it runs dry between the south end of the Dead Sea and the head of the Gulf of 'Aqaba. That, though, had been yesterday. What could I do to-day?

I was standing in the mouth of the rock-tomb in which I had passed the night. From the other side of the natural amphitheatre in which the city of Petra nestles, the faces of other rock-tombs were staring at me, and the Sun was just going to burst into view above the top of the crag out of which those opposite tombs had been chiselled. Should I climb to the Nabataean 'High Place' on the summit of that still higher crag there to the right, in the hope of seeing all the kingdoms of the World display themselves? Or should I turn back, half-way up, and make a dash for 'Aqaba? We should just have time, we had calculated, to get to 'Aqaba and back before the plane that had brought us from Beirut to Ma'an yesterday took off again. It would be imprudent to miss the plane; for, peering out of it yesterday as we wheeled over 'Amman, I had seen a demonstration going on in the main street of the city. Well, we ought to be able just to get back to Ma'an in time. So five of us opted for 'Aqaba.

Two hours later, I was walking up the Syk (say 'seek'), sometimes ahead and sometimes astern of the donkey on which my wife was riding (in the Syk there is not room for two travellers abreast). Where the boulders were big I had the advantage; on the shingle the donkey outpaced me. But how much easier it must have been for both man and beast when the torrent bed at the bottom of this fantastic, winding slit between towering red cliffs was paved, as it was in the days of the Roman Empire. Stepping out into the sunlight from the cool canyon, we rounded a corner and saw our car waiting for us at the road-head. But half an hour that we could not spare was now lost in resisting the driver's demand for a surcharge on the price previously agreed. Can we make it still? And what is happening in 'Amman by now? At last our wheels turn, and, after pausing for a drink from 'Ain Musa, where life-giving water gushes out of the rock, we have left the crags behind us and are jogging along southward over a rolling plateau.

The country to the east of 'Hollow Syria'—the Greeks' name for the Rift Valley to the north of 'Aqaba—is like a huge paving-stone that has been tilted out of the horizontal, so that it dips gently towards the River Euphrates and the Persian Gulf. It is featureless for hundreds of miles, and lifeless too, except for a narrow green belt along its western margin. East of that, it is just a bare, brown, gravel desert. Mother Earth seems to have been selfconscious about the dullness of this patch of her surface, for she has compensated for it by a series of extravaganzas along the great, dull paving-stone's western rim, where it breaks down into the Rift Valley. One of these freaks of Nature is the Arnon gorge (I had seen the less sensational upper reaches of it yesterday from the plane). Another is the Syk of Petra. As we trundled southwards over the plateau, I felt a pang of regret and misgiving. Had we made the wrong choice in tearing ourselves away from Petra's crags and clefts? The featureless landscape was here not even fertile, as the Hauran is. Its nakedness was not covered by the scanty tufts of prickly stuff on which occasional camels were browsing. Road and rail meandered side by side round the unexciting contours. Was it going to be like this all the way to the sea? And then, suddenly, there was a transformation scene. The rail stopped dead; the road acquired a first-rate surface; the plateau broke off short; and, from its ragged edge, we were gazing down into a wonderland of crags that made Petra seem tame by comparison. These surely must be works of art, not accidents of Nature. Prospero himself must have conjured them up. Are we driving into the Tempest?

The road plunged down to the foot of the escarpment, and then the crags closed and opened, opened and closed, threatening to catch us in a vice as we slipped between them. No dullness now, but no hint of the sea either. Can we have taken a wrong turning and swerved off into boundless Arabia? Suddenly we shoot out from between two rock-walls into the Wadi 'Araba, and catch the Rift Valley in the act of dipping below a blue arm of the sea. A thrilling panorama opens out around us: in front the blue water, to our left the white houses of the Jordanian port of 'Aqaba, with a merchant ship riding off-shore; to our right the Israeli port of Elath, with a warship at the jetty. Behind Elath, the west wall of the Wadi 'Araba runs northward in a line of cliffs. Those blue mountains beyond 'Aqaba are in Sa'udi Arabia, those opposite blue mountains beyond Elath are in Egypt. That is the strip of Egyptian territory that Israel was so reluctant to evacuate; and the shadowy island in front of an Egyptian headland must be the Ile de Graye, where the Crusaders had their southernmost castle. Do not be surprised at finding relics of the Crusaders here. The Crusaders were the Israelis of their day, and, en route from 'Amman to Ma'an, our pilot had circled over Castle Kerak and Castle Montréal.

And now our driver deserts the road into 'Aqaba and races westward along the shore full tilt towards Elath. Does this Arab patriot suppose that he can take Israel by storm with a conscript army of five Anglo-Saxon passengers, two of them female and one of the males past sixty-seven years old? But his destination is not Elath; it is the British Non-commissioned Officers' canteen just on the Jordanian side of the armistice-line. Hundreds of stalwart young men are splashing about in the sea, and I find myself, tray in hand, queuing up for sandwiches and Alsop's lager. This British Army bathing beach is as peaceful as Bridlington or More-cambe Bay.

'Aqaba takes its name from the steep passage over that first Arabian headland beyond the town, which Egyptian pilgrims bound for Mecca had to climb after rounding the head of the gulf. This sandy beach, on which I am standing, is the end of the Southern Sea; but it is not the end of the great rift that cleaves the World from Kenya to Palestine.

49. Saint Sergius and Saint Symeon

I mention them, as you see, in alphabetical order. I never did discriminate between them; and I am doubly careful now, after the lesson that I have been given. Who am I to judge the relative merits of these two star saints? Saint Sergius was martyred by Diocletian; Saint Symeon had to be his own persecutor, since he happened to be born into an age in which the Roman Government itself had turned Christian and so could no longer oblige a Christian saint by offering him a martyr's crown. The considerations that made me plan to visit Saint Sergius first were purely practical. I was trying to make shorter excursions alternate with longer ones; and, after a day's rest in Aleppo, it seemed better to choose the next day for the relatively long journey to Saint Sergius's city of Rusafa, and to visit Saint Symeon the day following, before taking the road from Aleppo to Damascus. No dis-respect to Saint Symeon was intended; but the redoubtable saint evidently did not see it that way. Without giving me a chance to explain, he went into action.

First the offended demigod turned himself into the Sun and raised huge rain-clouds out of the Mediterranean. Then he turned himself into the West Wind, and blew with all his might. By the evening of the day before I was due to set out for Rusafa, his breath was driving hurricanes of dust against the western face of Aleppo's city wall. Next morning I woke up to find it raining, though it was now some weeks past the date at which the rainless season normally begins. I realized at once that my projected visit to Saint Sergius was off. It was true that, whatever the weather, I could get within eighteen miles of him along the tarmac road that runs from Aleppo to Deir-ez-Zor; but those last eighteen miles were the crux; for they had to be traversed on a dirt track over the desert; and, if the rain went on, it would turn the gravel into mud in which a car might sink up to its axles. The rain did go on. In fact, it got steadily worse. So I made up my mind to reverse the order of my programme, I would visit Saint Symeon today, in the hope that, by tomorrow, the weather might have become more propitious again for venturing on to the desert's treacherous surface. Saint Symeon smiled grimly, but did not relent.

By the time we had crossed the Roman military road that runs from Seleucia Pieria to Qinnasrin, Saint Symeon's rain was coming down in torrents, and our hearts sank as we turned off the tarmac road that leads from Aleppo to Antioch on to the stony track that winds its way up to Qal'at Sem'an, the saint's magnificent acropolis. The rich deep ploughlands of Northern Syria are interspersed with rugged shields of limestone, which the Ancients turned to lucrative account by planting them with olive trees and vines; and one of these rock-islands in the sea of softer soil was the scene of Saint Symeon's career. The cultivation of the rock was remunerative because, in the days of the Roman Empire, there was a market for Syrian oil and wine in the great North-west. But, when the Arab conquest of Syria drew a perman-ent military front between these markets and their Syrian sources of supply, the industrious inhabitants of the Syrian rock-islands suddenly lost their livelihood. They had to abandon their beloved vine-stocks and olive trees and move down into the plains. The bedouin cut down the trees, and the rain soon denuded the rock to its present stark nakedness. The dead cities and shrines on the rock-islands—grandly built by pious hands out of the profits of an ingenious industry—stand today in the condition in which they were left, thirteen hundred years ago, when disaster overtook their builders. Qal'at Sem'an—Castle Symeon—is the most famous of them, but the saint made me pay dear for the sight of it.

As we stood and stared at the base of the column on which Saint Symeon is reputed to have spent the last forty-three years of his life, we were already wet through and chilled to the bone. 'Remember,' the saint was admonishing us, 'this is April; and, if your teeth are chattering in this mild April breeze and shower, you can imagine what I endured for forty-three Januaries on the top of this column.' Really, Saint Symeon, it is beneath your dignity to show off like this. You made your sensational reputation within your lifetime, and it has never depreciated from that day to this. Saint Symeon Stylites—Saint Symeon on the Pillar: your name has been world-famous for fifteen hundred years. You need not be so sensitive or so vindictive. Please do just grant me a break in the clouds, and give me a chance to inspect these magnificent buildings that your admirers have put up in your honour round the sacred pillar on which you perched for all those years. But the saint was obdurate. In the driving rain and howling wind we made a painful tour of 'the Castle': we visited the Octagon, with the four great churches radiating from it; we visited the Baptistery. But by now the mud was ankle-deep, and it was impossible for us to pay the saint his due by marching down the Sacred Way to the Deir, where the hostels still stand to welcome pilgrims who have defaulted for the last fifteen hundred years. If our visit was perfunctory, it was Saint Symeon's doing, not ours.

Well, so much for Saint Symeon. But I am not going to let him prevent me from visiting Saint Sergius too. As I shall not be able to reach Rusafa from Aleppo tomorrow, I will approach it from Palmyra in May. By May it must be beyond even Saint Symeon's power to turn the desert into mud.

It is the 5th May; the sun is shining; a cool, dry breeze is blowing from the south-east; and we are bowling gaily over the Syrian desert's firm dry gravel surface. Palmyra is behind us, and so is Qasr al-Khayr Sharqi, the easternmost of the Umayyad caliphs' two local hunting lodges. We are bearing down on Rusafa from the south, and the desert is alive with black tents, baby camels, foals, lambs, and enormous flocks of sheep. Abruptly, over the undulating horizon, Saint Sergius's city looms up at us, and, in triumph, we explore its vast cisterns, crumpled basilica, and arcaded ramparts. Then, on to the Euphrates over those last eighteen desert miles, and we are at last on the tarmac, heading west for Aleppo in the afternoon sunshine, hugging the south bank of the mighty river.

But what is happening in the western sky ahead of us? It is changing colour to an inky black, and the wind has veered round from south-east to south-west. Long before we reach Aleppo, it is pouring. Saint Symeon has been at it again; but this time he has been frustrated; for, this time, Saint Sergius, in his turn, has been roused. The military saint held his breath till the pillar saint had shepherded his new cloud to Saint Sergius's side of Qal'at Sem'an, and then he took a true aim north-westward—aiming first at the famous pillar and then, beyond it, at distant Spalato. 'Take that, you conceited old man,' said Saint Sergius, as he brought Symeon's rain down on Symeon's own head. 'Take that, you wicked old man,' as he drenched Diocletian working in his Dalmatian cabbage patch. Symeon, hoist with his own petard, actually begged for mercy; Diocletian fell into a rage; but, since the day when he put Sergius to death, Diocletian had abdicated, so now he was impotent. While Sergius was blowing Symeon's cloud back upon its maker, he was keeping an eye on the progress of our car over those last perilous eighteen miles. When our wheels touched the tarmac, he sat back. 'There, silly old man Symeon, you have failed to prevent these English people from visiting me, and you won't now be able to prevent them from reaching Aleppo before dark.'

Well, that is the story. And now, if you dare, please say which of the two saints you like the better.

50. Mount Lebanon and His Sly Sister

Mount Lebanon is aggressively masculine. He flaunts his snow-fields as a peacock flaunts his tail. In whichever direction you travel, he takes care to keep you dazzled with this glistering white glory; and, when he is robbed of it for a season by the summer sun, he fights furiously in defence of every threatened snow-feather. Today we are half-way through May, yet streaks of snow still dare the Sun to melt them. And then, when one tries to thread one's way between the mountain and the sea, the giant keeps on putting his foot down in front of one's wheels—just to force the traveller to clamber over his mighty instep. Mount Lebanon is full of wonders: the cliffs of Jezzin, where a prince once found refuge from his Turkish pursuers; and the cavern of Afqa, where the River Adonis bursts, with a roar, out of the bowels of the Earth.

This kingly mountain is the head of a family. He has two brothers on the east and a sister to the north. The brothers, Antilebanon and Hermon, have an obvious family likeness to their senior. They are perhaps half a head shorter than he is, but not so short as to fail to reach the snow line. Hermon's Arabic name is Jabal ash-Shaikh: 'Mount Whitehead'. His hoary pate had still not turned quite bald when we were travelling from Damascus to Beirut the day before yesterday. In sheer beauty, Hermon surpasses all his brethren.

But now take the northward road between Mount Lebanon and the Mediterranean, and surmount the last of

the promontories that bar your way to Tripoli. Suddenly you
find yourself in a different world. The mountain sheers off
from the coast; green lowlands open out; the mountain bows
and falls into the broad valley of 'the Great River' (Nahr
al-Kabir); and, to the north of this surprising gap in
Western Asia's ramparts, one can descry a tangle of green
hills. To an English traveller's eye they look rather like the
green hills of North Wales as one sees them from the English
side of the River Dee. These are the southernmost foothills of Mount Lebanon's northern sister, the Jabal Ansarieh.
How feminine she looks by contrast with her big brother's
frowning brows. One can see at a glance why Mount
Lebanon was able to offer shelter to victims of persecution:
Maronites, Druz, Shi'ites and the rest. But the Jabal
Ansarieh, too, has had her human protégés. She takes her
name from a community that pays a more than Islamic
respect to the Prophet Muhammad's cousin and son-in-law
'Ali. (How handsome the 'Alawi women are, with their fine
features, fresh colour, and auburn hair.) Surely the Ansarieh
people could never have found asylum in the bosom of this
mountain if she were really no more rugged than she looks
when one is treading on the fringe of her skirts. And then
there are the Isma'ilis who still hold castles that were seized
by 'the Old Man of the Mountain' in the scramble for
possession of Syria in the twelfth century. 'The Old Man's'
successor is known today as the Agha Khan, and his followers
as Khojas—peaceful shopkeepers in the ports of East Africa.
As for the castle of Qadmus, it has been turned into a sanator-
ium; yet it was a name of terror once; for this was one of the
eagles' nests from which the Assassins used to swoop down
to slay Muslim and Christian princes with an undiscriminat-
ing impartiality.

One of the southern foothills of the Jabal Ansarieh is
crowned by Krak des Chevaliers, the most magnificent of all
the castles built by the Crusaders. From the summit of its
highest tower one sees simultaneously the sea in one direction
and the Syrian desert in the other; but, even from this
vantage-point, one cannot espy the Isma'ilis' fastnesses.

When one pushes on north-westward to Borj Safita—'the White Keep' that is the Crusaders' legacy to a modern Christian town—the tangle of mountains grows denser; but from here, too, they still look smooth and green. I travelled on northward up the coast from Tartus to Lattaqieh, casting a wistful eye on Castle Marqab crowning the summit of a volcano. But it was not till the next morning, when we assaulted Castle Sahyoun, that the Jabal Ansarieh revealed the wildness of her inner recesses. The limestone strata stood on end, like a forest of giant stone needles. Two precipitous-sided ravines ran together; and on the tapering crag above their meeting-point stood the castle—severed from the main mass of the mountain by a fosse hewn out of the rock, with one slender rock-pillar left standing to carry the vanished drawbridge. What labour! What art! Yet Saladin took only four days to bring the valiant defenders to their knees. This was more than a victory over the invaders from the West; it was a victory over the mountain that had failed to save her protégés. In Saladin the Jabal Ansarieh met her match.

51. The Druz

In search of dead cities of the Roman age I had made my way into Jabal Druz—the isolated mountain that juts out into the North Arabian desert to the east of the undulating fields of the Hauran. There I had found myself among a hard-working people, still wearing their own distinctive dress and clinging tenaciously to a fastness which had given them asylum in a world that has been intolerant of minority religions. I longed to learn something of the inner spiritual life of this impressive but uncommunicative nation—for such the Druz virtually are, though they have no state of their own and speak no other language than Arabic. My desire was granted. I was hospitably invited to Mukhtara, the former political capital of the Druz community in the Lebanon. I was shown through a door, and suddenly found myself face to face with a row of majestic, grey-bearded figures that might have walked straight out of the world of the Old Testament. They were eminent doctors of the Druz religion—their neighbours call them Druz, but this is a plural coined from the name of the Caliph Hakim's apostle, Darazi. The Druz call themselves 'Unitarians'.

How does one become a Unitarian Shaikh? Apparently there is no set system of apprenticeship or initiation. An aspirant is accepted or rejected by the consensus of those who have found acceptance before him, and this is the means of access to all grades up to the highest. An unsystematized consensus gives the entrée. And what are the beliefs and ideals of which these accepted shaikhs are the guardians and exponents? Here I must borrow a tantalizing phrase that flows rather often from the pen of Herodotus: 'Though I know something about it, I am not going to say.' The shaikhs spoke to me with a generous open-heartedness, but the essential tenets of their faith are not made public. So I will speak only of what I am sure is already public knowledge.

This Unitarian religion has a vast intellectual and traditional background. Arising, as it did, in the eleventh century of the Christian Era, it is the heir of Islam, Christianity, Hellenism, and the previous faiths of Western Asia with which Hellenism coalesced. The Druz, by the way, would contend that the epiphany of Hakim in this world in the eleventh century was merely the beginning of the *visible* Unitarian church. The Unitarian religion had existed since the beginning of the World in the hearts and minds of saints who may not have been conscious of the faith that was in them.

One of the tenets that the Druz have derived from the Greeks or from the Hindus or from both is a belief in the transmigration of souls, but here the Druz have taken a distinctive line of their own. Most believers in transmigration, whether Orphics or Buddhists, have also believed that reincarnation is an evil and that the true end of Man is to liberate himself from the sorrowful wheel of rebirth. The

Druz believe that life in this world is good, and that the
series of rebirths is a destiny that ought not to be repudiated.
Even in the final age of the World, in which the Unitarian
religion will prevail on Earth, the rhythm of birth, death,
and rebirth will continue.

What is the future of this Unitarian religion which was
revealed in Egypt more than nine hundred years ago and
which is professed today in Syria and the Lebanon? What
is the future of other West Asian minority religious communities—for instance, the 'Alawis of Syria or the Yazidis
of 'Iraq? These formerly segregated peoples are now being
sucked into the vortex of modern life. They are being drawn,
by the pull of economic opportunity, to Beirut; they are
being drawn onwards overseas to Chicago and to São
Paulo. What is going to happen to their faith when they are
detached from their close-knit ancestral community and
are tossed into cosmopolis to sink or swim there? Certainly,
when they come back home, they come back changed. The
atmosphere of the present-day world is unpropitious to
traditional religion of any kind. On the other hand, the
modern world is becoming conscious of spiritual starvation.
Who knows whether some hitherto obscure sect may not
hold in its secret treasury the pearl of great price for which a
frustrated world is seeking?

A few days later I found myself climbing up a steep and
stony track above the village of Hasbeya in the south-eastern
Lebanon. I was making for the Khalwat al-Biyad, which has
been the spiritual centre of the Unitarian religion for the last
hundred and fifty years. This shrine is impressive in its
simplicity. A plain room, not very large, with the one word
'God' inscribed on the wall. A cluster of prophet's chambers
round it, in which any Unitarian shaikh from any part of the
World can stay, for as long as he wishes, to practise spiritual
contemplation in peace. The shaikhs took me up on to the
roof; and, if spiritual exercises can be aided by the sublimity
of the physical landscape, the Druz have been well advised
in the choice of the site for their holy of holies. On the east,
Mount Hermon rises to the sky. To the west the south end of

Mount Lebanon breaks down precipitously into the gorge of the River Litani. Above the gorge, the crusaders' castle Beaufort lowers menacingly. To the south one can see the Shi'ite mountain, Jabal 'Amil; and those more distant mountains beyond it must be the mountains of Galilee, now in Israel. All beauty and all history, happy or baneful, here combine. And here I leave the shaikhs in their communion with the One True God.

52. A Waxing Crescent

In the cities of the Arab World, people are debating whether Israel or Communism is the Arabs' Enemy Number One. Some are opting for 'positive neutrality', others for the Baghdad Pact. But most Arabs do not live in towns; they work in the fields or on the steppe; and Arab farmers today are dreaming, not of pacts and treaties, but of pumps and tractors. They are also translating their dreams into practical realities. The tractors and the pumps are already operating in large numbers. The big current event in the Asian Arab countries—an event that is certainly going to make history— is the renaissance of 'the Fertile Crescent'.

Only a few years ago, this historic birthplace of agriculture in the Old World was like a new moon shivered into half-a-dozen splinters. Today the Crescent is once again continuous, from the irrigated date-palm groves of Basra at its eastern tip to the rain-watered fields of Moab at its western tip; and now this reborn moon is waxing under the genial influence of petrol and the wealth that oil-royalties bring. It can hardly be expected to round itself out into a full orb unless atomic energy can be made, one day, to distil the sea and distribute it over the desert. But already the growing crescent has encroached on the desert as far, in places, as it ever stretched in the heroic early days of Man's still recent agricultural age; and here we are only at the beginning of a reclamation movement that is comparable in scale to the opening up of Iowa and Kansas a hundred years ago.

To give this agricultural revival the study that it deserves, one ought to travel round the Crescent from tip to tip—lingering longest in the Jazireh: 'the island' encompassed by the rivers Tigris and Euphrates above the point where they come within hailing distance of each other in the neighbourhood of Baghdad. In the northern Jazireh there is enough rainfall to bring crops to harvest without irrigation. This is the section of the Crescent which can be recaptured for the plough with the least amount of capital outlay. I have only just set foot in this immense land of promise. A few weeks ago I entered it on the Syrian side when I crossed the Euphrates from Rusafa to Raqqa on the river's left bank; and a few days ago I entered it from the 'Iraqi side when I drove out into the steppe, as far as the Parthian stronghold Hatra, from Qal'at Sherghat: the site of the ancient city of Asshur, perched above the right bank of the Tigris. Hatra lies on the extreme southern fringe of the belt in which a crop can be raised with the aid of rainfall alone. So I cannot claim really to have had more than an inadequate glimpse of the World's new bread-basket. Still, I have seen something of the Crescent's western horn from Moab to Aleppo, and of its eastern horn from Basra to the rolling wheat and barley fields of Assyria, on the left bank of the Tigris, opposite Mosul. I have certainly seen enough to realize how important this Arab agricultural renaissance may be going to be.

The Fertile Crescent holds a desert in its arms and is braced by a girdle of mountains running in a giant arc from near the head of the Persian Gulf to near the head of the Red Sea (Zagros, Antitaurus, Amanus, Lebanon, the hill country of Ephraim and Judah: all these are famous names). The foothills of the mountains surrounding the pit of this theatre of human history are now thought to be the region in which men—or women—first took to cultivating wild grasses. The pit, through which the Tigris and Euphrates flow in the last lap of their course to the sea, is certainly the

place where Man first developed agriculture on the grand
scale by mastering the art of irrigation.

The rainwater-cultivation zone accounts for most of the
Crescent's cultivable area. This zone extends continuously
from the plateau of Moab, south-east of the Dead Sea,
through the Hauran and the Rift Valley and the deep soils
of Eastern Syria across the Jazireh into Assyria between the
Tigris River and the mountains of Kurdistan. Homs, Aleppo,
and Mosul are the chief present agricultural centres; but
tomorrow they may be equalled or outstripped by Qamish-
lieh, Tell Afar and the other boom towns that are springing
up like mushrooms in the Jazireh. In the rain-belt, cultivation is cheapest; but it is most profitable in the irrigated
oases, and most remarkable in the isolated blocks of mountains that jut out into the dry heart of the steppe. There are
three notable oases: Basra, Baghdad, and Damascus. There
are two mountain citadels that harbour miraculous springs
and woods: the Jabal Sinjar, out in the steppe to the west of
Mosul, and the Jabal Druz, out in the steppe to the south-
east of Damascus.

The magic touch of running water in the oases is, of course,
sensational. 'Gardens with rivers flowing under them': the
oasis of Damascus gave the Prophet Muhammad his picture
of Paradise; the oasis of Baghdad and Babylon may have
been the reality behind the myth of the Garden of Eden.
I have steamed for one live-long day down the Shatt al-
'Arab between the Basra date-groves—interrupted only by
the oil refineries at Abadan; and I have driven about the
Ghutah of Damascus through leafy tunnels, with glimpses of
poplar groves and orchards and fields on either hand, and
with rills of water almost keeping pace with the car. But the
Baghdad oasis seems likely to have the greatest agricultural
future. It certainly has had the greatest past, and the 'Iraq
Government's oil-royalties are being partly devoted to the
enterprise of making this past come to life again.

In the early days of agriculture by irrigation, 'Iraq was
probably a going concern before Egypt was. After that, it
was Egypt's equal for at least four thousand years. It was not

till the thirteenth century of our era that the ancient irrigation system of 'Iraq finally went to pieces. Today it is being systematically restored; and, when the work is done, there will once again be a counterpart of Egypt in Western Asia.

The petrol age may go as fast as it came; but Man must always eat, whatever form of mechanical power he may be using. The Fertile Crescent is beginning once again to make a substantial contribution to Mankind's food supply. This is the really revolutionary event in the Arab World today.

53. The Reason for Assyria

Again and again I have found that one glance at a landscape with the living eye reveals the answer to riddles that cannot be read from a life-long study of maps and monographs. I had always been unable to grasp the causes of the power of Assyria. How had this country, which occupies so small a patch on the map, found the power to subjugate the whole of 'the Fertile Crescent', and Egypt and Elam as well? True, Assyria eventually exhausted herself by the effort; but how had she ever mustered the strength to succeed at all?

In a general way I had guessed that Assyria must have been stimulated by having perpetually to contend against the bedouin on the steppe with one hand and against the highlanders with the other. Yet the power of Assyria was still, for me, enigmatic. The puzzle has now been solved for me by three days' travelling by car: one journey from Asshur, Assyria's earliest capital, north-westwards into the steppe as far as Hatra; and two journeys from Mosul—dead Nineveh's living west-bank suburb—up to and over the rim of the mountains that run in an arc round Assyria's rolling ploughlands. North-westwards up the east side of the River Tigris, and south-eastwards as far as Erbil, the deep rich soil goes rolling on without a break for two and a half hours by car on a passably well-metalled road; and then, with a crash, you hit the mountains and immediately find yourself

caught in a labyrinth of sharply tilted ranges. Travelling
north-westwards from Nineveh I went over the pass to
Zakho in the broad green valley of the River Khabur, at the
foot of the snow-capped mountains that today divide 'Iraq
from Turkey. Travelling south-eastwards I beheld the plain
stretching on beyond Erbil as far as the eye could see, and
then I turned east and went over the first two ridges that
stand in the way of the road to Rowanduz. How fertile
those Assyrian fields are! How many tens of thousands of
Assyrian soldier-peasants they must have maintained to
cultivate them and to defend them! What covetous eyes must
have been cast upon them by the hungry inhabitants of the
highlands and the steppe! How fiercely their Assyrian
owners must have fought to keep their hold on so great a
treasure! Every further minute of gazing at the landscape
made the history of Assyria look less mysterious than it had
looked before I came to see it for myself.

Standing on the highest point within the inner city of
Asshur, and looking upstream along the western bank of the
River Tigris, I could see a couple of villages and a conspicuous white house. 'That house,' said my experienced
companion, 'was the headquarters of the late shaikh of the
Shammar. The tribe broke out of Central Arabia into the
Jazireh about two hundred years ago, but it was not till
within living memory that they made themselves masters of
cultivated land and thereby acquired peasant subjects. This
Shammar shaikh was the leader who made the landfall out
of the Desert into the Sown. That house is the abiding
monument of his achievement.' Today the Shammar have
been brought to a halt by a government armed with the
resources of modern civilization. But suppose the Shammar
had conquered those arid west-bank fields even as recently
as a hundred years ago: could anything have stopped them
then from crossing the Tigris and going on to conquer those
incomparably fertile east-bank ploughlands up to the foot of
the Kurdish mountain-wall? The answer to this question is
in the negative; for, four thousand five hundred years ago,
nothing did stop the Shammar's Assyrian predecessors from

pressing on as far as that arresting line. The Assyrians achieved the manifest destiny of any bedouin tribe that breaks out of the steppe to the west bank of the Tigris in the neighbourhood of Qal'at Sherghat, as the ruins of Asshur are now called.

When the Akkadian wave of bedouin broke eastwards out of the steppe towards the end of the first half of the third millennium B.C. the Assyrian tribe seemed to have been unlucky. The Akkadians themselves had acquired the vast irrigated oasis in the waist of Mesopotamia where the two rivers all but meet. The Assyrians had acquired nothing but one magnificent site for a fortress and those miserable fields at its foot, on the fringe of the barrenest tract in the whole of the Jazireh. But the Assyrians found for themselves a land as good as Akkad when they pushed their way up the Tigris and crossed to the east bank at Nineveh. In the course of centuries the whole of that fertile lowland country became theirs, and they turned and fought ferociously to hold it when a later explosion of population from the Arabian steppe brought the Aramaeans into the Jazireh in the Assyrians' wake.

In the next chapter of the Assyrian story, the Aramaeans were subdued by the might of Assyrian arms from the Tigris westward to the Euphrates, and from the Euphrates southward to the oasis of Damascus. The Aramaeans took an ironical revenge. They peacefully imposed on their Assyrian conquerors the Aramaic language and alphabet, since they had failed to hold their own in the ordeal by battle. The highlanders beyond those mountain ramparts, on the far side of Assyria's fertile fields, never went the Aramaean way. The Assyrians could march into the upland valleys, storm forts, gouge out the eyes of recalcitrant highland chieftains, or impale their wretched prisoners on stakes; but they could never finish the job. Their atrocities did not intimidate the tribesmen; they merely exasperated them into defying Assyria again. Mountain range rose up behind mountain range, century followed century, until this hostile conspiracy of space and time broke even stout Assyrian hearts.

Those huge mounds that once were palaces: Koyunjuk,
Nabi Yunus, Nimrud, Khorsabad; those immensely long
ridges of disintegrated unfired brick that were once the
ramparts of the city of Nineveh. When the ten thousand
Greeks passed that way in 401 B.C., these ruins were already
in the state in which we see them now. But before 612 B.C.
they had been the seat of government of the whole Fertile
Crescent. Only the highlanders had continued to bid
Nineveh defiance. From his pavilion at Nimrud or Khorsabad on a clear day, the Great King, at a time when his
dominions extended westward to the Mediterranean, could
still see peaks and ridges where his writ did not run. In the
long-drawn-out contest between steppe, field, and mountain,
the mountain was the winner.

54. Najaf

'The veil between us is very thin,' said the old mujtahid.
We had been talking for half-an-hour; but, for many years
before we had met, we had been feeling our way towards
each other unconsciously. We each had the same belief that
there was light in the other's tradition as well as in his own.
We each had the wish to make this friendly neighbour light
ours, and so, perhaps, to see a little farther into the mystery
of the Universe. The veil between us was thin, and light
was shining through it both ways.

When a Muslim, Christian, or Jew meets a Hindu or a
Buddhist in a spirit of charity on both sides, he is conscious,
here too, of an answering light streaming from a common
source. The veil is thin enough even between religions of
the West Asian and the Indian family. But, of course, the
affinity between the three West Asian religions is closer still.
All three see Ultimate Reality in the form of a God who,
like his human creatures, is a person, and who is merciful
and compassionate towards the beings whom He has
created in His image. Between Christianity and the Shi'ite

form of Islam the link is particularly strong. For, like Christianity, the Shi'ah dwells on the Passion of a holy hero; and Christ and the Imam Husain have a common prototype in the older god incarnate in the crops—Tammuz, Attis, Adonis, Osiris—who suffers a cruel death year by year in order to give life to the people.

The scene of the Imam Husain's martyrdom was Karbala, which I had visited twenty-eight years ago. For Husain's sake, Karbala is the emotional focus of the Twelve-Imam sect of Shi'ite Islam. Najaf is the burial-place of the Imam Husain's father, the first Imam, 'Ali son of Abu Talib, who was the cousin and son-in-law of the Prophet Muhammad and the fourth of the Prophet's successors in the temporal government of the Islamic state. 'Ali was buried at Najaf after being assassinated at his seat of government in the neighbouring city of Kufa—now a tiny village but once a cantonment whose Arab garrison shared with their Basran comrades-in-arms the command of all 'Iraq and all Iran. Najaf has become the intellectual focus of Twelve-Imam Shi'ism. Today it is a centre of Shi'ite theological studies; and these take the active form which the English poet Blake calls 'mental strife'. Ijtihad is an intellectual struggle to gain fresh spiritual light by re-interpreting the tradition. A mujtahid is a scholar-devotee who gives his life to this strenuous pursuit. The mujtahid with whom I was talking is one of the most senior and the most distinguished members of the learned fraternity at Najaf today.

Najaf is, in fact, the seat of a Shi'ite theological university; and, though the city lies in the Arab country of 'Iraq on the fringe of the Arabian desert, the doctors and students of the university are predominantly Persian. My old friend himself came, as his surname proclaimed, from the north-west Persian town of Zenjan. A student in one of the colleges, with whom I had a few words later on, came from Rudsar on Persia's Caspian coast. Shaikh Zenjani spoke in fluent Arabic; but my interpreters, who talked Arabic as their mother-tongue, told me that they could just detect the Persian accent in the old mujtahid's speech, though he had spent the greater part of his life in this city where Arabic was the language of everyday life. The three principal holy cities of the Twelve-Imam Shi'ah—Karbala, Najaf, and Kazimain, which has now become a suburb of Baghdad —all lie in 'Iraq, because it was here that the tragedy of the Shi'ite Holy Family was played out. The heroes and heroines were all Arabs of the Prophet Muhammad's house, and they are depicted as Arabs in the popular coloured prints that one can buy, all over Persia, in the bazaars. But the great majority of their present-day adherents are Persians, in consequence of a sudden and surprising revolution in the sixteenth century of the Christian Era, when the whole of Persia was more or less forcibly converted from the Sunnah to the Shi'ah by a Turkish-speaking Shi'ite empire-builder, Shah Isma'il.

A few weeks after my day in Najaf, I visited both Rudsar and Zenjan. Rudsar is as green as Bali or Ireland; Zenjan, in June, was almost as cool as northern France or southern Germany at the same season. Perhaps a Persian from the torrid gulf-coast might be conditioned by his native clime for life in Najaf. But how could a native of moist green Gilan or cool green Azerbaijan endure the dust and heat of the Arabian desert? One answer is that any place feels even physically delectable if it has a hold on one's heart; and Persian hearts are drawn to the holy cities of 'Iraq by their devotion to the Holy Family. Another answer is that the Persian genius has discovered how to evade the heat by changing one's altitude. In Persia one does it by climbing a thousand feet—and then another thousand and another, if the first thousand does not give one the degree of coolness that he requires. In Najaf and Karbala the Persian sojourners there secure the same effect by changing their altitude in the opposite direction. The date of my call on Shaikh Zenjani was no later in the season than the 24th May, so he received me in a room above ground. Had I come a month later, he would probably have taken me down one floor below ground, and two or even three floors below at the climax of the heat. In one of the Persian theological colleges at Najaf, I did go down to the third subterranean level. Going thirty feet downwards below the surface of the Arabian desert had about the same effect on the temperature as going a thousand feet upwards on the plateau of Fars. So in Najaf the blessed dead, in their underground tombs, enjoy a taste of the coolness that the Qur'an promises to souls in Paradise. In Najaf the dead far outnumber the living. It is a city of colleges and sepulchres. Both the dead and the living dwell in peace there, deftly eluding the Arabian sun's malice.

55. The Royal Road

The Greek historian Herodotus has recorded the stages and distances on a road which linked the eastern shore of the Aegean Sea with Susa, one of the four capitals of the Persian Empire. With characteristic Greek self-centredness, he calls this *the* royal road. But the north-west frontier of the Persian Empire, troublesome though it might be, never was the Imperial Government's principal anxiety. The tensest frontier was the north-east frontier, over against the Central Asian nomads. These had flooded over Western Asia before the Empire was founded, and they might try to break their bounds again at any moment. This was the frontier that the Persians were most concerned to hold. So *the* royal road *par excellence* was the road leading to this quarter. In Persian times the south-eastward terminus of this road was Babylon, the Persian Empire's economic capital. At the present day the termini are the two Shi'ite holy cities Najaf and Karbala; for today the Persians who travel along this road are pilgrims, not couriers or soldiers. Taking off from the plain of 'Iraq, this royal road charges, full tilt, at the Iranian plateau, mounts the successive mountain ramparts that cover its south-western flank, and then descends, south-eastward, into the plain of Soviet Central Asia. Push on from there and you will arrive in

China; incline to the right, and you will climb over the hump of Afghanistan into Pakistan and India.

In planning my present journey round the World, I had made a firm resolve to traverse this historic road on wheels, and not to let myself be persuaded to take the soft alternative of the flying carpet. In the end, I did travel from Najaf to Tehran on the ground, and only took to the air on the stretch between Tehran and Mashhad.

The first stage of the four days' journey to Tehran from Najaf was an easy one: the short stretch from Najaf to Baghdad, all on the level and all on tarmac too. But what a cluster of famous sites within a small compass! As if Najaf, with its golden dome and vast white graveyards, were not enough, here come the Euphrates and Kufa. The 'Iraqi Archaeological Service has been excavating the palace built by the Arab conqueror Sa'd ibn abi Waqqas; and there, at the door of the great mosque, is the spot where 'Ali met his death. On the southern horizon one can just descry faint traces of Kufa's predecessor Hira, the capital of the Sasanid Persian Empire's Arab wardens of the Arabian marches. These wardens failed to do their job. To the west lies Qadisieh, where Sa'd won his decisive victory. And now here comes the Euphrates again, and that mound in the distance on the left is Borsippa. The Euphrates for the third time, with the pleasant town of Hilla on its bank (the Euphrates divides into three branches in this section of its course); and next we are cutting across the eastern corner of Babylon. The great temple E Sagila, the dilapidated remains of the famous hanging gardens (if the archaeologists' identification is correct), and the mound that was once Nebuchadnezzar's summer palace flash past us on our left, and we are out in the open again. We pass the night in Baghdad on the west bank of the Tigris.

Crossing the Tigris next morning, we run on northwards over the level and, later, cross the Tigris's palm-fringed tributary, the Diala. The blanket of strata that covers the surface of the Earth is here still monotonously flat. When shall we come to the first of those great ruckles that have

been made in it by the Creator's imperious hand? The
ruckles begin unsensationally: first the rolling ridge of the
Jabal Hamrin and then a series of minor creases. At Qizil
Ribat we must be near the intersection of the road from
Babylon to Ecbatana with the road from Susa to Sardis.
Soon we are on Persian soil, and here the ruckling begins in
earnest. The strata writhe and twist; they stand up on end
and break off short, like a gigantic row of broken teeth. They
suddenly buckle down below the surface of the Earth and
plunge out of it again, leaving an unexpected passage for
roads and rivers to take, as a child's feet skip over a skipping-
rope. It is now afternoon, and we should be within easy
reach of our night's rest at Kermanshah, when, at Shahabad,
an unseasonable deluge overtakes us. Caught between a
mountainside and a cemetery, we watch the road being
washed away beneath our wheels, and the water rising half
way up the legs of the donkeys and horses in the fields. A
shepherd, dressed in the clothes of a clerk in a Western city,
takes off his trousers and wrings them out. Labour lost!
In an instant they are wet through once again. The road has
become a river. Will it bring our engine to a stop? We wade
out of the plain on to higher ground, but our troubles are
not over yet. At a fold in the mountains a torrent is strewing
boulders on the road, faster than a gang of frustrated truck-
drivers can remove them. We venture the passage, and get
through with the loss of our exhaust. So we do reach
Kermanshah after all, and are warmed by a friendly
welcome.

How shall I describe the glories of our third day's run,
which carried us from Kermanshah to Hamadan? At
Taq é Bostan a great river gushes out of a precipice, and in
an archway, carved out of the mountain, the Sasanid King
Khosrow Parviz, clad in chain mail from the head downwards, bestrides his plate-clad charger Shabdiz. For fifty
years I had been looking forward to seeing this famous
equestrian statue, but the thrill was surpassed by the thrill
of seeing Darius's bas-relief and inscription at Bisitun. The
rock soars up vertically like the towers of Cologne Cathedral.

The mighty work of an emperor is dwarfed by the far mightier works of Nature. And who is that man up there swinging dizzily in a cradle and taking squeezes of two of the columns of the inscription round the corner to the left? It turns out to be my old friend Professor George Cameron of the University of Michigan. What a marvellous mise-en-scène for an unexpected meeting.

Though the crag does dwarf the sculpture, Darius chose his site with marvellous skill. The traveller is bound at this point to hug the mountain's foot, because, at a few yards' distance from it, springs of water gush out of the ground and turn the plain into a marsh.

And so to Hamadan. What treasures may not the archaeologists lay bare when, one day, they raze the modern city and reveal the Ecbatana that lies beneath it?

The fourth day carried us out of authentic Persia into cosmopolitan Tehran. But this fourth day's journey was an anti-climax. I will not describe it.

56. The Goddess Anahita

On bas-reliefs of the Sasanian age one is shocked to find the goddess Anahita holding her ground beside Ormuzd, who is God Himself, and His prostrate adversary Ahriman. The Sasanid emperors were strict Zoroastrians, and Zoroastrianism is a severely monotheistic religion in theory. The Adversary is not God's peer, and, apart from the Adversary, no other divinity is left in the field. They have either been sublimated into attributes of Ormuzd or been degraded to the rank of demons. When the Iranians had come so near to monotheism, why did they fall away from it again? And why did the same fall happen twice? The later Achaemenids appear to have re-admitted the worship of Anahita, as the Sasanids did after them. Why was Anahita singled out, from the whole pagan pantheon, to reoccupy a place that no good Zoroastrian ought to have been willing to give her?

It is no accident that Anahita was the favoured pagan deity. Anahita is the goddess of water, and without water there can be no agriculture, and without agriculture no population. Zoroaster was a devotee of agriculture, and by implication he was a devotee of Anahita too, though no doubt he would have refused to acknowledge the force of the argument.

The Hindu god Shiva's consort is called Parvati, Our Lady of the Mountains; and the Persian goddess Anahita might fittingly bear the same title. In Persia, water is the gift of the mountains to Man. The mountains attract the rain-clouds, and store up the rain in their bosoms. The water gushes out in springs, and here comes Man's turn to play the creator's part. Man must conserve every drop of the life-giving water against loss by evaporation, and at the same time he must carry it over long distances, under a torrid sun, from the barren scree of the mountain-side to the fertile soil of the plain. In the course of five or six thousand years, Iranian Man has worked out a solution for this problem which is as ingenious as it is laborious.

The one thing to be said for flying over Iran instead of travelling on the ground is that, from the air, you can follow with your eye the lines of the qanats, radiating out from the foot of the mountains in all directions. A qanat is a Man-made subterranean water-course. It starts deep below the surface; the depth, at the take-off, may be as much as three hundred feet; and it eventually comes to the surface at the point where the water is to be used for irrigating trees and crops. To start at just the right depth to bring the water above ground at the point required demands a marvellous practical understanding of levels and gradients. A qanat may be twenty-five miles or occasionally even fifty miles long; yet the labour of constructing and maintaining qanats is enormous. What you see from the air is a line of immense mole-hills, stretching away into the distance till it ends in a patch of verdure. These hillocks are the heaps of spoil which a human mole, in digging the qanat, has thrown up at intervals of a few dozen yards. They serve as man-holes through which the maintenance-gang can make its way down into the qanat to clear it of silt and keep it in repair. This is dangerous work, and it calls for expert hands. The people of Yazd are famous for their skill in it; and they have reason to be; for Yazd is a Man-made oasis in Persia's dry heart.

The degree of skill and amount of labour that have been invested in qanats up to date is stupendous; but it is not too great an outlay for the results. It is hardly an exaggeration to say that, without qanats, the effective area of Persia would be confined to the Caspian provinces, Azerbaijan, and the northernmost strip of Khorasan. The southern three-quarters of the country would be as desolate as 'the Empty Quarter' of Arabia.

When the water is led on to the surface of the soil, a generous amount of it is allocated to maintaining trees. In Persia, trees are not a luxury. Quite apart from the value of the most characteristic Persian domesticated tree, the poplar, for providing a necessary building material, the presence of trees has a softening effect on the climate. And, in Persia, trees cannot be left to fend for themselves; for, in Persia, trees have four deadly enemies: charcoal-burners, foragers, goats, and drought. If the husbandman did not intervene in the battle on the trees' side, by planting saplings, bringing water to them, and fencing his gardens about with mud walls, there would soon not be a tree left in the land.

One of the characteristic features of the Persian landscape is the double avenue of poplars with a rivulet running between the two close-set lines of trees. These avenues intersect the cities and run for miles through the open country. They are one of the chief beauties of the Persian scene.

So hail, exuberant Anahita, Great Mother of the Medes. But hail thou too, thou ethereal goddess, whose name I do not know, the queen of all the thirsty land which Anahita's magic waters do not reach. Thy magic, unknown goddess, is greater than hers; for out of dry rock and parching dust thou knowest how to bring forth beauty. Thine are the wild flowers that are the glory of the Persian desert: wild hollyhock, white asphodel, bright blue thistle and that spiny scrub whose fragrance surpasses the fragrance of nectar and ambrosia. Even the oleanders and azaleas in Anahita's reedy river-beds are no match for thy lovely works. Hail, goddess of the drought, thrice hail.

57. Iran's Hidden Valleys

Plato, in one of his myths, imagines that civilization has been wiped out, many times over, by repeated catastrophes. The cities in the lowlands have been obliterated, and, each time, civilization has been set going again, from the beginning, by unsophisticated highlanders who have come through the catastrophes unscathed and have descended from their mountains to repopulate the plains. Plato's myth is Iran's history; only, in Iran, the catastrophes have been, not Nature's work, but Man's. They have not been deluges (for, though Iran does suffer from cloud-bursts, she is on the whole a thirsty land). Iran's calamities have been Manmade. They have taken the form of devastating invasions— worst of all, the incursions of the nomadic peoples of Central Asia. These nomads have been the arch-enemies of the Iranian farmer from the days of Zoroaster until the eighteeneighties, when Russia subjugated the last of the Türkmens. In the Arab countries, peasants and bedouin are business partners. The peasants employ the bedouin to look after their livestock and to lift their harvests on camelback. In Iran the latent antagonism between Cain and Abel is visible on the surface. It was visible even when the two brothers spoke the same language, as they still do in the Arab world. The mutual hostility is accentuated in Iran now that the nomadic tribesmen speak other languages than the standard Farsi: the kindred yet distinct Kurdish, Luri, and Baluchi dialects and the completely foreign Turkish form of speech.

When I was planning my visit to Khorasan, the north-easternmost province of Iran, which borders on the Central Asian steppes, I arranged to see two famous cities of the age of the 'Abbasid Caliphate: Tus, the home of the epic poet Ferdowsi, and Nishapur, the home of Omar Khayyám and Farid ad-Din 'Attar. But what did I find? At Tus nothing but a tiny hamlet; at Nishapur nothing but a small country town. Yet the records of the populousness of these two cities in the age before the Mongol invasion are borne out by the surviving vestiges of the city-walls. In both places the area contained within the four-square mud-brick enclosure is vast. Those decayed ramparts make it possible, with one's mind's eye, to reconstruct the two cities as they were in their prime.

Even when one has allowed for the fact that Nishapur and Tus have been replaced, in this post-Mongol age, by a new city that has grown up round the shrine of the Imam Reza at Mashhad, the permanent reduction in the density of Eastern Khorasan's population must have been enormous. The passage of more than seven centuries, since the date of the great calamity, has not availed to make good those grievous losses. The salvation of Iran has been her winding green valleys hidden in the folds of her mountains. The destructive floods of barbarian invasion have left these valleys unscathed. With cities to plunder and plains to ravage and depopulate, it has not been worth the invaders' while to raid these secluded spots; and, even if their cupidity did carry them so far, the lie of the land gave the highlanders a much better chance of repelling the attack than the city-dwellers had behind their mud-brick walls.

Iran's hidden valleys are legion, and I have been able to visit only a few of them: two in the folds of huge Elburz, two in the folds of Mount Gonabad, the giver of water to Mashhad and Nishapur, and half-a-dozen nestling round Mount Shir Kuh—the 'Lion Mountain', south-west of thirsty Yazd, which is still flecked with snow as late as the middle of June.

These highland paradises often take the traveller by

surprise; for the lower courses of the streams whose valleys the highlanders have turned to account are apt to run through precipitous-sided ravines which are too steep and too rocky to carry irrigation channels. You seem to be heading for a dreary upland desert, when suddenly, over the top of a ridge, tier upon tier of poplar plantations, vineyards, and fields bursts into view, with water-courses, cunningly led at many different levels, bringing life to trees and crops. I think, above all, of the village of Kharv, lying in the bosom of Mount Gonabad to the north-east of Nishapur, and the village of Banadk, lying in the bosom of snow-clad Shir Kuh. But, as I let my memory ruminate, these hidden mountain valleys melt into a single picture: the Happy Valley that has so often been the salvation of sorely-tried Iran.

But for these highland asylums, how could Iran have survived? She has repeatedly been the prey of nomadic invaders from Central Asia and Arabia, and of more civilized, but hardly less destructive, conquerors sent forth by Greece and Rome. In these age-long trials, her hidden upland villages have perpetually kept her alive.

58. Ispahan

When one visits, after long anticipation, some place with an established fame, there is always a chance that one may be disappointed; so, when, after all, the reality comes up to one's highest expectations, one is doubly grateful. For me, the beauty of Ispahan has been one of these happy experiences.

This is the more remarkable because Ispahan (say Esfahan) is hardly beautiful as a whole. There are some cities—for instance, Damascus, Shiraz, and Assisi—whose chief beauty consists in the ensemble. By contrast, large parts of Ispahan are dingy and dilapidated, and their sordidness is not redeemed by the quaintness of the old-fashioned industries that are still being carried on, by

traditional techniques, behind those crumbling mud walls.
The Great Mosque again—a house of many mansions built
at different epochs—is not so much beautiful as it is interesting from an antiquarian's point of view. It is the blazing
beauty of quite a few great works of art that makes Ispahan
one of the wonders of the World.

The Meidan, for example, to my taste, surpasses the
noblest piazzas that I have seen in Italy: the Piazza di
San Marco at Venice and the Great Piazza at Siena. And I
have seen no bridge, either at Venice or at Florence, that
equals in beauty the bridges that span Ispahan's river, the
Zayandeh. Part of the beauty of Shah 'Abbas's architecture
lies in its simplicity. With a couple of tiers of plain arcades,
his craftsmen can produce effects that elude the more
elaborate art of the Italian Renaissance. On the other hand,
the colours and patterns of the tiles on Shah 'Abbas's own
Masjid é Shah—and still more, those on the mosque of
Shaikh Lotfollah—are intricate almost to the verge of over-
ripeness. But they just stop short of going over the edge.
The tile-work of the Mongol, Timurid, and Türkmen
periods (Black Sheep Türkmens and White Sheep too),
which one finds, in a fragmentary state, in Yazd, Ardebil,
and other Persian cities, offers a wider gamut of artistic
possibilities than the masterpieces of the Safavi age. Yet the
Safavi workmanship, though relatively limited in its artistic
scope, is so exquisite in its execution that it takes the beholder
by storm.

How cunning, too, is the architectural design which, in
the lay-out of Shah 'Abbas's mosque, has reconciled the
alignment of the vestibule along the south-eastern end of the
Meidan with the orientation of the mihrab towards Mecca.

The River Zayandeh, which those noble bridges span,
would be nothing accounted of in well-watered Northern
Europe or Southern Asia; but in thirsty Iran it is a porten-
tous gift from a grudging Nature. As one watches its waters,
fed by snows melting on the Bakhtiari Mountains, swirl
past the city between the bridges' stately piers, one feels
almost indignant when one reminds oneself that, a few miles

off, this precious flood runs to waste in a swamp nicknamed 'the Cow House'. But never mind the river's imminent fate. In its march past Ispahan it is an ornament the like of which is not possessed by any other Persian city save those parvenus, Khorramshahr on the bank of the Karun and Abadan on the bank of the Shatt al-'Arab, and their elder sisters—Ahwaz, Dizful, and Shustar—on the plains of Khuzistan. As for lovely Shiraz, her river-bed is a wilderness of dry sand, without a single rill of perennial water. It is like an ugly scar slashed across some famous beauty's face.

But perhaps the greatest of all the graces of Ispahan is the oasis of fields and orchards to which the River Zayandeh gives life. This oasis may be small in extent by comparison with the rice-fields of Gilan and the pastures of Azerbaijan. It fades out into the desert long before the plain gives way to the mountains. Yet it has all the charm of the Ghutah of Damascus. It is an earthly paradise in a land that is elsewhere barren.

How fortunate that the lovely buildings of Ispahan came out intact from the great disaster of A.D. 1722, when Afghan adventurers snuffed out the Safavi dynasty and held most of Iran at their mercy. And how fortunate, again, that, since that day, Ispahan has never again been Iran's capital. Let modernism wreak its worst enormities on Tehran. Tehran can take it; for she has little beauty to lose. And to think that, but for an accident of history, Ispahan might have been turned into a standardized modern capital city! Why, the Meidan might have been dismantled to make room for an up-to-date speedway. The mere thought sends a shiver down one's spine. But fortunately it is Tehran that has taken the knock. The beauty of Ispahan has been saved—let us hope, for ever—by this ex-capital's political eclipse. The citizens of Edinburgh should take note of Ispahan's aesthetic good fortune. This might perhaps make them feel rather less unkindly than they do feel now towards upstart Glasgow and overbearing London.

59. A Land of Contrasts

Take the road from Ispahan and travel first one day's journey eastward to Yazd and then half a day's journey westward to Dastaneh, at the foot of the easternmost of the Bakhtiari Mountains' snow-clad ranges. You can hardly believe that these are neighbouring districts of one and the same country. On the road to Yazd you feel as if you were entering Arabia; on the road to Dastaneh you might be running into Switzerland.

Travelling eastward from Ispahan, you leave the oasis behind before you mount the first ridge; and from the top of this rising ground the desert slopes away in all directions. The mud-walled city of Kuhpayeh ('Mountain Foot') stands on the defensive against Türkmen raids that are now ancient history and against a perennial drought that is more difficult to subjugate than nomad brigands. The characteristic feature of the place is the series of steep flights of steps leading down to subterranean conduits. Kuhpayeh's lifeline is a qanat that brings water from a life-giving mountain. The people can be sure that they are not going to die of thirst. But, when they have drawn the minimum amount of water that is required for human needs, will there be enough left to raise sufficient crops to feed this number of mouths?

This question becomes more acute the farther east one travels. Nain, the junction of the roads from Ispahan and Tehran, can scrape a livelihood from the passing traffic. But Aqda, the next town on the road to Yazd, is fighting a losing battle with the niggardliness of Nature. The palm-groves below the houses are pitifully inadequate; and, indeed, half the houses are deserted and are falling into ruin. The ventilation towers give Aqda the appearance of some great fish that has been hauled out of the water and is now gasping its life away through its gills. The town could not survive if a large contingent of the able-bodied men did not spend part of the year earning wages in Yazd, Tehran, and other relatively prosperous cities.

Ardakan, which comes next into view, is struggling for life with rather more success. Lying in a trough between a nearby range of dry mountains and a more distant range of moist ones, it draws its water from the life-giving range in defiance of the distance that the qanats have to traverse. As one measures with a wondering eye the space between town and mountain, one sees line upon line of qanat-made mole-hills stretching away over the plain until they fade out of sight in the heat-haze.

Aqda's and Ardakan's manifest fight for life makes Yazd's existence seem miraculous. Here is a great city planted in the middle of the desert yet obviously thriving and apparently doing so with ease. But the miracle is an illusion. The city of Yazd is really the product of qanats and handicrafts, or, in other words, of human toil and ingenuity. We visited a Zoroastrian village on the outskirts of the Yazd oasis (Yazd is the home of the largest of the surviving Zoroastrian communities in Iran). From the roof of the village fire-temple we looked out, in the evening light, over irrigated poplar groves and orchards and fertile fields. But in the other direction the darkness was falling over a desert that crept right up to the village's mud walls. Like Aqda and Ardakan, Yazd is engaged in a daily struggle with Nature. Only at Yazd it is Man, not Nature, that has the upper hand.

And now travel with me from Ispahan towards the west. First comes Shah 'Abbas's model village Najafabad, with its running waters, shady avenues, and never-ending orchards. Then we swerve left and begin to climb. The winding ascent eventually brings us to an upper reach of the Zayandeh River, with the orchards of Saman overhanging the opposite brow of the ravine. By the time we sight the rapidly growing town of Shahr é Kurd, we have crossed an invisible water-shed. The waters that are now flowing under our wheels thread their way south-westwards through successive ranges of the Bakhtiari Mountains till they join the Karun

River and travel with it to the Shatt and thence to the Gulf. But it is not till we are within a few parasangs of our destination—the village of Dastaneh—that the first big mountains show their snowy heads. How many parasangs? Two and a half. We travel about three, and are then told that it is four more. At last, over the head of a pass across a low range of rocky hills, we see a green valley at our feet and, on the farther side of it, the first great snowy range. That zigzag track, up there, that climbs right over the top: can it really be true that, twice a year, the Bakhtiari tribesmen cross it with their flocks and herds and tents and women and children? Did the Bishop really convoy a party of British refugees across it during the First World War? And did the Bishop's wife make the same passage, as a child, on her way to school in England from her home in Ispahan? I have climbed many high passes in Greece with a knapsack on my back, but I should quail at this one, even if I were being carried in a litter.

Next day we are picnicking with our Bakhtiari host in a green valley that used to be the Bakhtiari khans' summer camping-ground. Spreading plane-trees, murmuring brooks, soft turf, and luxuriant vineyards: the landscape resembles the setting of Giorgione's picture 'the Fête Champêtre'. We might be in the Venetian foothills of the Alps. But no, we are in Iran, only a day's journey away from drought-racked Aqda. Truly this Iran is a land of contrasts.

60. Capital Cities in Fars

The habitable part of Iran is shaped like the capital letter Y. You must imagine that this particular Y has been overturned, so that the left branch of it now points ENE, the right branch SSE, and the stem of the Y WNW, like this: ≺. If history were determined by geography, the left branch would have been the historically important one; for this branch, which runs through the province of Khorasan, lies on the route from Europe and the Mediterranean to Afghanistan, India, Soviet Central Asia, and China. The right branch, which points SSE, is geographically a blind alley; for here the mountain ramparts of the Iranian plateau break down, in a series of gigantic steps, to the torrid shore of the Persian Gulf. A climate which is temperate at five thousand feet above sea-level, round Shiraz, turns semi-tropical, some two thousand feet lower, at Kazerun, and completely tropical at Bushire and in Baluchistan. Migrant peoples who have drifted into the south-eastern highlands of Iran have seldom made their way across Baluchistan into the Indus Valley ('When God made Baluchistan, He laughed'). And Alexander the Great is perhaps the only general who has ever led an army overland, along that fearful coast, all the way from Sind to 'Iraq. Kerman is the last of Iran's south-eastern highland provinces; Fars is the last but one. It is remarkable that Fars should have aspired on four occasions to make herself the metropolis of a great empire. It is still more remarkable that she should have succeeded no less than three times out of the four in fulfilling her apparently insensate ambition.

The natural site for the capital of Iran is at the fork of the ≺, where the letter's two branches diverge on either side of a central desert. The ideal site, on *a priori* geographical considerations, would be the city of Qom, where the road between Ispahan and Tehran skirts the desert's western fringe. And Qom is, as a matter of fact, the ecclesiastical capital of present-day Persia. The present political capital, Tehran, Tehran's predecessor, Ispahan, and Ecbatana (the modern Hamadan), which was the capital of the Median Empire, all lie in this neighbourhood. Yet the most famous capital cities of Iran have not been these that have enjoyed the geographical advantage of a central situation. They have been cities in Fars: Pasargadae and Persepolis, Gur (near the present-day Firuzabad), and Shahpur (near the present-day Kazerun). I made a point of visiting all four, to see whether a first-hand sight of the landscape would tell me why they had been selected to play their historic part.

Fars is a land of fantastically contorted mountain-chains alternating with upland plains which are as dramatically flat as the mountains are dramatically rugged. The mountains have a way of suddenly dipping and as suddenly raising their heads again. The dip creates a gorge, and rivers, meandering across the plains, scent out these gorges unerringly and joyfully plunge into them. Thus the rivers contrive to flow at right-angles to the direction of the mountain ranges. The gorges give them the opportunity; and, if a gorge is not too narrow to allow anything to pass except the river itself, it also offers an opportunity for human beings to make their way between plain and plain.

I found that all the four Farsi capital cities that I visited were sited on the edge of a plain in a position commanding the mouth of a gorge that was wide enough to serve as an important human thoroughfare. Cyrus II's capital, Pasargadae, on the edge of the plain of Morghab, commands the gorge (abandoned by the modern wheel-road) through which the River Pulvar threads its way to the plain of Marvdasht. In the throat of the gorge, where it debouches into Marvdasht, lie the ruins of a city, called Ishtakhr in the 'Abbasid age, which was the ecclesiastical capital of Fars in the time of the Sasanian Empire. And then, just round the corner, on a terrace overhanging the plain and backing on to a mountain, comes Darius I's capital Persepolis.

Shahpur stands in the plain of Kazerun at the exit from a gorge that gives passage to the Shahpur River. It was founded by the second of the Sasanian kings, Shahpur I, who brought the Roman emperor Valerian to his knees (the scene has been immortalized by the victor in a bas-relief here and in another at Nakhsh é Rustam, below the tombs of the Sasanids' Achaemenid predecessors). Gur, the capital city of Shahpur I's father, Ardashir, the founder of the Sasanian dynasty, stands in the plain of Firuzabad, commanding the exit from a gorge traversed by the River Tang é Ab. Ardashir built himself two palaces at two different stages of his career. When he was still a rebel satellite of the Parthian King of Kings, he constructed a palatial fortress on the

gorge's eastern brow. A wall ran down the mountain-side
from the fortress to the river-bank, and a would-be invader
would have to make himself master of these formidable
defensive works before he could pass. After he had over-
thrown his Parthian overlord Artabanus, Ardashir came
down into the plain and built an unfortified palace on level
ground just outside the exit from the gorge.

It is one of the curiosities of history that, in the nineteen-
twenties, two brothers—joint chiefs of the Kashgai tribe—
tried to make history repeat itself. They took the plain of
Kazerun as a base of operations for emulating Ardashir's
feat. Unfortunately for them, their suzerain was not Artabanus but Reza Shah, and their ambitious attempt to seize
the crown of Iran resulted in their defeat and death. They
did not live to build a palace; but they did leave as their
memorial a stately garden, in which two avenues of tall
cypresses, running at right angles to one another, stand
as mourners for the fall of the princelings who planted
them.

As for Pasargadae and Persepolis, the contrast between
them tells one at a glance that Cyrus's victory over the Medes
left the victor care-free, but that Darius was not reassured by
his more brilliant victory over a host of rebels. Cyrus's
little palaces lie in the open plain, unfortified, whereas
Persepolis is as much a fortress as it is a ceremonial centre.
Like the Hittite capital Boghazqalé, though on a smaller
scale, Persepolis is built in the shape of a chair. The platform
is the seat; the Mountain of Mercy (Kuh é Rahmat) is the
back. Climb the ridge of this mountain and you will find that,
like the citadel of Brescia in Lombardy, it is severed from the
mountain-mass behind it by a ravine at plain-level. The site
of Persepolis has been carefully chosen to make it defensible
by nature as well as by human art. From this palatial
stronghold Darius ruled far and wide—as far as the Panjab
on one side and Macedonia on the other. But the emperor
who had so nearly lost a throne that he had won by an
assassination was in no mood for taking chances. The iron
had entered into his soul. He was psychologically on the

defensive. Persepolis was built for a two-fold purpose: to impress the Great King's unwilling present subjects and to make a last stand against his successors' future conquerors. Darius must have had a premonition of Alexander.

61. Iran's Green North

Iran, like Turkey and Spain, is a plateau with a desert at its heart. The typical Iranian landscape is an irrigated oasis in an elsewhere barren waste, or a green valley lapped in a fold of a bare mountain. But, like Turkey and like Spain, Iran has her surprising green corner. Turkey has her Black Sea coast, Spain her Asturias and Galicia, Iran her Caspian provinces and Azerbaijan. I was determined not to leave Iran without having set eyes on this green patch, so at Kharej, on the Tehran-Qazvin road, I took a right turn into the gorge down which the Kharej River comes tumbling. The torrent loses itself, in the end, in the central desert's dreary salt pans; but, on its way to its death, it turns Kharej into a little paradise in the midst of a bald landscape. For the northward-bound traveller, this is a foretaste of what lies ahead.

The road from Kharej to the Caspian shore is a modern one, Shah Reza's impressive handiwork. The traditional route from Reyy to Rasht took the easier option of passing through Qazvin and then following the gorge of the Safid Rud. But, if you want to see the Elburz mountains in their glory, take Shah Reza's road and choose a season when the snow has retreated far enough to let you go over the top of the pass instead of worming your way through the tunnel. From the top you see a sight which the tunnel denies you: the glistening peaks of Takht é Suleiman and the still loftier white cone of Demavend.

When you come zigzagging down the steep Caspian slope, the trees suddenly begin. They thicken into a forest as you thread your way through the foothills, and they yield to orchards and rice-fields along the strip of coastal plain. If Mazandaran is green, its north-western neighbour Gilan is more so. Here, in the delta of the Safid Rud, you might imagine that you were in Japan or even in Java. The rice-fields are beautifully terraced; the foothills are planted with tea; and in tea-gardens and rice-fields a host of men and women—predominantly women—are at work.

On the morning of the second day, we set out early from the Caspian port of Bandar Pahlavi (once known as Enzeli). Our objective was to reach the Soviet frontier and thence push on, via Ardebil, to Tabriz. But were we really going to get there? Ahead of us, along the coast, we knew that there were ten broken bridges which had once spanned as many snow-fed rivers. And, last September, the British Ambassador, after crossing the first seven rivers out of the ten, had been stopped by the rising waters of the eighth. As we approached this eighth river, we kept our fingers crossed, but, for the traveller in Iran, June is a propitious month, and soon we found ourselves with all ten rivers behind us and only the Iron Curtain in front.

Turning westward now, with our backs to the sea, we began to climb a steeply winding, thickly wooded valley. I have never seen so dense a growth or such a variety of fresh green deciduous trees. In its luxuriance it beats the Dudden valley. The Persian road, on which we were travelling, wound along the valley's southern flank. Along the northern flank, a few dozen yards away, ran the Russian wire, with observation posts, on steel stilts, rearing their heads every quarter of a mile or so. The first two of these had stung the Persians into retorting by setting up two similar monsters on their side of the line. But, after having made this gesture, they had left the Russians to play the rest of the game alone. There was nothing on the Persian side that would have stopped a Soviet cow. You might have thought that Persia was care-free and that Russia was cowering in dread of a Persian invasion.

Before we had reached the head of the pass, the trees had stopped as abruptly as they had begun on the Caspian slope

of Elburz. They gave way to green pastures, studded with
cattle, and to wheat-fields fed by rain. We crossed the divide
and in a moment we were in another world. An upland plain
stretched away at our feet, and, beyond it, rose the magnificent peak of Mount Savalan—already famous for its
honey in the Greek geographer Strabo's day. The plain
was the plain of Ardebil, the cradle of the Safavi dynasty,
and I had long been eager to see the native land of a family
that had changed the course of the World's history. The
Safavis had started as Sunnite clerics; they had ended as
Shi'ite empire-builders; and, though their secular reign had
lasted for little more than two hundred years, they had left
an enduring mark on Iran. By converting her to the Shi'ah,
they had re-awakened in her the national consciousness that
had been dormant since the Arab conquest and the subsequent conversion of the country to Islam. The shrine of
Shaikh Safi in the city of Ardebil, and the shrines of his
forebears in the neighbouring village of Kalkhoran, deserve
a visit from the passing historian. And, if he passes that way
in June, he will enjoy the cool breezes of this invigorating
land.

'This used to be an Assyrian country; but, since the
Battle, we have been scattered,' said a voice in English (we
had heard little but Turkish spoken since we had crossed the
Talish mountains from the Caspian shore to Ardebil).
'The Battle': I knew what he meant. He was referring to the
Turkish invasion of Persian Azerbaijan in 1918, when the
Assyrian Christian inhabitants of the great green plain of
Urmieh, on the western shore of the lake, had been driven
from their ancestral homes and had fled for their lives, amid
terrible hardships, to the shelter of the British lines in 'Iraq.
That was now nearly forty years ago; but, in the speaker's
mind, it was still *the* Battle; for it had been the supreme
disaster in his people's history. We had paused in the street
of an Assyrian village at the southern foot of the pass leading
down into the Urmieh plain. Urmieh City has been re-
named Rezaïeh, but the past has not been obliterated
completely. Some of the former Assyrian inhabitants have

been allowed to return and resume possession of their fields, and this village (part Presbyterian, part Roman Catholic) was one of the present seventy Christian villages in the district.

Western Azerbaijan, between Lake Rezaïeh and the mountain chain that separates Persia from Turkey, is as green as Gilan or as Ireland; but, when you run on southward to Mehabad, everything changes. Green fields give way to rugged mountain-sides, the Turkish language gives way to the Kurdish, the Shi'ah gives way to the Sunnah. Forward to Maraghéh! But we were foiled in our attempt to return to Tabriz round the southern end of the lake. For, at Miandoab, there was a recently broken bridge over a river that, even in June, was still too deep for a car to ford. Let us be grateful for our good luck in getting as far as we did. We saw enough of green Persia for its greenness to be printed on our memories.

62. The Dome of Sultanieh

There it is at last: a tiny round protuberance breaking the level line of the horizon. For half a day and another half a day we had been travelling, south-eastwards, up the great north-westward road that had carried successive hordes of migrant nomads down from the steppes of Central Asia into Anatolia. Marianni and Mitanni, Cimmerians and Scythians and Turks, one after another they had all passed this way after breaking out of the steppe on to the Iranian plateau and squeezing through the narrow passage between the Elburz Mountains and the Central Iranian Desert. Last and worst of all had come the Mongols from the far north-east, and the particular Mongol horde that had conquered Iran and 'Iraq had established their seat of government at the place marked by that dome for which we are making. 'Seat of Government'—Sultanieh—there it is.

Between Bostanabad and Mianeh our road had dipped and

risen and dipped and risen again over an interminable series of alternate ridges and ravines. This morning the road had carried us through a gorge and then through a narrow valley. It was not till we had left behind us the theological academies of the city of Zenjan that the valley had broadened out into the flat green plain over which we were now travelling towards that no longer distant cupola. The nearer we came to it, the greener grew the land. The broken bridge at Miandoab had cheated me of a hoped-for view of the pastures of Maraghéh, where the Mongol conquerors of Iran had first encamped. Presumably they had judged the pastures of Sultanieh to be better, since they had shifted their capital to this plain and had built here this mighty monument to commemorate their final conversion to Islam. Now we were within eight kilometres of the soaring dome, and were turning off the high road on to a track that seemed to be wandering in the dome's direction. At first the track gave firm footing to our wheels, and we were counting on reaching our goal in a few minutes. But a sudden quagmire killed that expectation, and we jolted the rest of the weary way in a country cart. Yet, when we stood at last under the centre of the dome, we felt that our exertions had been worth while.

To a Londoner's eyes the height and diameter of this Mongol dome at Sultanieh seemed to be on about the same scale as Wren's work at St. Paul's. But you must imagine St. Paul's surrounded, not by a ruined city of big buildings, but by a living village of mud hovels. The great domed mosque was built by the Mongol Il-Khan Oljaitu Khodabandeh—'the Servant of the God' to whose faith the pagan prince had been converted—and, no doubt, in Khodabandeh's day the surrounding village was less shabby than its present successor. But perhaps there was never a city at Sultanieh if by 'city' we mean an Ispahan or a Shiraz. The Mongols, even those of princely rank, will have continued to live in their ancestral kibitkas: wooden-framed felt-covered huts that could be transported as easily as a present-day air-conditioned trailer. The cathedral mosque was a

memorial of the Mongol Il-Khan's revolutionary conversion
to Islam. Between mosque and camp there was room for a
modest bazar, where Persian merchants would provide their
barbarian masters with the elementary apparatus of civilization. What mattered to the Mongols was not the contents of
the bazar but the quality of the pasture; for this would
determine the condition of their horses; and the condition of
their horses might decide whether they were going to keep
their empire or to lose it. They lost it within a hundred
years of winning it, though the quality of the pastures seems
still first-class today.

Standing inside the dome at Sultanieh, one marvels at
the grand simplicity of its structure. Looking at it from a
distance, one marvels at its present loneliness. Might
St. Paul's look like this one day, if it survived a third world-
war fought with atomic weapons? I fancied myself pacing
the Spaniard's Walk on Hampstead Heath, and seeing
nothing but the dome of St. Paul's between me and the
Surrey hills. The city of God endureth when human empires
pass away. The solitary dome at Sultanieh speaks volumes.

63. The Cedars

The Cedars of Lebanon! We had shrunk from making the
conventional trip from Beirut, partly because it had become
such a hackneyed piece of tourist routine, and partly because
we feared that we might be disappointed at seeing the
scraggy remnant of a noble cedar forest fenced in for show
like a gang of caged lions and tigers in a zoo. We had reconciled ourselves to giving the Cedars a miss, and were
taking a short rest at Baalbek, when, one evening, two young
men made their appearance in the hotel. Where had they
come from? Why, from the Cedars. How had they come?
Well, over the top of Mount Lebanon. What was the road
like? Hair-raising. We went out and gazed at the mountain
in the clear evening light. It rose like a sheer wall, with

flecks of snow still clinging to its crest and one long curving
band in the shape of a white stocking. At this distance the
road over the top was not visible. Meanwhile we had made
up our minds. We would visit the Cedars after all, and reach
them from this side. We hired a car in the village of Shlifa
and made an early start.

From Baalbek to Shlifa our road ran across the gently
sloping plain of the Baqaa—the section of the Great Rift
Valley that intervenes between Antilebanon and Lebanon.
The unimpressive source of the Litani River was on our left,
the mysterious solitary Roman column on our right. The
wheat was white (yes, really white, not yellow) unto the
harvest. The country people were reaping it with sickles; and
camels, hired for this purpose from the bedouin, were
carrying huge loads of it to the village threshing-floors.
But at Deir al-Ahmar, the Red Convent, we left the fields
behind and began to wind our way up among Mount
Lebanon's rocky, scrub-covered outworks. Suddenly we
found ourselves zigzagging down into a deep valley with a
ribbon of fields in its trough, and from the farther side rose
Mount Lebanon itself: that sheer wall that we had been
gazing at from Baalbek, on the far side of the Baqaa.

Here, in the village of 'Ain 'Ata, at Lebanon's foot, we
saw, for the first time, the next stage of our road. A faint
scar zigzagged, unconvincingly, up the mountain's side and
disappeared over the top. Can we really get by? Yes, we
can. The surface is strewn with boulders, like a torrent-bed;
but the road itself is skilfully aligned and gently graded.
It carried us up and up till we arrived at the head of the pass;
and here what a sight had been awaiting us! The toe of the
white snow stocking, which we had seen, far away, from
Baalbek, was now within a few yards of our wheels, and
below us lay the white harvest fields of the Baqaa on one
side and the blue waters of the Mediterranean on the other.
From this unique point of vantage, we could see them both
at once.

The Cedars were not yet visible; but now we were winding
down into a vast natural amphitheatre, encircled by the

highest heights of Lebanon on the north as well as on the east. This amphitheatre breaks down into the apparently bottomless gorge of Qadisheh; but the alpine slopes above the brow of the cliffs are seamed with cultivation terraces and studded with villages. This North Lebanese fastness was the earliest asylum of the Maronite Christians. The impregnability of the stronghold gave its rocks an inestimable value for a persecuted minority, and this, in turn, gave an inestimable value to every patch of cultivable soil on the mountain-side. Each additional terrace would feed a few more mouths, and the problem for these refugees in the highlands was to win security without incurring starvation.

The Cedars! We had forgotten them; but here they were, in sight at last round this corner of the mountain, though still far below us. Seen thus from far above, they looked as insignificant as we had expected: just a straggling patch of dark green trees that hardly broke the monotony of the expanse of grey limestone. But, when you sit under their shade and look up at their spreading branches, your feelings change. Each tree is a noble creature. Cedars are the lions and eagles of the arboreal world. There are still about four hundred of them here; and, on the steeper slopes of the amphitheatre, hundreds more have recently been planted by a Lebanese Government that has adopted the Cedar as the Republic's national emblem.

So we have seen the Cedars after all; but our day's journey is not yet over; for our objective today is a double one: the Cedars of Lebanon and the source of the River Orontes. So we re-cross Mount Lebanon, wind our way down again into the Baqaa, and then race northwards as, one day, the Pharaoh Ramses II raced along the same road till he ran into the Hittite ambush at Qadesh.

At last we turn off leftward from the road that leads to Hermel, and follow a track that dips down into a ravine. It dips steeper and steeper till we have to leave the car and slither the rest of the way down on foot. But the toilsome descent is worth while. From the base of a semicircular limestone apse, volumes of water are welling out into a pool that must be twenty feet deep. The water is so clear that we can see the pebbles glistening on the bottom; and it is so abundant that, before it leaves the pool, it has already made a river. Singing and foaming, the new-born Orontes courses down the ravine, impatient to set the great water-wheels turning at Hama.

64. The King and the Jinn

'Arabian American'! Desert and oil-field! Even as recently as thirty years ago, the boldest flight of imagination did not put two and two together. What concern could the United States of America ever have with the Arabian Peninsula— or 'Arab Island' as it is called by the Arabs themselves, ignoring the Isthmus of Aleppo that intervenes between this virtual island's Mediterranean coast and its river-front along the Euphrates? A few romantic-minded American missionaries, fascinated by the lure of Bible lands, might have bowed their devoted shoulders to Psyche's task of trying to convert Muslims to Christianity. But what American business man in his senses would reckon that he could earn dividends in the land of Ishmael? Business does, no doubt, boom when Uncle Sam makes his annual masquerade as Father Christmas, but who has ever yet heard of his playing the jinn? Oil? If Pennsylvania and California do not satisfy Gargantua's needs, are there not also Oklahoma and Texas? And does not Venezuela lie just across the Caribbean? America and Arabia! Never the twain shall meet. Yet this inconceivable meeting is now an accomplished fact. The insatiability of the West's demand for oil and the genius of an Arabian empire-builder have worked together to bring this miracle about.

Fifty-five years ago, in the second year of this century, Arabia was still languishing in her age-old poverty and anarchy. Her coasts were divided between the Turkish and

the British Empire; the interior was dominated by the House
of Rashid. Besides his own ancestral domain—the Jabal
Shammar in north-western Najd—Ibn Rashid held in his
grip the domain of the rival House of Sa'ud, which lay
between the Jabal Shammar and Arabia's 'Empty Quarter'.
The Ibn Sa'ud of the day, a young and untried man named
'Abd-al-'Aziz bin 'Abd ar-Rahman, had grown up as a
'displaced person' in Kuwait, at the head of the Persian
Gulf. The sub-continent was, in fact, in its usual state of
disunity and unrest.

The first step towards the establishment of the present
American oil industry in Arabia was taken, not by any
American prospector or promoter, but by young 'Abd-al-
'Aziz ibn Sa'ud when, in 1902, with only a handful of
fighting-men behind him, he made a surprise attack on his
ancestral capital, Riyadh, and wrested the town out of the
hands of Ibn Rashid's garrison. Within less than a quarter
of a century from that epoch-making stroke, Ibn Sa'ud had
united under his rule the whole of Arabia except the south-
western principality of the Yaman and the British possessions
and protectorates along the southern and south-eastern
coasts. By that time he had proved himself to be a wise statesman as well as a victorious soldier. He had persuaded the
rest of the Muslim World to acquiesce in his conquest of the
Hijaz, though the Hijaz is the Holy Land of Islam and Ibn
Sa'ud and his people are adherents of the severely puritanical
Wahhabi sect. Again, when the exasperating ruler of the
Yaman had committed an act of aggression against him, he
had brought the offender to his knees in a seven-weeks' war
and had then heaped coals of fire on his head by granting
him generous terms in the name of Arab fraternity.

This was a brilliant twenty-five years' record, but it was
the beginning, not the end, of the Sa'udi empire-builder's
task. Empires had been built in Arabia before, only to collapse on shifting sands. The real problem was one, not of
building, but of maintenance, and the arch-enemy of
political stability in Arabia was her poverty. The border
tribes raided the Fertile Crescent; the interior tribes raided

the border tribes; every man's hand was against his neighbour's. The only possible remedy for this chronic anarchy
would be some alternative source of livelihood; and where
was this to be found? In the profits from the annual pilgrimage? The number of pilgrims was fluctuating and the
profits from them were precarious. In an extension of
agriculture? Ibn Sa'ud set himself to harness Wahhabi zeal
to this economic objective. But what were Arabia's reserves
of untrapped underground water? How raise the capital for
sinking artesian wells? And how wean away the bedouin from
their ancient and well-beloved pastoral and warrior way of
life?

As he was musing on these problems at the crisis of his
career, the latter-day Solomon inadvertently rubbed his
ring. Instantaneously there was a whirr of aeroplane
propellers from the far side of the Frankish Ocean, and a jinn
—unknown and gigantic—was standing at attention in the
king's presence. 'May it please Your Majesty,' said this
impressive visitant ever so politely—'May it please Your
Majesty to let *me* do your digging for you. I shall be digging,
not for water, but for a much more valuable liquid. And
I shall not ask to be paid for my trouble. On the contrary,
I shall expect to pay to Your Majesty a handsome share of
the profits of the enterprise. And, whatever may be the
percentage on which we shall agree, I can assure you that
this will relieve you of your financial anxieties.' —'Done,'
said the King. And he cast his ring into the oil-field, as the
Doge of Venice used to cast his into the sea. Once again, a
poverty-stricken land had made a fruitful marriage with a
wealth-giving element. The American oil industry and the
Kingdom of Sa'udi Arabia have been partners now for
twenty-four years. Neither party regrets the bargain. The
Arabian American Oil Company has been a profitable
business for them both.

65. An American Tripolis

Tripolis, triborough: the most famous cluster of three cities in the world today is Greater New York, tied together by its three-way bridge. There was an older trinity in Phoenicia: Tyre, Sidon, and Arvad. For an age, this consortium of three Phoenician cities was the World's workshop, market-place, and port. It is commemorated in the name of the present town of Tripoli in the Lebanon, which was the place where the representatives of the three cities met to deal with matters of common concern. But the Phoenicians, according to the legend, were late-comers on the Syrian shore of the Mediterranean. They had served their apprenticeship, it was said, on the Arabian shore of the Persian Gulf. The archaeologists have not yet found any material evidence to confirm this legend. But, if you visit the eastern province of Sa'udi Arabia today, you will find a tripolis there now in full swing —not a Phoenician but an American one. Abqaiq, Ras Tanura, Dhahran: the names are Arabic, but the three cities—planted though they are on the Arabian desert— are as American as New York itself. America in Arabia: this is one of the wonders of the present-day world. I could not imagine it before I set eyes on it. Shall I be able to convey this extraordinary spectacle in mere words?

Climb with me into the Arabian American Oil Company's plane on Beirut airfield. When we have soared over Lebanon and Antilebanon and have left the last vestiges of Damascus's oasis behind us, we head south-east, sight the Abqaiq-Sidon pipe-line, and then fly on over it, always south-east-wards, for four more hours (a thousand miles). On that long flight there is not a sign of life below us except an occasional pumping-station. Neither on the outward journey nor on the return one did I spy a single black tent, and the desert itself is monotonous. When the dark volcanic wilderness, east of Damascus, is behind our tail, the rest is an expanse of tawny gravel, rarely diversified by a patch of those yellow sand-waves that are the conventional picture of the desert in the Western imagination. Even when you are having the thrill of peering down at Arabia for the first time in your life, the sensation gradually subsides from excitement into boredom. And then, at the end of the journey, the scene changes again as abruptly as it changed at the beginning. Dhahran springs up out of nowhere as suddenly as Damascus vanished, and, as we glide down, the Sun is smiting another glittering sea. We have crossed 'the Arab Island' diagonally from the Mediterranean to the Gulf.

How shall I describe these three outposts of America in the Arabian wilderness? There is a division of labour among them. Abqaiq extracts the oil; Ras Tanura refines it; Dhahran administers the astonishing enterprise. Ras Tanura lies at water's edge on the promontory from which it takes its name. Dhahran lies among a host of miniature mountains (this is what the word 'dhahran' means). Abqaiq stretches its limbs in the open desert. Abqaiq has acquired a satellite town, and will, no doubt, become a mother of many such, for the oil-field on which she stands has no known limits so far. Prospecting parties continue to explore the desert, and still they find oil beyond oil. All three cities are equipped with fantastic technical installations, but, in this, Ras Tanura excels her sisters. If H. G. Wells had lived to visit her, she might have inspired his chef d'œuvre. In all three cities, green lawns, thick hedges, and pleasant air-conditioned houses, schools, hospitals, theatres, clubs, and offices hold their ground between the Wellsian erections on one side and the desert on the other. If you are acquainted with Los Angeles or Pomona, you can picture the scene—with the water-sprinkler fighting its victorious but never-ending battle against the searing drought.

'A pillar of cloud by day and a pillar of fire by night.' On the oil-field of eastern Sa'udi Arabia, such pillars are as numerous as the pagan deities of pre-Islamic 'Times of Ignorance'. The natural gas, disengaged from the oil, is unwanted; so it is disposed of in this drastic way. Travel by night on any of the roads that link the three Arabian American cities together. The whole landscape seems to be aflame. The wavering hell-fires of the nether world flare up into a deep blue sky set thick with stars. At the peak of the day the temperature may rise—this is July—to 120 degrees Fahrenheit in the shade. But, during the last hour before midnight, it is cool enough for the mind to meditate. This astonishing feat of Western technology and organization; this exotic setting in which the American drama is being performed! The three cities think nothing of distance. Their hill stations are in the Lebanon and in Eritrea. Their hospital nurses are brought from India, their taxi-drivers from Somaliland. Quo vadimus? What lies hidden in the future? May the God who is the God of both Muslims and Christians guide Man's racing feet out of the paths of destruction.

66. An Incredible City

I had pictured the Najd as a high steppe clothed in at least a thin coat of grey-green camel-feed. But I saw nothing like the Najd of my imagination from the plane between Dhahran and Riyadh, the capital of Sa'udi Arabia. It is true that one was seldom out of sight of dots of scrub. But most of the landscape was bare, and all of it was empty. During that two-hours' flight I saw not one house or field, and only two encampments of black tents; and then, without warning, the incredible city rose up and hit me in the eye.

This rising city of Riyadh is born of oil, as truly as the American tripolis on the oil-field. If the oil-royalties should cease to flow into the Sa'udi Government's coffers, the fabulous building activity in the capital would stop as dead as the tower of Babel. One does not often see a whole city being built at one moment, but this is what is happening here. Apartment houses, blocks of government offices, schools, hospitals, hotels, power stations, and, not least, palaces and palatial private mansions—all designed in the most modern style—are sweeping out of existence the lovely city of chocolate-coloured and cream-coloured mud walls that King 'Abd-al-'Aziz won back for his house by his historic coup de main, fifty-five years ago. On the outskirts there stands unchanged 'the Needle's Eye'—a little mountain with a hole through it—where Ibn Sa'ud and his companions took cover during the night before that victorious assault which changed the course of history. But, if they could come back to life to repeat their exploit today, they would hardly recognize the city that was their cynosure. Just enough of it still remains to make the visitor marvel at their achievement. Every surviving block of the old city is a fortress. The towers and curtain walls are in the Assyrian style; the houses perched on the walls have as many storeys as a modern Arab house in the Hadramaut or an ancient Phoenician house in Tyre or Sidon.

The new style of building bears witness to the arrival of a new kind of people in this Arabian capital city: Lebanese contractors, Egyptian labourers and hotel managers and schoolmasters, Palestinian clerks. But the makers of the new Riyadh are not, of course, all foreigners. The surging tide of modern life is buoying up Sa'udis too. After all, the Hijaz is a part of Sa'udi Arabia, and, thanks to the Pilgrimage, the Hijazis have always been a cosmopolitan and sophisticated people, in touch with what is going on in the great world whose routes converge on Mecca. But ultramodern Riyadh lies in the heart of the once ultra-conservative Wahhabi country. Are the people of Ibn Sa'ud's ancestral domain being swept along, too, in the formidable stream of swiftly solidifying reinforced concrete? You have only to stroll through some of the suks of the new city, and you will see that Riyadh's native Najdis are not letting themselves be left behind in the breakneck race.

You can build on mineral oil, but you cannot eat it or drink it. So what does modern Riyadh live on? At lunch in the city I had been feasted on canned roast turkey imported from the United States, but this could hardly be the population's staple diet. In answer to my inquiries on this point, my host obligingly drove me out of the city to the date-palm groves of the Wadi Hanifeh, and, on the way back to Dhahran, the pilot made a detour to carry me over the famous gardens and fields of Al-Kharj, about twenty minutes' flying distance from Riyadh in the direction of 'the Empty Quarter'. Here indeed were ribbons of green in an almost Persian profusion, and I heard of all the good things that are being raised for King Sa'ud in Al-Kharj by the Texan agricultural experts who manage the royal farms there. Yet, what are these oases compared to the vast encompassing desert? And what must 'the Empty Quarter' be like if the quarter that I did see counts as an inhabited, or anyway a habitable, country?

Well, the surroundings of Riyadh are not more inhospitable than those of Petra and Palmyra. And, if modern Riyadh were to enjoy the same measure of prosperity as those two caravan cities enjoyed in their day, Riyadh could count herself fortunate.

67. The Gardens of Hofuf

It was the hottest hour of a July day, and, even on the short drive across the open desert from the east gate of the city of Hofuf to the nearest stand of date palms, the Sun's rays had battered us till we felt as if we had been beaten with a flail. But here, under a triple tier of shade, it was as cool as it would have been at the same season in Northern Europe. The crowns of the date palms received the sunshine's first assault, and any shafts that broke through the palms' defences were stopped by the peach-trees and the trellised vines. As we stood eating the sweet purple grapes and the softly ripe peaches that our host was plucking for us, I wondered for a moment whether I was experiencing Adam's and Eve's primal state of felicity. But no; the Garden of Eden is fabled to have yielded its fruits without exacting any preliminary human labour, whereas this garden in Arabia, like the English one that delighted Andrew Marvell, was the work of 'the skilful gardener's' toil and art. It is true that God gave the water that is this Arabian garden's life; but Man led this precious liquid through a thousand channels, cunningly graded and aligned; Man planted the trees and set the rice in the paddies and the alfalfa in the fields. Without Man's intervention, the welling water might have begotten a marsh or even a jungle but never a garden yielding 'the luscious clusters of the vine' and 'the nectarine and curious peach'. The gardens of Hofuf are what Man has made of the opportunity that God has given him.

Arabia is like a huge rough-hewn paving-stone which has been slightly tilted so as to dip towards the south-east. The geologists say that the water which bubbles up to make the oasis of Hofuf has been captured by the Earth somewhere in the distant north-western uplands of the Najd and has been conveyed, all this way, by gravity, underground—thus escaping evaporation and rising, at last, to the surface with its volume undiminished. The volume is large. In this L-shaped oasis which supports Hofuf and its twin city Mubarraz, there are thirty-six greater springs and about a hundred and twenty lesser ones. The runnels that watered my host's garden took off from a stream that was one of three branches of a river fed from a single source. The three combined, my host declared, had as big a flow of cubic feet as the famous River Barada which makes the oasis of Damascus; and this mighty Arabian spring has thirty-five sisters of equal power. No wonder that the Hofuf oasis is—or was till the meteoric rise of Riyadh—the most populous area in all Sa'udi Arabia, not excluding Mecca, Medina, and Jiddah.

Hofuf is forty or fifty miles from the nearest American oil-city, Abqaiq, so the pull of the oil-field is not as strong here as it is at Qatif, which is caught in a vice between Dhahran and Ras Tanura. The pull is strong enough to have

drawn the administration of the Eastern Province of Sa'udi
Arabia out of the palace at Hofuf into an air-conditioned
office in Dammam—the new business centre on the coast,
next door to Dhahran, which has been conjured into
existence by the purchasing-power of American house-
wives. So far, however, the attraction of alternative and more
lucrative occupation on the oil-field has not led to any
diminution of the care with which the gardens of Hofuf have
been tended from time immemorial. In the gardens of
Qatif, on the other hand, an increasing neglect is sadly
apparent. The runnels are silting into stagnant pools; the
dates are unharvested, the trees are dying. Why should one
labour for small returns as a husbandman or a fisherman or a
pearl-diver or a shepherd if one can earn more money in a
new kind of job that also carries with it the prestige of being
unquestionably 'modern'?

Yet even in the thick of the American oil-cities, on the
road from Damman to Ras Tanura, I found a Palestinian
farmer who had made the desert blossom like the rose by
bringing water to the surface and irrigating a soil that lacks
none of the chemical requisites for fertility. This magician,
who was transforming a once bare countryside, had been a
prosperous landowner in Palestine till his citrus plantations
had been taken from him by the Israelis. He had had the
spirit to start again from the beginning in an unfamiliar
climate and terrain. Probably he will die a richer man than
he would ever have been if he had not been robbed of his
Palestinian home and property. To be turned into a 'displaced person' is one of the severest ordeals that can over-
take a human being. The victims who rise to the occasion
are heroes.

'A green thought in a green shade': 'such was that happy
garden-state' in which I found myself in the oasis of Hofuf.
But the angel with the flaming sword was on the watch for
me. The hour at which I was billed to give a lecture in
scorching Abqaiq drew nearer and nearer, till at last we had
to uproot ourselves from our green felicity. As we left the last
protective row of palm-trunks behind us, the shade turned

into a glare in a blinding flash. The Sun's flail-strokes came battering down again upon our heads and shoulders. Can five yards really make all the difference between Paradise and Purgatory? Ask Adam and Eve. They ought to know.

68. The Spell of Palestine

Countries have characters that are as distinctive as those of human beings. There is an extraordinary difference in the effects that they produce on human feelings. There are countries that can make your fortune for you without gaining any hold on your affections. You may have spent a lucrative working life in one of these; yet, as soon as you are able to retire, you carry your earnings away with you to some more congenial clime, without feeling any twinge of regret for the prosaic land that has done so much for you. There are other countries that offer you no flesh-pots but win your heart so completely that you feel yourself an exile anywhere else in the World. You may be prised out of the beloved country by economic pressure or be driven out of it by military force, but you will never reconcile yourself to being divorced from it. In the land of exile, your feelings and thoughts, your life and work, will be governed by one master passion: a determination to make your way home again at the earliest possible date. To insure against the chance that you yourself may fail to achieve your heart's desire, you will indoctrinate your children with the feelings that glow in your own breast, and you will enjoin it upon them to indoctrinate their own children in their turn, so that your resolve to regain your homeland will be perpetuated from the generation that has experienced the pangs of exile to generations that have never set eyes on the beloved land. The attachment created by a compulsive tradition may become even stronger than the original tie between the land and its children who lived in it in the flesh.

Such spell-binding countries are, of course, rare. Among the countries of Europe perhaps Poland and Ireland come nearest to Palestine in producing this hypnotic effect. No doubt, even the most entrancing country will leave some hearts unmoved. Few Irishmen, Poles, or Jews who have become citizens of the United States show much desire to return in person to their ancestral homes; and the original Israelis cannot have felt the spell of Palestine very strongly either, or they would not have become the 'lost' ten tribes. As we know, the recent settlers in Palestine who call themselves Israelis today are descended, not from the historical Israel, but from the historical Judah. Of all the peoples who have come and gone in Palestine since civilization began at Jericho eight or nine thousand years ago, the children of Judah, so far, have been the classic victims of Palestine's spell.

Historically speaking, being a Jew means being derived, by descent or adoption, from the people of the little Palestinian Kingdom of Judah that was extinguished by the Babylonian empire-builder Nebuchadnezzar in the sixth century B.C. But one may generalize the meaning of the word 'Jew' to signify any former inhabitant, or any descendant of any former inhabitant, of any part of Palestine who has lost his Palestinian home but has refused to resign himself to losing it. If we agree to give the word 'Jew' this psychological meaning, we shall find that the rôle of being 'the Jews' is changing hands today under our eyes. The people who have been 'the Jews' since they were exiled from Palestine in 587 B.C. by Nebuchadnezzar and in A.D. 70 by Titus and in A.D. 135 by Hadrian are now ceasing to be Jews, while a new community of Jews is being bred by a repetition of the experience of being exiled from the beloved land.

It can already be foreseen that both the modern Israelis in Palestine and the modern 'Dispersion' of historical Jews in the countries of the Western World are going to be de-Judaized as a consequence of the establishment of the present state of Israel on Palestinian soil. Psychologically, a Jew is an ex-Palestinian, or a descendant of one, who is determined to return to Palestine but has been unable to return so far; and neither the present-day Israelis nor the present-day 'Dispersion' answer to this psychological definition. The Israelis do not answer to it because they have translated the hope of returning into achievement; the Diaspora because they have decided not to return now that it is within their power to attain the traditional Jewish goal. In carving out for themselves a territorial state on Palestinian ground, the latter-day Israelis have transformed themselves from Jews into gentiles. If present-day Israel survives, it will become just another of the World's hundred parochial states: a new Denmark or Nicaragua or New Zealand or Cambodia. If the 'Diaspora' survives, its members will become American, French, British, or Dutch citizens of Jewish religion, which is quite a different thing from being a Jew in the traditional sense. How can one remain a Jew psychologically if, when one recites the annual pious hope, 'Next year in Jerusalem', one does not really mean it? Any Western Jew who wants to return to Palestine nowadays can return at any moment. His journey will be financed for him if he cannot pay for it himself. In deciding not to return now that the door is at last open, he is doing the same thing as the Israeli in another way. He is giving up being a Jew and is turning himself into a gentile.

Meanwhile, the classic experience of losing a Palestinian home is creating a new Jewry out of the nine hundred thousand Palestinian Arab refugees. When you ask them, 'What do you call for and hope for?' the answer is: 'Justice. We have been wrongfully deprived of our homes, lands, and property. Reinstatement is the only thing in the world that we will accept.' Reinstatement? This looks chimaerical when, from the unlost portion of the village of Beit Safafeh, near Bethlehem, you stare across the barbed wire at the lost land on the other side. These former fields and orchards, which are still legally the villagers' property, are now as if they lay in the Antipodes, with the whole diameter of the globe between them and their rightful owners. The stolen ground is now planted thick, not with barley or vines or

olives, but with tenement houses inhabited by Israelis. The
impression is that of a Martian invasion of our planet.
Regain the lost ground from that crushingly stronger power?
A non-Palestinian observer, not personally exposed to
Palestine's spell, might have asked the same question in the
same sceptical mood if, in the second century of the Christian
Era, he had been gazing at Aelia Capitolina: Hadrian's
gentile city, garrisoned by a Roman legion and dedicated
to pagan gods, which had been planted—a veritable
abomination of desolation—on the site of David's and
Solomon's holy city of Jerusalem. 'The Jews did return
from their Babylonish captivity, but this Roman extirpation
of Jewry is irreversible,' the second-century observer would
have commented. Yet, eighteen hundred years after Hadrian's 'definitive' extermination of the Jews in Palestine, a
Jewish state was founded in Palestine again by the never-
despairing descendants of the Jews whom Hadrian had
crushed. It was only ninety years after the conquest of
Palestine by the Crusaders that the Muslims won the dis-
puted Holy Land back again. So what are the nine years
during which the present-day Palestinian Arab exiles have
been waiting so far? As I watched the faces of refugee school-
girls singing a song declaring their determination to return
and refusing to renounce their rights, I was witnessing a new
Jewry in the making.

I have witnessed the same thing, in a more constructive
form, in many parts of the Arab World. The dire fate of exile
breaks the hearts of most of its victims, but it stimulates a
few of them to a constructive response, and these heroes
become the salt of the Earth. A 'Dispersion' of Palestinian
refugees is already playing a notable part in the Arab
World's current renovation. It is Palestinian enterprise
that has developed Jordan's once rustic capital 'Amman into
a modern city; and Palestinian teachers and technicians are
busy in the oil-bearing Arab countries: 'Iraq, Kuwait,
Sa'udi Arabia. On the oil-fields of Sa'udi Arabia's Eastern
Province, within sight of the Persian Gulf, I came across
that new oasis conjured out of the desert by a refugee

Palestinian citrus-fruit planter. Here was the familiar invincible Jewish spirit at work. The new Jews are following in
the old Jews' footsteps. How long will these Arab victims of
the spell of Palestine have to wait for their return? Fifty
years? Ninety? Eighteen hundred? And how many times
is the tragic Palestinian drama going to repeat itself?

69. The Gaza Strip

As we stepped into the plane that was to convey us from
Beirut to Gaza, we were presented with a sample of the
world government of the future. Our fellow travellers included a New Zealand colonel representing the Armistice
Commission in the Gaza Strip sector, and an Indian N.C.O.
and a couple of Brazilian privates from the United Nations
Expeditionary Force (UNEF), returning to duty from leave
in the Lebanon. All civilians in the plane, apart from us,
were officers of the United Nations Relief and Works
Agency (UNRWA).

As we flew southwards offshore, I could not keep my eyes
off the unfolding panorama. Sidon and Tyre: I had seen
these already from the ground. But here comes 'the Ladder
of Tyre', which is now the seaward end of the armistice line
between the Lebanon and Israel; and everything beyond
that cape is new to us. Acre, Mount Carmel: how thrilling to
set eyes on them for the first time. And next come alternate
patches of bright yellow sand-dunes and dark green orange-
groves. This big built-up area must be Tel Aviv and Jaffa.
And now we are veering south-eastwards over the coast. A
town, with masses of hutments north and east and south of it,
flits by beneath our descending wings. That must be Gaza
with its thorn-crown of refugee camps. We are touching the
ground and coming to rest. The end of the runway lies, they
tell me, only a few yards away from the dividing line between
the Strip and Israel. That house and that horse, just over
there, are in Israeli territory.

While my eyes had been drinking in the landscape, my mind had been pulling out of its pigeon-holes some of its previous associations with the region that I had come to see. Gaza, refugees, Philistines: were not the Philistines refugees who had trekked by coasting-boat and bullock-cart all the way from the Aegean Isles to the Nile Delta and had then settled in the Strip after they had been flung back from Egypt? Was not Gaza the southernmost of the five Philistine cities? The sites of the other four must be in Israel today. Gaza: here it was that captive Samson pulled down the pillars of the theatre—content to die himself in the act of bringing death upon his Philistine enemies. And here it was that the Macedonian Christian fanatic, Saint Porphyrius, tore down the temple of Our Lord, Gaza's tutelary god, after having pulled the necessary wires in the Imperial Palace at Constantinople. Ominous episodes of local history; for there are plenty of fanatics and plenty of prisoners in the Gaza Strip today. Their tempers are on edge; and I would not put it beyond them to attempt some desperate act of demolition that might bring, not just a single temple or theatre, but the whole of civilization tumbling in ruin about the ears of the human race. It is a relief to switch one's mind from Gaza to Rafa and to recall the battle, fought there in 217 B.C., in which Indian and African elephants met for the first and last time in history. (The Indian elephants won. The Africans were bigger, but they were not so well trained or so well led.)

From Rafa to Gaza the Strip is, at most, twenty-five miles long. Its width varies from three miles, at the northern end, to five. Along the coast there is an almost continuous belt of sand-dunes. Inland the landscape turns to desert as one travels south. Behind Gaza itself there are stretches of green fields and orange-groves fenced in with huge hedges of some evergreen shrub, casuarina or something of the kind. But on the southward road there comes a point where this gives way to hedges of prickly pear and where the desert sands show through the furrows. Before the catastrophe of 1948, the population of the Strip was about 90,000. Today it is about 100,000, while the refugees in the

Strip amount to twice that number. The permanent population is hard put to it now; for some of their best lands are on
the Israeli side of the armistice line. But at least they still
have something to live on and something to do. The refugees
have nothing to do but to brood over the injustice that has
been done to them. The Germans wronged the Jews, but the
Arabs, not the Germans, have been made to pay for what the
Germans did. This has been the act of the Germans' victorious British and American adversaries. In Arab eyes this
looks like a conspiracy among the Western nations to salve
the West's guilty conscience towards the Jews by compensat-
ing the Jews at the Arabs' expense. In the refugees' hearts
the reaction is to insist obstinately on a righting of the wrong
done to them. They must be reinstated in their own homes
and fields under a non-Israeli régime. What is to happen to
the Jewish settlers on Arab land that has been seized forcibly,
and without being paid for, since 1948? 'England and
America created the problem; it is for them to solve it' is the
Arabs' logical but unconstructive reply.

Within each camp the refugees maintain their former
village organization—each village under the leadership of
its headman (mukhtar). These headmen still have the
influence to set the tone of the rank and file, and they tend
to set it hard, because it is they who have suffered the most
painful change of fortune. Some of them own four or five
hundred acres of ploughland, with fruit trees besides, on the
other side of the line. Yet now they are paupers on the dole.
Inevitably they are bitter; and, in present circumstances,
their passions are not curbed by the responsibility that used
to rest on their shoulders before they lost their homes.
Today the responsibility for keeping the refugees fed,
housed, clothed, medically tended, and educated lies with
UNRWA and its staff.

This United Nations agency is doing a fine job under
perpetual difficulties, financial, political, and psychological.
Its budget is derived, not from UN's general funds, but
from contributions paid by individual member states (the
U.S. pays the lion's share, and Britain the next largest share,

as is just). UNRWA's moves to re-settle the refugees permanently elsewhere than in their own homes are opposed by the governments of the Arab states in whose territories the refugees are camped (the Gaza Strip is administered by the Egyptian Government). There is also opposition among the refugees themselves. They feel that to acquiesce in resettlement would be tantamount to renouncing their title to restitution. One may point out to them that Western Germany has absorbed the East German refugees into her economic life—and has won prosperity and power by so doing—without renouncing her title to the German territories that Poland and the Soviet Union have annexed. But this apparently pertinent example makes little impression on Arab minds. As they see it, the maintenance of their title requires them to reject proposals for resettlement in the meanwhile.

UNRWA has two budgets: one for the refugees' subsistence; the other for their rehabilitation. The first is too small to give the refugees more than about 1,500 calories of food in summer and 1,600 in winter; the use of the rehabilitation fund is blocked by the political opposition of the Arab governments. In this quandary, UNRWA is doing well. The rations may be inadequate, but they are efficiently and fairly distributed, and, for a selected group consisting of children, old people, and the sick, they are supplemented by a hot midday meal. The health service is excellent (the maternity work is particularly striking). Mothers are being educated into bringing their children to the camp clinic at an early stage of any complaint. The rehabilitation fund, which cannot yet be used for resettlement, is being drawn upon for education. The refugees' standard of education, like their standard of medical attention, is probably higher now than it was before they were uprooted. There can be few other Arab communities in which so high a percentage of the girls is at school. These measures are a credit to UNRWA, but what is going to be the end thereof? The refugee population is increasing rapidly and is being educated in large numbers—for what? What have they to look forward to when their education is over—especially the abler minority that has gone on to the secondary schools? Perhaps the most encouraging institution in the Strip is UNRWA's vocational training centre. Technicians, even if refugees, do seem to have a prospect of permanent employment. But what are these among so many?

If the nine hundred thousand Palestinian Arab refugees are a bomb, the two hundred thousand of them who are languishing in the Gaza Strip are this bomb's explosive warhead. Here is a risk to the World's security as well as a challenge to its conscience. This urgent human problem cannot be solved without painful sacrifices on the part of all parties concerned: Israel, the Arab states, and the refugees themselves. The World's duty is to insist on negotiating a settlement and to pay handsomely to alleviate its hardships. Among all the nations of the World, the heaviest responsibility lies on Great Britain and the United States. On this point, at least, the Arabs' contention is unanswerable.

70. Three Pisgah Sights

As we stood on the western edge of the Greek Orthodox Christian monastery on Mount Nebo, the famous panorama unfolded itself before us. The mountain juts out like a headland over the Great Rift Valley, with a twin headland to its left, and from here the eye can sweep the horizon in every direction except eastward. Due west, below us, the Jordan was pouring its muddy waters into the clear Dead Sea, and, west of that again, when one lifted one's eyes to the hills, one could just make out the Mount of Olives breaking the level of the long ridge of the hill country of Judah and Ephraim. Below us, to the left, the blue waters of the lake stretched away southwards into the haze, while to the right the river, like a writhing snake, lashed the sides of its narrow dark green trough, with the desert floor of the Rift Valley showing up yellow on either side, and a patch of green under

the lee of the western mountains to mark the site of Jericho.
On a bluff at the foot of the same mountains, above the
western shore of the Dead Sea, we could make out the ruins
of the mysterious monastic settlement at Khirbet Qumran
—original source of the Dead Sea Scrolls—which we had
visited the day before. It was a marvellous view, but not the
view that I was most intent upon seeing. For me, not Judaea,
but Galilee, was the heart of the Holy Land and the goal of
the pilgrimage that had brought me to Jordan from England
travelling westward across two oceans and one continent.
I could not bring myself to return home without having set
eyes on the Sea of Galilee and Nazareth; but Galilee lies on
the Israeli side of the armistice-line, and Israel was one of the
many countries that were not on my agenda. How were my
Pisgah sights of Galilee to be won?

The next afternoon, at about the same hour, I was standing on another headland with a westward view and with a
glimpse of a lake far down below; and this time the blue
waters were those, not of the Dead Sea, but of the Sea of
Galilee, while the headland was the site, not of Moses'
legendary vision, but of the historic Greek city of Gadara.
I was standing on the topmost row of the basalt seats of
Gadara's west theatre. (In the orderly and opulent Roman
age, every self-respecting Greek city in Palestine made it a
point of honour to possess more theatres than one.) Behind
and around me the living village of Umm Qais was strewn
with the dead Greek city's débris: drums and capitals of
columns and blocks of masonry, some of them inscribed.

Gadara was the seat of a number of distinguished Greek
men of letters. The most famous of them was the poet
Meleager, who put together one of the earliest anthologies
of Greek elegiac verse, and prefaced it with a 'garland'
poem of his own which he wove out of the names of his
predecessors. But Meleager, sitting here in this theatre,
would have had no eyes for the view that had caught and held
mine. Gadara rides aloft on what Plato calls 'the true surface
of the Earth'. What did this Olympian home of Hellenism
care for those fanatical barbarians on the farther shore of

that sultry water-logged hollow? The Gadarene city-state's territory was broad. It included a lake-frontage. The Greek ascendancy's native swineherds were welcome to pasture their animals there, but this was no fit ground for a free Greek farmer to till or for a cultivated Greek gentleman to visit. Gadara stands on the crown of her headland, joined by an isthmus to a foreland with a level fertile top. The city shields the foreland; the foreland feeds the city; the two together make an impregnable Hellenic fortress towering above a hostile barbarian land. When Meleager lifted his eyes from the stage, he did not gaze northwards, as I was gazing, along the western shore of the Sea of Galilee towards Capernaum and Chorazin and Bethsaida. He looked north-westwards, between the lake shore and Mount Tabor, towards the Galilaean highlands, and, beyond these, he saw, with his mind's eye, Tyre, his birthplace, and, beyond Tyre, Paphos, Rhodes, Delos, Athens, Delphi. He was a citizen of the world-wide Hellenic republic of letters; and this extended, in his day, from Taxila in the Panjab to Rome in Italy. What had he to do with the crude barbarians beneath his feet?

As we reluctantly turned our faces towards Irbid and 'Amman, the flat summit of Mount Tabor rose up against the sunset and the grim ravines descending from the Gadarene ridge to the gorge of the River Yarmuk caught the evening light on their jagged western flanks. A sinister landscape and an ill-omened name; for it was in this neighbourhood that, seven hundred years after Hellenism beyond Jordan had received the Roman peace from the hands of Pompey and Gabinius, a Roman army, posted to cover the road to Damascus, was driven westwards into the broken country and hurled to perdition over the cliffs by the invading Muslim Arabs. On that fateful day, Meleager must have turned in his Gadarene grave.

And now, three days later, I am taking the last of my three Pisgah sights—the one that, for me, is the most precious of all. I am standing on the tell of Ta'annak, one of the commanding positions on the low and easily traversible chain of

hills that separates the maritime plain of Sharon from the
hill-girt plain of Esdraelon. The levels of Esdraelon stretch
away northwards below my feet, thick-set now with solidly-
built Israeli tenement houses. Mount Gilboa soars up over
my right shoulder. Megiddo must be just round the corner to
my left, and Mount Tabor somewhere on my right front.
Both are screened from my sight by intervening heights; but
no matter, if only I can descry Nazareth. It is a hazy July
morning and the southern face of the Galilaean highlands is
blurred. But one of my companions used often to cross the
plain to Nazareth from Jennin in the days before the plain
was partitioned by an impassable military front. She is
familiar with the landscape, and there, high up on the
distant hillside, far higher than I had expected, she points
out to me a faint white streak. That is Nazareth; I have seen
Nazareth; the goal of my seventeen months' long pilgrimage
has been attained; I am content now to be catapulted back
from the heart of the World to my remote native London.

71. Jordan's Cities

Jordan is a small country. If you lop off her desert fringes
she becomes very small indeed. From her capital, 'Amman,
you run straight out into the desert if you drive east, and,
driving north or west, you reach the Syrian frontier or the
Israeli armistice-line in a few hours. Yet, within these
narrow bounds, Jordan contains more famous cities than the
largest of the other countries of the present-day world.
Jerusalem and Samaria, Bethlehem and Hebron, Nablus
and Shechem, Jerash and Umm al-Jemal, 'Amman inter-
twined with Philadelphia, and Jericho without a peer: what a
roll-call! And this is only the first batch. The catalogue could
be doubled and trebled.

Jerusalem and Samaria—respective capitals of the
Kingdoms of Judah and Israel—are like one another in two
points: both cities are built on heights, and both are laid

out on the grand scale. Either would have served as the capital for one of the biggest empires of the last millennium B.C. As you wend your way round them it is hard to believe that they were founded as the ambitious capitals of two small highland principalities. The Phoenician cities—Tyre, Sidon, Arvad—were wealthier and more civilized than the rustic states in their hinterland; yet, compared with either Samaria or Jerusalem, their areas are minute.

The contrast between present-day Samaria and present-day Jerusalem reflects the contrast between the reactions of Israel and Judah after they were carried into captivity. Samaria has shrunk to the dimensions of a village that hangs on the huge hill's south-eastern flank. The citadel is now an orchard of olive trees and fig trees; the forum is a threshing floor. The whole population of the village, both human and animal, was busy there, threshing and winnowing, on the July afternoon when we passed that way. The colonnaded street, following a contour half-way down the southern slope, has now dwindled into a country lane. Only the view from the crown of the hill—capped by the remains of a temple dedicated to Augustus—still remains as it was. From this vantage-point you look westward over descending ridges to a shining sea. And today, as in the days of Omri and Ahab, that visible sea-coast is in foreign hands. Like the present-day Kingdom of Jordan, the ancient Kingdom of Israel was a land-locked state with no sea-board on the Mediterranean and with only a precarious access to the Gulf of 'Aqaba.

At Jerusalem, unlike Samaria, the historic heights are still covered by a living city with standing walls; but, since David's day, the walled city has gradually crept northwards, leaving the original site outside the present circuit, but embracing the traditional sites of Golgotha and the Holy Sepulchre. The modern walled city is the work of two of the World's most indefatigable builders, the Idumaean king Herod the Great and the Roman emperor Hadrian; and the authentic remains of their structures are the most impressive monuments of antiquity that Jerusalem has to show. Herod has immortalized himself in the vast platform of the Haram ash-Sharif and in the pavement and cisterns of Castle Antonia. The Antonia still survives, from the pavement (scene of Christ's scourging) downwards, beneath the present-day convent of the Ladies of Zion. The Haram, levelled up to carry Herod's temple, now carries the Umayyad Caliph 'Abd al-Malik's beautiful Dome of the Rock, as well as the later and more common-place Jami al-Aqsa.

But, for the historian, the most interesting piece of ancient Jerusalem is the narrow shelving ridge that he sees below him if he looks southward over the southern wall of the Haram, or over the present southern wall of the city near the Gate of the Maghribis. This is Mount Ophel, the site of the Jebusite city which David captured. That low spur, dominated by Mount Zion as well as by Mount Moriah? How could it ever have been defended? Why should it have been a town-planner's first choice? It was easily defensible in the days when the longest range of missile weapons was a bowshot. It was chosen because it commands two perennial springs: Siloam at its south-western foot, and the Fountain of the Virgin under its eastern flank. When Jerusalem was threatened with an Assyrian attack, King Hezekiah of Judah, fearing that the Virgin's Fountain might prove untenable, cut a tunnel through the rock beneath Ophel to lead the waters of the Virgin's Fountain down into Siloam, which was safely inside the circuit of the eighth-century B.C. city-wall. These two springs were the parents of the historic city whose two present-day poles are the Sepulchre and the Rock.

The Jebusite stronghold held out on the border between an intruding Judah and an intruding Benjamin. Drive southward to Bethlehem and Hebron, and you are in the heart of Judah itself. Yet even this tiny hill country of Judah displays contrasts that are embodied in its two cities. Bethlehem is the traditional birthplace of Christ; Hebron, the traditional burial-place of the Hebrew Patriarchs. Bethlehem is distinctively Christian, Hebron distinctively Muslim. Yet piety overleaps the barriers between rival exclusive-minded religions. A party of Persian Muslim pilgrims, whom we had met first in the Mosque of Abraham at Hebron, turned up later on the same morning at Bethlehem in the Church of the Nativity. (They put us to shame by reverently taking off their shoes before setting foot on this Christian holy ground.)

Judah is as hard a country as Attica. A land flowing with milk and honey does not stand thick with corn. This is a land of rocks and scrub, fit only for rough pasture, except in so far as it can be planted with fruit-trees. There are plantations round Bethlehem; but Hebron is the peak of Judah's altitude and fertility.

The catalogue of Jordanian cities runs on, but my space is almost used up. Quickly travel with me through the east-west pass between Mount Ebal and Mount Gerizim. At the eastern mouth of the pass, commanding the broad cornfields on that side of the two holy mountains, stands the ancient city of Shechem, now being excavated by American archaeologists. In the throat of the pass lies the formidable city of Nablus—Neapolis, a Roman foundation—with a watered, tree-filled valley running down from the city north-westwards in the direction of Samaria. And now stand with me on the southern rim of the citadel of the Greek city of Philadelphia, and look down on the Roman theatre in the vale of the blue River Jabbok, and round about you at the present-day city of 'Amman, fast choking the ravines and clambering up the mountain-sides. 'Before Philadelphia was, I am,' 'Amman might boast. For this is Rabbath Ammon, the capital of a Hebrew people that was the cousin and the enemy of Israel. The Greek city was as ephemeral as its name; the Semitic city lives and grows.

Jerash and Umm al-Jemal: each is a vast field of ruins in the desert; both flourished in the same age: the first four centuries of the Christian Era. Yet the contrast of aspect and atmosphere is extreme. Jerash is jolly; Umm al-Jemal is glum. Jerash bestrides a valley between naked limestone hills. But their nakedness is offset by the ribbon of green trees along the banks of the perennial stream that trickles down the valley's bottom. Umm al-Jemal sprawls over a level waterless desert. From a distance it looks like an oasis of dark green trees; but, as you approach, the dark patch proves to be a wilderness of basalt-built walls. Its life depended on its cisterns, and one of the biggest has lately been reconditioned. The camels and donkeys drinking there, and the ancient pavements now being used as threshing floors, are this gloomy city's only graces.

Even present-day Jerusalem is not unique. It has been split, like an atom, into two mutually hostile cities which stand, and grow, side by side without meeting. But the same fate, after all, has overtaken Berlin. Jordan's unique city is Jericho: the birthplace of civilization, nearly eight hundred feet below sea-level. As you stand on the brow of Miss Kenyon's great trench, you see at the bottom a solidly-built round stone tower. This is one of the bulwarks of a city built in the Early Neolithic Age—an age which had already seen the invention of agriculture, but not yet the invention of pottery. Now turn round till you face east instead of west, and you will find yourself looking down on the spring that waters the Jericho oasis. This 'Ain as-Sultan is for Tell as-Sultan, the mound of Ancient Jericho, what Siloam is for Ophel, the nucleus of Ancient Jerusalem. The perennial flow of living water made it possible to found a permanent human settlement. The spring below the mound at Jericho is literally the source of human civilization.

72. The Shocking Umayyads

One of the greatest ironies of all history is the fate of the house that Muhammad built. Muhammad had a great fall. The unsuccessful prophet succumbed to the temptation to succeed as a statesman and a strategist. Yet, in seeking and winning worldly success in Medina, Muhammad was un-wittingly working for his adversaries in Mecca. When it came to a competition in Realpolitik, the merchant princes of Mecca were more than a match for their queer fellow-townsman, and far more than a match for Muhammad's gallant but incompetent cousin and son-in-law 'Ali. After Muhammad had successfully cut Mecca's trade-route to Syria, the Meccans capitulated on the easy terms that the sentimental Meccan exile offered them; but, in outwardly submitting to Muhammad and to Islam, the Banu Quraish had their tongues in their cheeks. They had no intention of being permanently deposed from power. Now that they had failed first to suppress Islam and then to repel it, their only alternative was to run away with it after capturing it by the stratagem of a nominal conversion. They bided their time till in 'Ali they found their victim and in Mu'awiyah their man of destiny.

Mu'awiyah was one of the greatest masters, known to history, of the artful, patient type of statesmanship. He ranks with Augustus, Philip of Macedon, Liu Pang, and Cavour. Poor 'Ali was utterly outmanoeuvred by him. Within twenty-nine years of Muhammad's death, the state that Muhammad had founded, and that his successors had swiftly expanded into a vast empire, became the undisputed spoil of Mu'awiyah the son of Hind: that redoubtable Meccan merchant-princess who had been Muhammad's bitterest enemy. Unlike Muhammad, Mu'awiyah founded a dynasty —the House of Umayyah—which lasted for ninety years and ruled the world from Multan and Tashqand to Aden, and from Aden to Gibraltar and Narbonne.

Mu'awiyah and his successors performed a valuable service for their subjects. By tact, rather than by force, they kept the turbulent Arab ascendancy more or less in order, and so gave unity and peace to a large part of the human race. Being practical business men, they levied a large commission to compensate them for their trouble; and, being un-repentant pagans in all but name (save only for one sincere Muslim, the Caliph 'Umar II), they went to the limits of discretion in flouting Islam by indulging in the worst abominations of civilization. They were wine-bibbers, and they decorated their palaces with mosaics and paintings in the Hellenistic style that had been endemic in Syria for the last thousand years. They revelled in breaking the Islamic tabu on the representation of living forms. They employed Christian artists who were adepts in this line; and they were not content with representations of animals and men. Their favourite orders were for pictures of women—preferably naked, or at least naked down to the waist.

How did they manage to get away with this indecency and impiety for as long a time as ninety years? When Jezebel and Ahab flouted the orthodox worship of Yahweh, retribution was swift; and, like the Kingdom of Israel, the Realm of Islam had its fanatics. The Kharijites were not less militant than the Rechabites. So how, one asks again, did the Umayyads contrive to fare so much better than the House of Omri? One may not like or admire the Umayyads, but their adroitness does command our reluctant respect, and one cannot help being grateful for the works of art that they have bequeathed to us.

Come and see the Umayyad Caliph Hisham's palace in the Rift Valley, a little to the north of Jericho. Here you will find the largest surviving Hellenistic mosaic floor in the World. The greatest curiosities are the stucco statues of Hisham himself and his half-naked houris, now lodged in the museum at Jerusalem. But the thing of beauty is the smaller mosaic in the room where the roué used to rest from his profligate labours. Here the Tree of Life still blooms, with its fruits glowing on its waving branches, while peace and war, good and evil, confront each other below. On the left side of the trunk the peaceful deer are nibbling at the lowest leaves; on the right side one of them, in agony, is being mauled by a springing lion. No finer work of art in this medium can ever have been executed, even in the heyday of the Hellenistic civilization. The Umayyads' patronage gave Hellenistic art a glorious sunset.

The most surprising legacy of the Umayyads is their palaces in the desert. 'Abd al-Malik's mosque in Jerusalem, Walid's mosque in Damascus, Hisham's winter palace in the warm Rift Valley: these are just what one would expect of a race of sophisticated Meccan townsfolk who had suddenly acquired the sovereignty over a great rich empire. But why did they also build mansions for themselves out in the wilderness? The Umayyads were anything but bedouin. To manage and exploit the bedouin was one of their hereditary professions, but they themselves were as urban as if they had been born and bred in Antioch or Alexandria. Yet half-a-dozen elegant hunting-boxes in the great open spaces still stand to bear witness to their apparent nostalgia for the Arabian Steppe. Was this cult of the simple life an affectation, like Marie Antoinette's pose of playing the dairy-maid in her toy village? In May I had visited two northerly Umayyad desert palaces—Castle Handsome West and Castle Handsome East—en route from Palmyra to Rusafa. In July, finding myself in 'Amman, I took the opportunity to visit three of the southern group: Qasr al-Mushatta, Qasr al-Kharaneh, and Qasr al-'Amra. The third of these three, like Hisham's palace in the Rift Valley, was originally decorated with paintings. The picture of the Caliph, with four discomfited kings lined up behind him, has faded out. The houris and the Signs of the Zodiac are still visible.

On this July day the desert was alive. Huge herds of camels had gathered round the rare water-holes, and at our farthest point eastward, Qasr al-Azraq, there was vegetation on the fringe of the pools, and a mighty spring was welling up from beneath a long ago congealed flow of basalt. At this famous watering-place we were hospitably entertained by five men and boys and two sheep. (In Western Asia, sheep have human rights and are conscious of being full members of society. If you do not realize this, you will not be able to appreciate the imagery that the Gospels draw from the relation between the sheep and their shepherd. In Asia, sheep are not driven, as they are in Europe; they are led; and the flock, as well as the sheep-dog, answers to the shepherd's call.)

Qasr al-'Amra: what a charming little palace, with its painted walls and dome, perched on the bank of the dry Wadi Botof. In July there is not a trace of water there on the surface; yet up through the shingle-bed spring trees with bushy heads like the trees in a child's Noah's Ark. What life and beauty in the midst of the wilderness: how well the Caliph chose his site for his Petit Trianon, and how beautifully he adorned it. The picture of Qasr al-'Amra, in its desert setting, is printed indelibly on my mind; and, when I enjoy the pleasure of recalling it, I cannot think unkindly of the dynasty that conjured it up. The Umayyads were shocking, no doubt; but then I am neither a Kharijite nor a Rechabite, so I do not have to be indignant. On the other hand, I am a Philhellene, so I appreciate the Umayyads' enlightened patronage of the Hellenistic art which they found still a going concern in the former Roman provinces in which they made themselves at home. Moreover, these Umayyads were not only cultivated; they were tolerant. So God be merciful to them and to Jezebel and to good King Herod too (good, I mean, as a builder; for he was not so good as a man). As for Abu Muslim and Jehu and Jehonadab, I am not going to pray for them. The fanatics can fend for themselves.

73. The End of a Journey

As we drove back, yesterday evening, from Byblos to Beirut, we saw the sun sink into the Mediterranean again. It might have been any day in our itinerary. We seemed still as far away from England as when we were in Indonesia or Japan. Yet, this morning, here we are back in our house in London. At the London Airport, an hour ago, five small smiling faces were peeping round the door of the customs bay, waiting for us to clear our baggage; and, two hours before that, when the Sun rose upon us again after having made one of his mighty subterranean return-voyages from west to east, he was shining upon the snow-covered peaks of the Alps, and the Matterhorn was receding behind my left shoulder.

It is difficult to realize that we have travelled round the globe more or less 'according to plan'. Before we started—now more than seventeen months ago—we had been occupied for at least a year and a half in working our itinerary out; and all this calculation and correspondence had felt more like some academic exercise in staff-work than like genuine preparations for a journey that was actually going to be accomplished. On Saturday the 28th April, 1956, should I really find myself climbing on board the S.S. *Rangitata* as she steamed through the Panamá Canal? Would my wife really be in that cabin that we had booked? And then on Sunday the 19th May, 1957, at 4 a.m., should I really be de-training at Asshur from the Baghdad-Mosul night mail? In advance this seemed improbable. So one started with one's heart in one's mouth, and a good part of the long programme had to be successfully put behind us before we began to feel any confidence that the rest of it would follow suit. There have been, of course, both losses and gains. I lost Bolivia through falling sick, but gained Sa'udi Arabia and the Gaza Strip through unlooked-for hospitable invitations. On balance, the gains have exceeded the losses, and this is something quite beyond our expectations.

When one sets out to plan a seventeen-months' journey, one imagines, in advance, that this will give one time enough to see the whole World and to see it at leisure. When one gets down to details, one discovers that one may hope to see a fraction of the surface of the globe if one makes an industrious use of every hour and every minute. The surface of a globe is boundless; and, however far one may push one's way in any direction, there will always be some tantalizing objective still just beyond one's reach. Think of having to turn back at Pomata, when, over there, across the Peruvian-Bolivian frontier—only just out of sight—there lies Tiahuanaco: the city that threw the great disturbing stone into the quiet pond of early Peruvian civilization. And think of standing on the Kohat Pass, and gazing south-westward into Waziristan, without having time to beat the bounds of the North-west

Frontier from here to Quetta. In the course of a journey one is excruciated, all the time, by the consciousness of how much one is missing. At journey's end, one discovers how big a cargo of new knowledge one has brought home. All the same, in these seventeen months, we have not set foot on Africa or on a single Polynesian island, and we have seen, but not entered, China, Afghanistan, and the Soviet Union. (We saw China from the New Territories of Hongkong, Afghanistan from the western end of the Khyber Pass, and the Soviet Union from the north-western tip of the leafy Persian province of Gilan.) This sounds as if we must have idled away our time. Yet, from beginning to end, we have been on the run, and we have managed to see something of many of the countries of Asia.

Most travellers, I suppose, travel in order to arrive somewhere, and these are the people for whom the transportation services cater. If one belongs to the minority that travels in order to see what is on the way, one has two deadly enemies to contend with: the capital city and the aeroplane.

'The better the milling machinery, the less nourishing the bread; the better the conveyance, the less instructive the journey.' High-powered American machinery grinds the vitamins out of the flour. High-powered British aeroplanes carry the passenger so high above the clouds that he cannot see the countries over which he is being hurled. For the traveller whose object in travelling is to see the World, the best conveyance is shanks's mare.

As for the World's capital cities, they are all growing bigger, growing more like one another, and growing more magnetic. They draw you into their spider's web (all transportation services conspire with them); and, when once they have caught you, they will not let you go. They cannot conceive that you can really wish to escape from them into the countryside. Yet, even today, the countryside still remains the real world. Every capital city is more or less unrepresentative. I myself am a Londoner born, and I have lived in London all my life. But, if ever I wanted to make a serious study of my native country, I should flee from

London and steep myself in Huddersfield and Warrington. This unrepresentativeness of the capital is one of its generic defects, but it comes to a climax in those countries—and they are a majority of the countries of the World—that in our time are in process of modernization. For modernization begins in the cities, and it standardizes urban life on Western lines; so that, in Latin American and Asian countries, the gulf between capital and countryside is now extreme and is steadily growing wider. When you enter Tehran, for example, you feel as if you were leaving behind you the country of which this is the official capital. If some joker jinn were to dump Tehran where Lima stands, and Lima where Tehran stands, overnight, the Iranian and Quechuan peasants, coming into market next morning as usual, would probably fail to notice that there had been any change. Neither Lima nor Tehran could be more exotic anywhere else than each of them is in its own country, and they are as like one another as two peas. If one's object is to see the World's standardized capital cities, one might as well save oneself the trouble of packing one's bag. Wherever one may be, one cannot fail to collide with this typical creation of our modern age.

Much—too much—of my precious seventeen months has been spent on languishing in capital cities. Too much of it has been spent on being catapulted in aeroplanes. Yet my running fight against these two traveller's banes has not been altogether a losing battle. I have skimmed over the tree-tops of the Amazon forest in a hydroplane; I have ridden up one of Iran's hidden valleys on donkey-back; I have threaded my way through the Syk at Petra on foot. Such glimpses of the real world are gleanings of priceless value. Now that I have harvested them, I must do my best to turn them to account.

A.J.T.'s Itinerary

March	28	Trujillo – Fanfán – las Guitarras – Chiclayo – Lambayeque – Túcume – Purgatorio – Chiclayo (road)
	29	Chiclayo – Trujillo (road)
	30	Trujillo – Lima (road)
April	8	Lima – Arequipa (air)
	9–10, night	Arequipa – Juliáca (rail)
	10	Juliáca – Puno (rail); Puno – Pomata – Puno (road)
	11	Puno – Juliáca – Cuzco (rail)
	11–14	in and around Cuzco
	14	Cuzco – Machu Picchu (autocarril)
	15	Machu Picchu – Ollantaytambo (autocarril); Ollantaytambo – Pisac – Cuzco (road)
	16	Cuzco – Lima (air)
	18	Lima – Pucallpa (air); Pucallpa – Yarinacocha (road)
	18–21	in and around Yarinacocha (hydroplane)
	21	Pucallpa – Lima (air)
	22	Lima – up the Rimac Valley to Viso – Lima (road)
	23	Lima – La Cantuta – Lima (road)
	25–26, night	Lima – Guayaquil – Panamá City (air)
	27	Panamá City – Colón (road)
	28	Colón – Cristóbal (road); Cristóbal – S.S. *Rangitata* (launch); Cristóbal – Balboa, through Panamá Canal, on S.S. *Rangitata* with V.M.T.; Balboa – Panamá City (road)
	29	Panamá City – Balboa (road)
April 29–May 19		Balboa – Auckland, on S.S. *Rangitata*
May	9	anchor off Pitcairn Island
	11	pass south of Rapa Island
	19	reach Auckland
	19	Auckland – Rotorua – Lake Taupo – the Chateau (road)
	20	the Chateau – the Desert Road – Bulls, near Palmerston North (road)
	21	Bulls – Wellington (road)

May 21–24	in and around Wellington
24	Wellington – Auckland (air)
25–30	Auckland – Sydney, on S.S. *Monowai*
May 30–June 12	in and around Sydney
June 10	Sydney – Bowral – Wollongong – Sydney (road)
12	Sydney – Newcastle (air)
14	Newcastle – Brisbane – Cairns (air)
14–18	in and around Cairns
15	Cairns – Green Island – Cairns (launch)
16	Cairns – Atherton Tableland – Cairns (road)
17	Cairns – Kuranda – Cairns (rail)
18	Cairns – Brisbane (air)
18–21	in and around Brisbane
21	Brisbane – Sydney – Tamworth (air); Tamworth – Armidale (road)
21–26	in and around Armidale
24–25	Armidale – Wallamumbi – Armidale
26	Armidale – Tamworth (road); Tamworth – Sydney (air)
26–28	in Sydney
28	Sydney – Canberra (air)
June 28–July 9	in and around Canberra
June 29–July 2	tour of Snowy Mountains Scheme (road)
July 8	Canberra – Winderadeen – Canberra (road)
9	Canberra – Melbourne (air)
9–18	in and around Melbourne
15	Melbourne – Bendigo – Melbourne (road)
18	Melbourne – Hobart (air)
18–24	in and around Hobart
19	Hobart – Mount Wellington – Hobart (road)
21	Hobart – Port Arthur – Hobart (road)
24	Hobart – Launceston (road); Launceston – Melbourne (air)
24–27	in and around Melbourne
27	Melbourne – Adelaide (air)
28–30	Adelaide – Port Pirie – Port Augusta – Kalgoorlie – Perth (rail)

July 30–August 6	in and around Perth
August 4–6	Perth – Manjimup (big trees) – wheat country – Perth (road)
6–7, night	Perth – Adelaide (air)
7–14	in and around Adelaide
11	Adelaide – Murray Bridge – Coonalpyn – Adelaide (road)
12	Adelaide – Barossa Valley – Angaston (Yalumba) – Kapunda (Anlaby) – Adelaide (road)
14	Adelaide – Melbourne (air)
14–18	in Melbourne
18	Melbourne – Adelaide – Alice Springs (air); Alice Springs – Hermannsberg Mission (road)
19	Hermannsberg – Haast Bluff – Derwent – Mount Wedge – Aileron (road)
20	Aileron – Warribri Reserve – Tennent Creek (road)
21	Tennent Creek – Darwin (air)
21–23	in and around Darwin
22	visit uranium mine at Rum Jungle, near Batchelor, and rice cultivation project on Alligator River (road)
23	Darwin – Djakarta (air)
24	Djakarta – Bogor – Bandung (road)
24–26	in and around Bandung
26	Bandung – Djakarta (road)
26–29	in Djakarta
29	Djakarta – Jogjakarta (air)
29–31	in and around Jogjakarta
30	Jogjakarta – Borobudur – Mendut – Jogjakarta – Prambanan – Jogjakarta (road)
31	Jogjakarta – Semarang (road); Semarang – Surabaya (air)
August 31–Sept. 2	in and around Surabaya
September 1	Surabaya – Modjokarta – Majapahit – Surabaya (road)
2	Surabaya – Den Pasar (air)
2–4	in Bali
3	Den Pasar – eastern crater lake – Den Pasar (road)

September 4	Den Pasar – Surabaya – Makasar (air)
4–6	in Makasar
6	Makasar – Surabaya – Djakarta (air)
6–8	in Djakarta
8	Djakarta – Medan (air)
8–13	in Sumatra
9	Medan – Parápat, at S.E. corner of Lake Toba (road)
10	Parápat – Medan (road)
11	Medan – Padang (air); Padang – Bukatinggi – Padang (road)
11–13	in and around Padang
13	Padang – Palembang – Djakarta (air)
14	Djakarta – Singapore (air)
15	Singapore – Johore – Singapore (road)
16	Singapore – Johore – Singapore (road)
Sept. 17–October 1	Singapore – Yokohama, on S.S. *Cambodge*
September 19	reach Saigon
19–22	at Saigon
20	Saigon – Tây Ninh (Caodai temple) – Saigon
22	visit Catholic refugees' camp near Saigon
22	leave Saigon
24	touch at Manila
26	reach Hongkong
26–27	in and around Hongkong
27	leave Hongkong
October 1	reach Yokohama; Yokohama – Tokyo (road)
October 1–Nov. 30	based on the International House of Japan, Tokyo
October 8	Tokyo – Nikko (rail); Nikko – Kegon Falls – Chusenji Lake – Tachiki Kannon Temple – Ryuzo no taki Falls – Yunoko Lake – Nikko (road)
9	Nikko – Tokyo (rail)
13	Tokyo – Kamakura – Odawara – Hakone (road)
13–15	in and around Hakone

October	15	Hakone – Tokyo (road)
	16	visit prehistoric sites E.N.E. of Tokyo
	20	Tokyo – Osaka (rail)
	21	Osaka – Uji Yamada – Ise shrines (rail); Ise shrines – Shima Kanko (road)
	22	Shima Kanko – Uji Yamada (road); Uji Yamada – Osaka – Kyoto (rail)
	22–26	in and around Kyoto
	26	Kyoto – Mount Hiei – Miidara – Kyoto (road, funicular, footpath, funicular, road)
	26	Kyoto – Kobe (rail)
	26–27, night	Kobe – Imabari (sea)
	27	Imabari – Beppu (sea); Beppu – Kokura (rail); Kokura – Fukuoka (road)
	28	Fukuoka – Saga – Nagasaki (rail)
	29–30	Nagasaki – Saga – Fukuoka – Moji – Shimonoseki – Hiroshima – Kobe (rail)
	30	Kobe – Himeji Castle – Kobe – Osaka – Kyoto (road)
	31	Kyoto – Osaka (road)
November	1	Osaka – Koya San – Osaka (rail)
	2	Osaka – Nara (road)
	2–6	in and around Nara
	4	Nara – Horyuji – Nara (road)
	5	Nara – round Mounts Kasuga and Wakakusa – Nara (road)
		Nara – Tenri City – Nara (road)
	6	Nara – Sakai – Kyoto (road)
	7–8	Kyoto – Tokyo (rail)
	8–11	in Tokyo
	11	Tokyo – Omiya – Utsunomiya – Fukushima – Sendai (rail)
	12	Sendai – Aomori (rail); Aomori – Hakodate (ferry)
	13	Hakodate – Otaru – Sapporo (rail)
	14	Sapporo – Naganuma – Toasa – Shiraoi – Noboribetsu (road)
	15	Noboribetsu – Hakodate (rail); Hakodate – Aomori (ferry); Aomori – Owani Springs (rail)

November 16	Owani Springs – Odate – Akita – Niitsu – Niigata (rail)
17	Niigata – Niitsu – Miyauchi – Yuzawa – Shinizu Tunnel – Minakami – Takasaki – Tokyo (rail)
17–30	in Tokyo
Nov. 30–Dec. 1, night	Tokyo – Hongkong (air)
December 1	Hongkong – Bangkok (air)
1–12	based on Bangkok
2	Menam River and canals (launch)
5	Bangkok – Siem Réap (air)
5–8	in and around Siem Réap (Angkor)
8	Siem Réap – Bangkok (air)
9	Bangkok – Ayuthia – Bangkok (road)
12	Bangkok – Rangoon (air)
12–23	based on Rangoon
14	Rangoon – Mandalay (air)
14–18	in and around Mandalay
16	Mandalay – Sagaing – Mandalay (road)
17	Mandalay – Maymyo – Mandalay (road)
18	Mandalay – He Ho – Rangoon (air)
19	Rangoon – Syriam – Rangoon (river and road)
23	Rangoon – Calcutta (air)
December 23–Jan. 4 1957	based on Calcutta
December 26	Calcutta – Patna – Benares (air)
26–28	at Benares
28	Benares – Gaya (rail); Gaya – Bodh Gaya – Gaya (road)
28–29, night	Gaya – Howra (rail)
31	Calcutta – Dacca (air)
Dec. 31–Jan. 3 1957	in and around Dacca

1957

January 1	Dacca – Comilla – Brahmanbaria – Mymensingh – Randina – Brahmaputra River – Mirzapur – Dacca (air: round trip without landings en route)
3	Dacca – Calcutta (air)
4	Calcutta – Bhubaneswar – Vishakapatnam (air); Vishakapatnam – Woltair (road)

January	5	Woltair – Bimlipatnam – Woltair – Vishakapatnam (road); Vishakapatnam – Bezwada – Guntur (rail)
	6	Guntur – Nagarjunakonda – Guntur (road); Guntur – Tenali (road)
	6–7, night	Tenali – Madras (rail)
	7–25	based on Madras
	8	Madras – Mahabalipuram – Pondichéry – Anamalainagar and Chidambaram – Gangaicholapuram – Anamalainagar (road)
	9	Anamalainagar – Coleroon River – Anamalainagar (road)
	10	Anamalainagar – Pondichéry – Arikamedu – Wandiwash – Conjeeveram – Madras (road)
	14	Madras – Bangalore (air); Bangalore – Nandi Hill – Bangalore (road)
	15	Bangalore – Seringapatam – Mysore – Krishnarajasagar Reservoir Hotel (road)
	16	Krishnarajasagar Reservoir Hotel – Seringapatam – Sravana Belagola – Hassan – Belur – Halebid – Sakleshpur – Ossoor Estate (road)
	17	Ossoor Estate – Halebid – Banavar – Bangalore (road); Bangalore – Madras (air)
	18	Madras – Jaffna (air); Jaffna – Elephant Pass (road)
	18–24	in Ceylon
	19	Elephant Pass – Vavuniya – Mihintale – Anuradhapura – Habarane – Sigiriya (road)
	20	Sigiriya – Minneriya tank – Polonnaruwa (road)
	21	Polonnaruwa – Dambulla – Matale – Kandy – Peradeniya (road)
	22	Peradeniya – Colombo (road)
	22–24	in Colombo

January	24	Colombo – Trichinopoly (air); Trichinopoly – Tanjore – Kumbakonam – Madras (road)
	25	Madras – Hyderabad (air)
	25–27	in Hyderabad
	26	visit Golconda
	27	Hyderabad – Bombay air port (air); Bombay air port – Karli Caves – Poona (road)
	28	Poona – Kharakwasla (National Defence College) – Poona (road)
	29	Poona – Bombay (road)
January 29–February	3	in Bombay
February	3	Bombay – Aurangabad (air); Aurangabad – Daulatabad – Khuldabad – Ellora Caves – Aurangabad (road)
	3–10	in and around Aurangabad
	5	Aurangabad – Ellora – Aurangabad (road)
	6	Aurangabad – Paithan – Aurangabad (road)
	7	Aurangabad – Ajanta – Aurangabad (road)
	10	Aurangabad – Indore – Bhopal – Gwalior (air)
	11	Gwalior – Agra (road)
	11–14	in and around Agra
	12	Agra – Fatehpur Sikri – Agra (road)
	14	Agra – Máthura – Delhi (road)
	14–27	in and around Delhi
	22	Delhi – Panipat – Karnal – Nilokheri – Thanésar – Kurukshetra – Delhi (road)
	27	Delhi – Amritsar (air)
	28	Amritsar – Lahore (rail)
February 28–March	3	in and around Lahore
March	2	Lahore – Harappa – Lahore (road)
	3	Lahore – Rawal Pindi (air)
	4	Rawal Pindi – Taxila – Rawal Pindi (road)
	5	Rawal Pindi – Taxila – Attock Bridge – Peshawar (road)
	6	Peshawar – Warsak Dam – Khyber Pass to Afghan frontier – Peshawar (road)

March	7	Peshawar – Charsadda – Dargai – Malakand Pass – Swat Valley (as far as Mingaora) – Peshawar (road)
	8	Peshawar – arms factory – Kohat Pass – Peshawar (road); Peshawar – Rawal Pindi – Lahore (air)
	9–10, night	Lahore – Rohri Junction (rail); Rohri Junction – Sukkur – along Rice Canal – Larkana – Mohenjo-daro – Larkana (road)
	11	Larkana – Mohenjo-daro – Larkana – Sukkur (road)
	12	Sukkur – Rohri Junction (road); Rohri Junction – Karachi (rail)
	12–17	in and around Karachi
	16	Karachi – Tatta – Indus Ferry – Karachi (road)
	17	Karachi – (over) Horn of Arabia – (over) Abadan – (over) Basra – (over) Najaf – (over) Damascus – Beirut (air)
March 17–August 2		based on Beirut
March	21	Beirut – Byblos (Jbail) – Beirut (road)
	22	Beirut – Baalbek – Beirut (road)
	23	Beirut – Sidon (Saida) – Beirut (road)
	30	Beirut – Byblos (Jbail) – Aqura – Afqa – Beirut (road)
	31	Beirut – Saida – Jezzin – Beit ed Din – Bhamdoun – Beirut (road)
April	2	Beirut – Saida (Sidon) – Sur (Tyre) – Tibnin (Toron Castle) – Bint Jbail – Meis Jabal – Adeiseh – Marjayyun – Khiam – Marjayyun – Beaufort Castle – Saida – Nabatieh – Beirut (road)
	5	Beirut – Damascus (road)
	5–9	in and around Damascus
	7	Damascus – Deraa – Bosra (road)
	8	Bosra – Suweida – Athil – Shahba – Suweida – Kanawat – Suweida – Izraa – Damascus (road)
	9	Damascus – Beirut (road)
	13	Beirut – (over) Damascus – (over) Shahba – (over) Jabal Druz –

April	13 *(cont.)*	'Amman – (over) Kerak Castle – (over) Shobek (Montréal Castle) – (over) Udhruh (Roman fort) – Ma'an (air); Ma'an – Wadi Musa (road); Wadi Musa – Petra (horse-back)
	14	Petra – Wadi Musa (feet); Wadi Musa – Ma'an – 'Aqaba – Ma'an (road); Ma'an – (over) Hijaz Railway – 'Amman – (over) Jabal Druz – (over) Damascus – Beirut (air)
	18	Beirut – Tripoli – Tell Kalakh – Qal'at al Husn (Krak des Chevaliers Castle) – Monastery of St. George (road)
	19	Monastery of St. George – Borj Safita – Tartus – Ruad Island – Tartus – Lattaqieh – Ras ash-Shamra – Lattaqieh (road)
	20	Lattaqieh – Qal'at Sahyoun – Lattaqieh – Jisr ash-Shoghur – Idlib – Aleppo (road)
	20–23	in and around Aleppo
	22	Aleppo – Qal'at Sem'an – Aleppo (road)
	23	Aleppo – Hama – Shaizar Castle – Hama – Homs – Nebq – Ma'lula Monastery (road)
	24	Ma'lula Monastery – Seidnaya Monastery – Damascus – Beirut (road)
	27	Beirut – Mukhtara – Beirut (road)
	28	Beirut – Saida – Nabatieh – Marjayyun – Nahr Hasbani bridge – Springs of Jordan – Hasbeya – Khalwat al-Biyad – Upper Hasbani Valley – the Baqaa – Beirut (road)
April 28–May	1	in Beirut
May	1	Beirut – Damascus (road)
	2	Damascus – Qasr al-Khayr Gharbi – Palmyra (road)
	2–5	in Palmyra
	5	Palmyra – Sukhneh – Qasr al-Khayr Sharqi – Qom – Rusafa – Raqqa – Meskeneh – Aleppo (road)

May	6	Aleppo – Hama – Apamea (Qal'at Mudiq) – Hama – Homs – Damascus (road)
	7	Damascus – Beirut (road)
	11	Beirut – Damascus (road)
	12	drive round the Ghutah; Damascus – Beirut (road)
	16	Beirut – (over) Damascus – Baghdad (air)
	16–25	based on Baghdad
	18–19, night	Baghdad – Jernaf (rail)
	19	Jernaf – Qal'at Sherghat (Asshur) – Hatra – Gayara – Mosul (road); Mosul – Nineveh – Mosul (road)
	19–21	in and around Mosul
	20	Mosul towards Khorsabad (stopped by mud); Mosul – Erbil – Salaheddin – Shaqlawa – Salaheddin – Erbil – Mosul (road)
	21	Mosul – Zakho – Mosul (road)
	21–22, night	Mosul – Baghdad (rail)
	22–25	in and around Baghdad
	24	Baghdad – Babylon – Hilla – Kufa – Najaf – Kufa – Baghdad (road)
	25	Baghdad – Khanaqin – Khosrovi – Qasr é Shirin – Sar é Pol – Shahabad – Kermanshah (road)
	26	Kermanshah – Taq é Bostan – Bisitun – Kangavar – Hamadan (road)
	27	Hamadan – Takistan – Qazvin – Kharej – Tehran (road)
May 27–June 1		in and around Tehran
May	30	Tehran – Shahr Reyy – Narses' palace – Shahr Reyy – 16 kilometres along Khorasan road and back – Tehran (road)
	31	Tehran – 56 kilometres along Qazvin road – Tepe Mil (road)
June	1	Tehran – (over) Sabzavar – (over) Nishapur – Mashhad (air); Mashhad – Tus – Mashhad (road)
	2	Mashhad – Husainabad – shrine of an Imamzade at a spring – Nishapur – cenotaphs of Farid ad-Din 'Attar and Omar Khayyám – Kharv – Mashhad (road)

June	3	Mashhad – Vekilabad – Tordabeh – Mashhad (road)
	4	Mashhad – Tehran (air)
	6	Tehran – (over) Qom – Ispahan (Esfahan) (air)
	6-14	in and around Ispahan
	9	Ispahan – Kuhpayeh – Nain – Aqda – Ardakan – Yazd (road)
	9-11	in and around Yazd
	10	Yazd – Taft – Bala Deh – Tezirjan – Banadk (Bunafti) – Dara – Fakhrabad – Hamza – Tezirjan – Bala Deh (Hedesh) – Taft – Yazd (road); Yazd – Qasimabad – Yazd (road)
	11	Yazd – Ispahan (road)
	12	Ispahan – Najafabad – bridge over Zayandeh Rud – Saman – Shahr é Kurd – Kharaji – Dastaneh (road)
	13	Dastaneh – Qal'ah Mamika – Choghar Khor – Uregun (the Bakhtiari khans' former summer camping ground in the Chahar Mahall) – Urujan (*alias* Burujan) – Shah Reza – Ispahan (road)
	14	Ispahan – Shiraz (air); Shiraz – Persepolis (Takht é Jamshid) – Nakhsh é Rustam – Persepolis (road)
	14-16	in and around Persepolis
	15	Persepolis – Pasargadae – Persepolis (road)
	16	Persepolis – Shiraz (road)
	16-20	in and around Shiraz
	18	Shiraz – Kazerun – Shahpur – Kazerun – Shiraz (road)
	19	Shiraz – Firuzabad – Shiraz (road)
	20	Shiraz – Ispahan – (over) Qom – Tehran (air)
	21	Tehran – Kharej – Kharej gorge – over the pass, not through the tunnel – Chalus – Ramsar – Rasht – Bandar Pahlavi (road)
	22	Bandar Pahlavi – Astara – Ardebil – Kalkhoran – Ardebil – Bostanabad – Tabriz (road)
	23	Tabriz – Marand – Khoi – Shahpur – Rezaïeh (road)

June	24	Rezaïeh – Mehabad – Qumqal'a – Rezaïeh (road)
	25	Rezaïeh – Shahpur – Khoi – Marand – Tabriz – Mianeh (road)
	26	Mianeh – Zenjan – Sultanieh – Takistan – Qazvin – Tehran (road)
	26–29	in and around Tehran
	28	Tehran – Kharej – part way up the Kharej gorge (road) – side valley eastward and back (donkey-back) – Tehran (road)
	29	Tehran – Baghdad – (over) Damascus – Beirut (air)
June 29–July 3		in Beirut
July	3	Beirut – Baalbek (road)
	3–7	in and around Baalbek
	6	Baalbek – Tell Ahmar – 'Ain 'Ata – crest of Mount Lebanon – the Cedars – Besharré – Tell Ahmar – Lebwe – Springs of Orontes – Hermel Monument – Baalbek
	7	Baalbek – Zahle – Mruje – Bois de Boulogne – Shweir – Beirut
	7–11	in Beirut
	11	Beirut – Dhahran (air)
	11–17	in and around Dhahran
	12	Dhahran – Khobar – Dammam – Qatif – Dhahran
	14	visit tomb at Jawan
	15	Dhahran – Riyadh – Dhahran (air); Dhahran – Ras Tanura – Dhahran (road)
	16	Dhahran – Mubarraz – Hofuf – Abqaiq – Dhahran (road)
	17	Dhahran – Beirut (air)
	19	Beirut – Gaza (air); visit Maghazi refugees camp (road)
	19–22	in and around Gaza
	20	visit Beach Camp – Vocational Training Centre – Jabalieh camp – Nuseirat camp (road)
	21	Gaza – former agricultural experimental station on northern edge of the Gaza Strip – Rafa – Gaza (road)

July	22	Gaza – Jordanian Jerusalem (air);
	22–24	in and around Jerusalem (on the Jordan side of the armistice-line)
	23	Jerusalem – Mount of Olives – Gethsemane – Hebron (Khalil) – Ramat al-Khalil – Bethlehem – Jerusalem (road)
	24	Jerusalem – Khirbet Qumran – Musa al-'Allami's farm school for orphan refugees – Hisham's palace – Tell es Sultan (Old Jericho) – Allenby Bridge over Jordan – Salt – 'Amman (road)
	24–29	in and around 'Amman
	25	'Amman – Madeba – Zerka Ma'in hot springs – Mount Nebo – 'Amman (road)
	26	'Amman – 'Ajlun – Qal'at Ribat – Jerash – Tell er Ramit (?Ramoth Gilead) – Irbid – Umm Qais (Gadara) – Irbid – Mafraq – 'Amman (road)
	27	visit 'Amman citadel; 'Amman – Mushatta – 'Amman (road)
	28	'Amman – Muwaqqar – ancient tank reconditioned by Point Four – Qasr al-Kharaneh – Wadi Botof – Qasr al-'Amra – Qasr al-Azraq (spring and pools) – pool – Qasr al-Hallabat (Roman fort) – Mafraq – Umm al-Jemal – Mafraq – 'Amman (road)
	29	'Amman – Salt – Damiya Bridge over Jordan – Jiftlik – Nablus – Jennin – Tell Ta'annak – Nablus – Sebastieh (Samaria) – Nablus – Ramallah – Jerusalem (road)
	30	Jerusalem – Beit Jala – Bethlehem – Beit Safafeh – Diheisheh refugees camp – Battir – Jerusalem (road)
	31	Jerusalem – (over) Salkhad – (over) the Lejah – over N.E. end of Mount Hermon (Jabal ash-Shaikh) – Beirut (air)
August	2	Beirut – Byblos (Jbail) – Beirut (road)
	2–3, night	Beirut – London (air)

INDEX